BLACKBELT IN BLACKJACK

PLAYING 21 AS A MARTIAL ART

For K

_____

ACKNOWLEDGMENTS

Thanks to those who have stuck with me.

Abbot Avarrisa
Sam Case
Moe Cash
Cellini
Cotton
Mark Dace
Darryl
Steve Forte
Dan Gordon
James Grosjean
Honcho
Tommy Hyland
Bob Loeb
Munchkin
98%
Phil
Sal Piacente
Radar
Max Rubin
Pennie Ruchman
Howard Schwartz
Stalker
Bill Zender
Mango
Mookie
Ti
Whitey

Finally, thanks to Avery Cardoza for keeping the faith, and to Sara Cardoza for editorial diligence and patience.

BLACKBELT IN
BLACKJACK

PLAYING 21 AS A MARTIAL ART

ARNOLD SNYDER

CARDOZA PUBLISHING

Cardoza Publishing is the foremost gaming and gambling publisher in the world with a library of more than 200 up-to-date and easy-to-read books and strategies. These authoritative works are written by the top experts in their fields and with more than 9,000,000 books in print, represent the best-selling and most popular gaming books anywhere.

THIRD EDITION
2nd Printing

Copyright ©1983, 1998, 2005 by Arnold Snyder
All Rights Reserved

Back Cover Photo: Howard Schwartz

Library of Congress Catalog No: 2004101410
ISBN: 1-58042-143-1

Visit our website at www.cardozapub.com or write for a full list of books and advanced strategies.

CARDOZA PUBLISHING
PO Box 1500, Cooper Station, New York, NY 10276
Toll Free Phone (800) 577-WINS
email: cardozapub@aol.com
www.cardozapub.com

ABOUT THE AUTHOR

Arnold Snyder is the world's foremost authority on blackjack and one of its greatest players. Snyder is the author of nine books and advanced strategies on the game including *The Blackjack Formula*, the groundbreaking work which revolutionized the ways professional card counters attacked the games, and of course, the best-selling classic, *Blackbelt in Blackjack*. For 23 years, he was the publisher of the highly respected *Blackjack Forum*, a quarterly journal on gambling for professional players.

In January 2003, in recognition for his contributions to the game, Arnold was elected one of the seven charter members of the Blackjack Hall of Fame. Arnold is a high-stakes professional player who has been writing about casino blackjack for well over two decades.

TABLE OF CONTENTS

SECTION ONE
EARNING YOUR WHITE BELT

Big Secrets
Psychic Gamblers

No-Bust Blackjack
Player-Banked Blackjack
Summary

SECTION THREE
EARNING YOUR BLACK BELT

1

INTRODUCTION

I'm going to show you how to beat the casinos at blackjack. This is something I know intimately, because I have been doing it for 30 years. I've also spent the past 25 years teaching other players how to beat the casinos. I'm on a mission. I can't help myself! It's not that I hate the casino industry; I just love taking their money. There's nothing more fun than walking out of a casino with a few thousand more bucks in your pockets than you walked in with. Free money! Watch out! It's addictive! It makes you wonder why anyone goes to work at a regular job.

The only reason you're not doing this right now is that you don't know how to do it yet. Maybe you've read other books on card counting, and you can't figure out why it's not working. Read this book. I guarantee you this book is different. You're going to find a lot of information here you won't find in any of the other books, including all the books by self-proclaimed "experts" who have never in their lives filed their taxes as professional gamblers. They're hack writers, hack mathematicians, and hack blackjack players. Read this book. I wish I had this book when I started playing in 1977. I would have gotten out of my post office job a lot sooner!

I have completely revised and updated *Blackbelt in Blackjack* to conform to today's games and have included information I have never before revealed to a general audience.

This book is a step-by-step complete course on how to beat the casinos at blackjack. Everything you need to know to win money at the game, from the basics of play and the rules of the game, to the most advanced systems used by the pros—it's all within these pages. You'll learn playing strategies, basic and advanced betting techniques, optimal single and multiple-deck play, simple card counting systems you can use to beat most games, plus advanced techniques known only by a handful of pros.

To guide you on your way, I have divided the book into three sections to help your progression from amateur play right up to the top pro level. There are many secrets revealed in these pages that the casinos don't want you to know, and for good reason: They are the strategies professionals use to make their living at the casinos' expense!

In the first section, Earning Your White Belt, we cover the rules and basics of blackjack, and why you can beat the game—with the odds! You'll also learn the basic strategies needed to beat single and multiple-deck games, plus easy-to-use card-counting strategies that are perfect for the realistic conditions you'll actually face in the casinos. You'll learn about the Red Seven, Hi-Lo Lite, and Zen counts, simple ways to increase your edge against the casino, table conditions that influence profit margins, and key bankrolling decisions that are vital to your success.

In the second section, Earning Your Green Belt, we take an in-depth look at professional betting strategies as well as table-hopping, playing multiple hands, and the principles the pros use to decrease flux. We also cover depth-charging, opposition betting, deception, camouflage, surviving surveillance, and more insider secrets.

The third section, Earning Your Black Belt, is for the very serious player. The key topics here are known by few players and are covered in great detail: shuffle tracking, team play and all the issues associated with it—the gorilla (big player), bankroll risks, polygraph testing, investment deals, spotter teams, casinos that cheat, traveling with cash, milking the casino comps, and much more—plus the many secrets professional players use to remain anonymous in the casinos that would bar them from play if they knew who they were.

Remarkably, more than forty years after Edward O. Thorp's *Beat the Dealer* (1962) was published, the game of casino blackjack offers greater profit opportunities to intelligent players than at any time in the history of the game. Few would have predicted this back in 1962, when the only state in the union where you could legally play casino blackjack was Nevada, and blackjack was a distant second to craps in popularity. But, Ed Thorp didn't just write a book in 1962; he transformed an industry and altered the consciousness of literally millions of casino players throughout the world.

If you're a serious blackjack player who wants to beat the casinos for serious money; if you're considering a career as a professional player, this is the book for you. Let's get started.

Why This New Edition?

With this expanded edition of *Blackbelt in Blackjack,* my goal is to make it the single best, and most comprehensive, book on card counting available. I will cover every important topic and concept, in order to provide an overview and a working knowledge of how to do it, how to get away with it, and how to advance from amateur to professional, if that's your plan.

For most players, who are not looking for a professional career at the tables, this book should provide all the information you need to succeed as a card counter. You will learn how to count cards at the same level as the top pros, how to judge profitable games and avoid unbeatable ones, and how to disguise your skills from casino pit bosses and surveillance agents in order to take the money and keep the welcome mat out for your return. If your ultimate goal is to do this at high stakes, playing blackjack for a living and soaking the casinos for megabucks, then this book is your launching pad. You may use it as a guide to take your blackjack career as far as you want to go.

I have attempted to organize the material so that even if you consider yourself a rank beginner, you may start your education here. In the opening chapters, I assume that you do not even know the rules and procedures of how to play the game. You'll find that I have followed this initial primer on the game with the simplest card counting system that can beat most games, and as you get deeper into the material, as increasingly advanced strategies are provided, I have attempted throughout to present explanations of not only how these strategies may be employed, but why they work, and which types of games they may be used in.

What's New?

This 2005 edition of *Blackbelt in Blackjack* is a major expansion of the 1998 edition. Part I, "Earning Your White Belt," contains, in addition to a full explanation of three different card counting systems, discussions on "phony" systems as well as problem gambling. Neither of these topics are covered by most books on card counting, but I feel they are of prime importance to those who are new to advantage play, and especially to those who are considering investing serious time and money.

In Part II, "Earning Your Green Belt," I have greatly expanded the discussion on "table conditions," or how to choose a profitable game. In the past seven years, many forms of "pseudo-blackjack" have been appearing in casinos. Some of these new variations on the game are patented "scams," with names like "Spanish 21" or "SuperFun 21," where the rules seem so liberal as to be almost too good to be true; others are just sneaky forms of traditional blackjack with seemingly "minor" changes, such as blackjacks paying 6 to 5 instead of 3 to 2, or the game is a "fake" single-deck or two-deck game, where the decks are actually being removed from a larger six- or eight-deck shoe. I have also augmented the information on bet-sizing, answering another question that concerns all card counters: How much should I bet in any given game?

There's a lot more information on camouflaging your play, avoiding detection by casino surveillance, and many of the legal issues that concern card counters. If you are considering playing casino blackjack for high stakes, either as a career or simply as an adventure, you must always keep in mind that this can be a risky business. Card counting is legal, and the biggest problem most counters ever have is being barred from the tables if their skill is discovered; but for those who play at the highest levels, the hazards are greater. The casinos sell gambling to the public as "fun," emphasizing the possibility of *winning money from the house*. In fact, the casinos expect *every* player to lose money at their games in the long run. All that glitz and glamour is simply there to lure in the fish, and if they think you're going to walk out with their money, your action will not be welcome.

Just because a casino may offer a game that can be beaten with skillful play does not mean that skillful players are welcome. In fact, using those cameras in the ceiling bubbles, they monitor every big bettor at their tables in order to detect those who might be playing the game with unusual ability. When they find such a player at a high-stakes game, the reaction is swift and not always pleasant; in many cases, the casinos have violated laws themselves in dealing with professional gamblers. Because these types of incidents have become more frequent and more severe in the past few years, I think every book on card counting should provide players with information on how to handle these types of problems. What if you are kicked out of a casino? What if casino security wants to escort you to a "back room?" What if they refuse to cash out your chips? You should know your rights and how to handle some of the common situations that advantage players encounter.

In Part III, "Earning Your Black Belt," I've added more material on playing on teams or with a partner, taking advantage of casino promotions, hustling comps, playing in foreign countries, playing on the Internet, traveling with large amounts of cash, and protecting yourself from dealers who cheat—and, yeah, some of them do.

A Little History...

Little is known of the original blackjack counting systems. In *Beat the Dealer,* Ed Thorp discusses a number of the first systems developers who had colorful names like "Greasy John" and "Stem Smitty." They had privately worked out crude but effective blackjack strategies that they used to win their livelihoods from the Las Vegas blackjack tables. Until the early sixties and the publication of Dr. Thorp's book, most casinos felt that blackjack systems were like all other gambling systems, a lot of bunk. Prior to Thorp, the only "card counting" system that was recognized by the casinos as valid was "casing the aces," in which a player would markedly increase his bet (say from $5 to $500) in the second half of the deck if no aces had been dealt in the first half. Crude as this counting technique was, it was effective and the casinos knew it. Unfortunately, it was extremely easy for the casinos to detect. Because it was such a weak method, and because the players who used it rarely followed anything resembling proven basic strategy, a huge betting spread was necessary for the system to gain an advantage over the house.

Then, in 1956, a group of mathematicians led by Roger Baldwin tediously applied the methods of statistical analysis to the game of blackjack and developed a basic strategy which they published in a technical journal for mathematicians. This strategy, if followed rigorously, would narrow the house edge, making blackjack close to a break-even proposition for the player over the long run. Though a colloquial version of this paper was later published in book form, few gamblers took notice. Gamblers wanted winning systems, not "break even" systems.

One person who took particular note of this technical paper was Dr. Edward O. Thorp, a mathematician. He saw that Baldwin's strategy had been devised on old-fashioned mechanical adding machines, but he had access to what, in the early sixties, was a sophisticated computer. He wrote a more precise program than had been used by the Baldwin group, and subsequently developed a more accurate strategy.

Blackjack is a difficult game to analyze mathematically because the depletion of the deck constantly alters the makeup of the remaining cards, constantly altering the probabilities of winning or losing. It occurred to Dr. Thorp that using a computer he could analyze just how the makeup of the deck affected the possible outcomes of the various hands. His method was unique. He wrote a program to analyze the best strategy and what a player can expect in the long run, assuming various cards had been removed from the deck. He noted that the player's chance of winning was dramatically increased when fives left the deck. In fact, to remove any of the "low" cards—2, 3, 4, 5, 6, or 7—worked in the player's favor in varying degrees. On the other hand, if tens or aces were removed, the player's chances were badly hurt.

Thorp's first winning strategy was based on counting fives. He recommended betting heavily when they were depleted, and also playing a slightly different strategy when no fives were in the deck. His next innovation—upon which most winning card counting systems in use today are based—was called the "ten-count." In this system, tens and non-tens were counted separately. Larger bets were placed as the proportion of tens to non-tens in the deck became larger.

The ten-count system, as Thorp created it, was not easy to learn or apply in a casino. It required keeping two separate "backward" counts, and computing the ratio of tens to non-tens prior to betting and strategy decisions. Thorp played his system with what today would be considered a wild betting spread, sometimes jumping from a table-minimum bet of a dollar to a table-maximum of $500. Casinos were unaware of the power of Thorp's system, especially when they saw some of the "unusual" plays he made—like splitting 8s vs. dealer up-cards of tens and aces—and many continued dealing their single-deck, hand-held games to him down to the last card. Players able to use Thorp's system had an enormous advantage over the house, and players capable of following even a crude approximation of the strategy could win big if they used even a moderate betting spread in the deeply dealt single-deck games that predominated.

Once the Vegas casinos realized a legitimate winning system was being employed at their blackjack tables, they took drastic action, changing the rules of the game. This was in 1964, eight years after the first publication of the relatively accurate basic strategy, and two years after the advent of Thorp's *Beat The Dealer.*

The rule changes did not last long because, to the casinos' dismay, players stayed away from the tables rather than play against the new rules.

Casinos began losing a lot of money. So, bracing themselves for the worst, they changed back to the original rules.

The worst never came; in fact, the opposite occurred—blackjack became the most popular table game in U.S. casinos. Everyone, it seemed, believed they could beat the game, but few put in the time and effort to learn a legitimate system. Many blackjack systems were sold that were not mathematically valid, and players who did have valid systems often had no understanding of normal fluctuation. They overbet their limited bankrolls and tapped out before they ever had a chance to see the long run profits. Most importantly, casinos learned to recognize card counters by their playing styles.

Card counters jumped their bets suddenly, they paid inordinate attention to everybody's cards, they were quiet, they concentrated, and they didn't drink or socialize. They were often young collegiate types who didn't fit in with the normal run of tourists and vacationing businessmen.

Once spotted, a suspected card counter would be silently observed by the pit boss or "eye in the sky." If suspicions were confirmed, the dealer would be signaled to "shuffle-up" on the counter. If the suspect changed tables, the "heat" would follow him. If he did not leave the casino, he would be asked to leave the blackjack tables, and ultimately ordered to leave the casino. Thus, the casinos weeded out the few competent players and let hoards of fools who thought they could beat the tables with sloppy play and invalid systems play to their hearts' content.

The Game Today

A small number of card counters have still managed to profit from the game of blackjack. Two factors contribute to the success of the present day counter. First of all, he knows the basic math of the game—he has studied valid systems and has a realistic attitude about his long and short run expectations. Secondly, he knows the basic psychology of the casino environment. He understands how casinos detect counters and disguises his play. He is an actor; if he senses heat, he leaves, maybe returning later when different casino personnel are running the show. He doesn't take chances. There are lots of casinos.

Although four decades have passed since the first valid card counting system was published, many casinos still offer beatable blackjack games, and the math of card counting is easier than ever. The systems presented in this book are among the easiest-to-learn professional level systems ever devised. This does not mean that you can learn to beat the game of blackjack in an hour. If you are serious about playing for profit, you should plan to spend quite a bit of time studying and practicing. I will say this, however: Any person with average math ability could learn to count cards at a professional level.

The difficulty of making money as a card counter isn't in the arithmetic, but in the psychology. Some people are good actors; some are not. Some are adept at reading attitudes and manipulating people, and some aren't. To make it as a card counter, you must often be friendly to dealers and pit bosses, while at the same time deceiving them into thinking you're just another dumb gambler. Most card counters who experience any long-term success thrive on this exhilarating espionage-like aspect of the game. You must be part rogue and part charlatan. You must be cool under pressure. You must have enough money behind you to weather losing streaks without financial worry. You must thrill to beating the casinos at their own game. If you're not in it for the fun as much as for the money, you'll never make it as a counter. Card counting is boring, once mastered. It's work. Few who try card counting stick with it. It's like most games—chess, tennis, even the stock market; many people "know how to play," but only a few become masters.

I realize that most of the readers of this book will not go on to become masters of blackjack strategy. With this in mind, you'll find many simplified, albeit less powerful, methods that the casual player may use to win at the blackjack tables. I will also attempt to provide clear explanations of the more powerful techniques so that the casual player will at least understand how and why the advanced systems work. By understanding these concepts, a beginning player who has not developed the skill to apply them will, hopefully, realize his limited abilities, and will not entertain false visions of himself as an unbeatable player.

One thing you must remember: Casinos don't give money away; you have to take it. And contrary to appearances, casinos are holding on to their money with both fists. You've got to be slick to take them on for high stakes, and walk away with your shirt.

SECTION ONE

EARNING YOUR WHITE BELT

2

THE GREAT BLACKJACK HOAX
An Irreverent Overview of Card Counting

Forty-five years ago, the top casino table game in this country, in terms of gross revenues, was craps. Craps was an all-American pastime during World War II, and after the war the state of Nevada provided a way for old war buddies to get together and shoot dice through the years.

Today, thanks to Ed Thorp, casinos make their money from blackjack players. They make a lot of money from bad card counters as well. Authors and system-peddlers also make a lot of money from blackjack players who are, or want to be, card counters. It's a big business, but the people who make the most money from it are not the counters themselves but the casinos. Card counters, on the whole, are losing money on their investments. Players who actually profit from card counting form a small, elite group.

A Card Counter Is Born

I am a card counter. I got hooked on blackjack thirty years ago to the point of obsession. I love the game; there's nothing as exciting as beating a casino and walking out the door with more money in your pockets than when you entered. To walk in with the ability to beat the house, knowing the casino will do everything it can to stop you, gives a James Bond, Spy-vs-Spy flavor to the experience. The heart races. The feeling is not unlike that which I recall from my childhood when all the kids in my neighborhood would choose up sides for "cops and robbers." I'd forgotten how much fun it was to hide, sneak, run, hold your breath in anticipation...

Then I discovered card counting. It took me a year of weekend trips to Nevada, some dozen books on card counting, and another half-dozen books on mathematics, to learn that I didn't have enough money to play the game professionally. Prior to the 1980s, many blackjack authors seemed to neglect the risk factor, and didn't provide much guidance on bet-sizing according to bankroll. The counter's edge is small, and the fluctuation of capital is huge. If you don't have enough money, you won't last.

I'll never forget my first trip to Nevada as a card counter. I was driving a car that was 15 years old and over the hill—it guzzled gas and leaked oil. Winding up through the Sierra Nevada Mountains on my way to Lake Tahoe and the casinos of Stateline, I had to stop twice to add a quart of oil and give my overheated wreck a rest. I was with a friend, and we were splitting the cost of the trip. The way we figured it, after paying for gas, oil, motel room and meals, we'd have about $55 left over to play at the $1 blackjack tables.

When I pulled over to the shoulder of the road for my second oil stop, I said to my friend, "It's hard to believe that we're on our way to becoming wealthy. I hope my car makes it up this damn mountain."

"A year from now," my friend responded, "you'll look back on this day and laugh. This is just the beginning."

One year and a dozen trips to Nevada later, I thought back to that first trip and I laughed. I was again on my way to Stateline, this time alone. My car had long since broken down, beyond repair, and I didn't have the money to replace it. I was traveling by bus, and the way I figured it, if I was ahead by twenty-five bucks the first day, I could get a motel room and stay for another day. Otherwise, it was back to the Greyhound station that night. About that time I started to realize I'd been fooling myself into believing I'd get rich easily at this card game.

Why Blackjack Is So Popular

Blackjack is the casinos' best moneymaker precisely because people believe the game can be beaten. Casinos are forever bemoaning their losses to card counters, and constantly changing their rules and dealing procedures to make their games tougher for these feared blackjack experts. Casino floormen, with increasing frequency, unceremoniously bar suspected counters from their tables. Promoting this paranoia is one of the most successful advertising campaigns ever developed. Not one person in a thousand has what it takes to make any significant amount of money playing blackjack, but hundreds of thousands of people have given it a try.

Card counting is not difficult for the dedicated practitioner, but few people are dedicated enough, and, as most players discover the hard way, there is more to being a successful card counter than the ability to count cards.

In cynical moments, I see the American public being taken for a ride by the strange bedfellows of the casino industry and the blackjack systems sellers. A tremendous effort is being made to convince people that card counters can get rich quick at the casino blackjack tables.

I don't mean to imply that all blackjack system sellers are trying to bilk the public—I am a system seller. I'm the author of nine books on casino blackjack, and have written operating manuals for two home computer blackjack programs, and articles on card counting for numerous magazines, and I've acted as informal consultant for a number of high-stakes international counting teams. I know the game can be beaten. I have played professionally for many years myself, and I know many full- and part-time card counters who regularly take the tables for piles of money. I know a few players who have made fortunes playing blackjack.

But the successful pros are few and far between. Their dedication to the game is beyond that of the average counter—they live and breathe blackjack. They devour every written word on the subject; they drill and practice until they count cards in their sleep. They know professional blackjack as a dog-eat-dog business.

Some blackjack system authors have been honest about their negative experiences at the blackjack tables. Most publishers, however, aren't so forthright, and the media in general isn't any better. It's not newsworthy to say, "Gambler loses money." Advertisements for blackjack systems promise everything from instant wealth to private airplanes and priced-to-move personal islands.

The average player has no way of knowing that the author of his system objects to the publisher's advertising claims, and sometimes to large portions of the ghostwritten text. In fact, publishers, promoters, and imitators have abused the most respected names in the field of blackjack.

Compound all of this misinformation about card counting with the dozens of books on the market that teach totally inaccurate count strategies, "money management" systems, strategies so weak as to be a complete waste of time or too difficult for anyone to master, and you can begin to fathom why card counting is the best thing that ever happened to the casino industry in this country.

The Great Blackjack Myth

In New Jersey, in 1982, representing himself before the state supreme court, the late Ken Uston, renowned author of numerous books on card counting, won a landmark case against the casinos. Today, the fourteen Atlantic City casinos may no longer bar skillful players from their tables. The immediate response of the casinos to this law was to stop dealing a game that card counters could beat. This is, and always has been, a very easy thing for the casinos to do. Converting their 6-deck shoes to 8-deck shoes, the dealers were simply instructed to deal out only four decks between shuffles. Voilà! Card counting became a waste of time!

Within a few months, however, the A.C. casinos threw in the towel and reverted to their prior practice of cutting off only two decks. In an unofficial boycott reminiscent of what happened in Nevada eighteen years earlier when some Las Vegas casinos tried to change the rules of the game to thwart Thorp's followers, the players again forced the casinos to loosen up or lose it all.

Never forget that blackjack exists as a beatable game only because the casinos choose to keep it that way. They do not need mechanical shuffle machines, or electronic card readers, or any other high-tech contraptions to eliminate the potential profits that card counters might extract from the tables. A simple change of rules or dealing procedures could make every blackjack game in the world unbeatable by any card counting system, no matter how advanced, in an instant. But the casinos simply cannot afford to let that happen.

To this day, however, the 8-deck shoes still predominate in Atlantic City, making them some of the most difficult blackjack games in the world. Many Nevada casinos, as well as casinos in some two-dozen other states and around the globe, currently offer blackjack games that are unprofitable for card counters, primarily due to the large betting spread necessary to get a small edge. In most cases, casinos protect their games from counters with poor deck penetration. The casinos, naturally, want players to believe that every unbeatable sucker trap, just because it is called "blackjack," is still a game of skill. It is common knowledge among casino executives that hopeful but incompetent and self-deluded card counters, like other "system players," are a major source of income. If card counters actually stopped playing blackjack in the lousy Atlantic City games, the casinos' blackjack profits would nosedive.

What many people—including most card counters, system sellers, dealers, pit bosses, and the media at large—fail to comprehend is that being a successful professional card counter takes no less ability, study, dedication, time, and luck than any other profession. Card counters attempt to inconspicuously, legally, and consistently siphon large sums of money from a multi-billion dollar industry, which utilizes the most advanced surveillance techniques this side of the Pentagon.

Most card counters believe in the Great Blackjack Myth that flatly states that *a card counter can beat the game of casino blackjack.* The truth is that some card counting strategies can beat some blackjack games, depending on the number of decks being shuffled together, the number of players at the table, the number of cards being dealt out prior to reshuffling, the rule variations, the betting spread being employed, the size of the counter's bankroll, the actual skill of the player at applying the system, and so on. In casinos outside of New Jersey, the threat of being barred causes many counters to kill their own chances of winning. In Atlantic City, despite the no-barring law, card counters must still hide their skill because the casinos may enforce other betting restrictions on suspected counters, which eliminate the potential profits from counting cards. So, counters seek out more crowded, less conspicuous tables. They hold down their betting spreads, and they make occasional "dumb" playing decisions. All of these camouflage tactics cut into, and often kill, the counter's small potential edge.

Card counters, as a subculture, have developed a unique jargon. One term that all counters understand is "heat," which means that a pit boss is sweating your action, dealers shuffle the cards any time you raise your bet, or, worst of all, a floorman reads you your rights: "You may play any of the casino games except blackjack; if you attempt to place a bet at any blackjack table, you may be arrested for trespassing."

Many counters think they're getting away with murder when they don't get heat from casinos. The truth is that the casinos are swarming with counters, and most are easily detectable. By standing behind crowded blackjack tables, and counting down the cards as they are dealt, I can spot many obvious card counters in the course of a few hours. If I can spot them so easily, you can be sure the casino counter-catchers can spot them. Most counters follow obvious betting schemes, and to be sure, most counters are likely to get heat at one point or another in their playing careers, especially if they don't camouflage their play, although most of the time counters are not bothered by casino personnel. If the casinos actually gave heat to all the card counters at their tables, they would lose hundreds of customers, and their money, every busy night.

I'm not trying to give the impression that dealers and pit bosses are talented con artists who can act like they're afraid of card counters while knowing most counters are losers. Lower-level casino employees, such as dealers and pit bosses, know very little about card counting, and even those few who are trained to count cards in order to recognize their adversaries, often believe that all card counters pose a real threat to their profits.

There is no reason for the upper management of the casinos to educate dealers and pit bosses about the realities of card counting. Dealers and pit bosses, like many in the gambling subculture, are often highly superstitious, and ignorant of the mathematics of any of the games themselves. Counters love to share stories about superstitious pit bosses, and to most, casino management is dumb. This reminds me of Lenny Bruce's "Religions, Inc." bit where the fire-and-brimstone preacher is accused of being dumb. "Yeah, I'm a big dummy," he responds to his detractors. "I've got two Lincoln Continentals, that's how damn dumb I am!"

The Future of Blackjack

So, where is this all going? Are the days numbered for card counters? Many players fear this may be so, especially considering all the technological countermeasures that have been developed in the past decade.

Automatic shuffling machines are being introduced on more and more tables. These devices make shuffle tracking impossible, and they make it faster, and cheaper, for the dealers to shuffle more frequently. The new continuous shuffle machines make card counting itself impossible. Various types of "auto-peek" devices are now extensively employed to read the dealers' hole-cards, eliminating the possibilities of most legal hole-card strategies—tell play, warp play, first-basing.

Surveillance software that analyzes the skill levels of blackjack players is now used in many major casinos. Counters who have fooled the pit bosses for years suddenly are called up on a computer. Prototypes of "smart" blackjack tables—equipped with shoes that can read the cards as they're dealt, keep track of the players' hands and strategies, and record the players' betting histories via magnetized chips—are now being introduced in Nevada.

Even more ominous than these technological horrors are the legal problems card counters face. In Nevada, the Gaming Control Board is supposed to be an agency that protects the rights of both the casinos and the players, ensuring the fairness of the games. To the consternation of blackjack players, this official state agency has officially taken the position that Nevada's cheating statute, which prohibits the casinos from altering the table games in a way that would change the frequency of the payouts, does not apply to blackjack. Because of this ruling, many Nevada casinos now train their dealers in hand-held games to count cards and shuffle up any time the game favors the players, only dealing when the cards favor the house.

In New Jersey, the state supreme court has ruled that players whose civil rights have been violated by the casinos—even if those players are cheated at the tables—may not sue the casinos for damages. They must settle their differences with the Casino Control Commission, a state agency which claims no authority to order monetary reparations to casino patrons.

Card counters must accept the fact that the state gaming regulatory agencies are often corrupt. These "protective" agencies are in fact puppets of the casinos, controlled by that immensely wealthy industry. As a result, one of the most rewarding aspects of card counting is taking money from some truly evil entities. The dealers, pit bosses, shift managers, hosts, and most of the people a card counter will actually come into contact with in the casinos, are not themselves corrupt; they're worker ants, in the same way that people who work on the assembly line at a cigarette factory, or a munitions plant, are just people who have found a job to do, and they try to do it well in order to pay the rent and raise their families.

But lurking in the shadows of this gambling business are some truly slimy bastards. If you get into card counting with any serious amount of money, you will learn firsthand what a nasty business this is. Though it has been shown over and over in the courts that card counting is perfectly legal—nothing more than using your brain to play your hands—counters are viewed within the industry as parasites, cheats, and enemies to be eliminated by whatever means necessary.

Casinos throughout the world keep "mug books" of card counters' names and photographs, and these photos are hawked and sold on the open market. Despite the fact that these blacklists might violate various consumer laws, the Fair Credit Reporting Act, civil rights, laws against libel, slander, and the invasion of privacy, the state courts and police agencies throughout the U.S. and around the world systematically use these mug books to harass card counters and deny them access to the gaming tables.

The mega-corporations that have taken over the casino industry have money and political power; professional gamblers, on the other hand, are nobodies, and lawmakers know which side their bread is buttered on. The majority of the American public is ignorant of the issues, and the small handful of professional players who see their civil rights being trampled are like a small voice in the wilderness.

When Bill Bible, the Chairman of the Nevada Gaming Control Board, was appointed by President Clinton to the new Federal Commission on Gaming in 1997, the American press reported extensively on the opposition to this appointment by the religious right. The debate centered on the pro-gambling vs. anti-gambling issues, with Bible portrayed by the right wing as the penultimate pro-gambling apologist. Ironically, all the professional gamblers I knew were more vehemently opposed to Bible's appointment than the anti-gambling lobby, as he is held by many to be personally responsible for the Nevada casinos' right to violate the state's cheating statutes at blackjack.

So, is this forty-plus-year war with the casinos almost over? Is this the beginning of the end? Hardly. Despite the technology, politics, legal persecution, and immense financial strength of the casino industry, I remain optimistic. With legal blackjack games now being offered in more than 25 states, there are more profit opportunities for card counters today than at any time in the history of card counting. Despite four-plus decades of stupid, sometimes illegal, and often very costly countermeasures, the casinos are not so stupid as to give up all their profits from their biggest moneymaking table game.

Blackjack as a Sport

People enjoy taking risks, and gambling, of any type, is a rush. Casino blackjack combines this run for the money with a competitive angle, a game of wit and subterfuge. Every turn of the cards is a cliffhanger. Blackjack has become popular not because most people think they can get rich playing it, but because it has been shown to be a game of skill. Card counting is more interesting than picking a number on a roulette wheel, more challenging than pulling the handle of a slot machine. Many people who play blackjack have little interest in any of the other casino games, and most do not seriously dream of getting rich at the blackjack tables. Like myself, they are often people who had never entered a casino until they'd discovered that one of the games could be beaten by applying an intelligent, systematic strategy. It's unfortunate that so many gurus, authors, and publishers believe that people have to be tantalized by great wealth to interest them in casino blackjack. You don't have to make a hundred thousand dollars to make this game exciting. If you're dedicated and you practice hard, you'll come out ahead of the game in the long run. Why risk your life savings? For most people, the reward is in the play, not the pay.

Many years ago, I realized that the fastest way to make money from card counting would be to open my own casino. Unfortunately, my $300 savings was not sufficient seed capital for this venture. I did the next best thing—I started selling inside information to other players. I set up a network of professional players, mathematicians, and computer experts to share facts, experiences, and research, and started publishing a quarterly technical journal. But, I never stopped playing the game for fun, mostly for "nickel" ($5) chips. In the past few years, my connections with professional blackjack teams and big-money players have enabled me to play a lot more at higher stakes, but the game has remained just that for me, and the challenge still means as much as the money.

I wouldn't advise any new blackjack enthusiast to quit work and hock his car in order to stake his million-dollar fantasy. If, as you practice basic strategy, you feel the urge to dream about piloting your own airplane to your private island in the Caribbean, think of these reveries in the same way that thousands of chess players imagine going head-to-head with Garry Kasparov, or the way a tennis player might fantasize about playing Roger Federer. The fact that only a handful of tennis players will ever be professionals does not keep millions of amateurs from playing with true passion.

If you have a passion for blackjack, and you apply yourself diligently, the game will likely pay you dividends in both money and enjoyment. There are, to be sure, a handful of blackjack legends who have made a fortune from the tables, and there are many more unknowns who have done the same, steadily, quietly, and unsung. I suspect a few readers of this book may ultimately join those professional players; I know a few readers of the last edition did. For all I know, you may be among the pros by the time the next edition of this book rolls off the press.

For me, a major joy of this game, however, will still come from discovering, analyzing, and revealing its secrets. Over the next fifteen years, I expect to see shuffle-tracking strategies expounded upon by other authors. I feel sure that "lite" strategy tables—simplified strategy charts that are easy-to-use—will gain popularity. I expect to see more running-count systems with accurate "Kelly" betting strategies, and further variations on my simplified methods of true count adjustments. I also expect the casino industry to continue moaning and crying, as a small handful of players get smarter, the games get tougher, surveillance gets more high-tech, and the majority of card counters keep losing their shirts, due to their own sloppy play and general incompetence.

The information that follows is the information you need to keep a few steps ahead of the casinos. Study it. Learn it. And give 'em hell.

3

HOW TO PLAY CASINO BLACKJACK

Before learning any winning strategy, it's important that you familiarize yourself with the game of blackjack, as played in a casino, including all its rules, procedures, and options.

Blackjack is one of the easiest casino games to play. After an hour of practice with a deck of cards, following the procedures in this chapter, you will find that you can comfortably play blackjack in any casino. You cannot beat the game this easily, but the rules and procedures are simple enough that anyone could understand and play the game with this small amount of practice.

The Deal

The cards are dealt from the dealer's left to right, thus the designation of the first seat on the dealer's left as **first base**. The last seat is referred to as **third base**.

Blackjack was originally dealt from a single 52-card deck of standard playing cards. Many casinos now shuffle together anywhere from two to eight decks. If more than two decks are used, the shuffled cards are placed into a specially designed box on the table called a **shoe**, which facilitates dealing.

The object of the game is to get a total of 21, or as close to it as possible, without going over 21, or **busting**, and beating the total of the dealer's hand. Players do not play against each other, but rather against the

33

dealer, who follows house rules in playing his hand. If a player and dealer tie, it is called a **push**, and neither wins. If the player busts, he loses even if the dealer busts.

In totaling the hands, cards valued 2 through 9 count exactly at their face value, while cards valued 10, jack, queen, and king each count for 10. The ace may count as either 1 or 11, whichever the player prefers.

A card's suit is irrelevant. Any two-card hand that consists of one ace and one ten-valued card is called a **blackjack**, or a **natural**, and is an automatic win, paid off at the rate of $3 to every $2 bet, or 1 1/2 to 1.

The Table

This is how a casino blackjack table appears from the top:

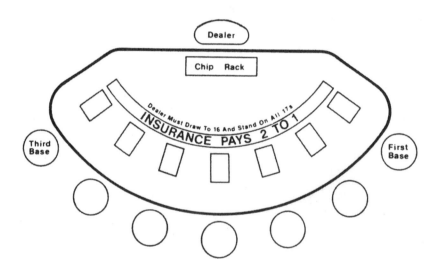

The large circles represent the seats, which can accommodate one to seven players. The small rectangles represent the marked areas on the table where players place their bets. There is usually a **limit** sign posted on the table, which states the minimum and maximum bets allowed. Table minimums may run from $1 to $100, and maximums may run from $25 to $10,000. $5 minimum tables are most common, and some states, such as Colorado, have $5 maximums. Some casinos, but not all, also post the rule variations for their games on the table.

"Hard" Hands and "Soft" Hands

> ## SOFT HAND:
> Any hand in which an ace can be counted
> as 11, without busting, is a soft hand.

Example: You hold an ace and a 7, totaling a *soft 18*. Another example: You hold an ace, a 9, and an 8, which is a *hard 18*. In this case, if you counted the ace as 11, your total would be 28, a bust. It's important that you be able to read your hand's total value, hard or soft, quickly and effortlessly. When you begin to learn winning strategies, you'll find that hard and soft hands require different decisions. (Remember, any hand with no aces is always considered a hard hand.)

The Play of the Hands

The dealer shuffles the deck or decks, and then offers the shuffled cards to be cut by a player. Sometimes, in hand-held games, games where the dealer physically holds the cards in his hands when he deals, this cut is done exactly as in any home game. The dealer sets the cards on the table, and a player simply cuts a portion of the cards from the top of the deck onto the table. In all shoe games, games where the cards are kept in a plastic device known as a shoe, however, and in most hand-held games, a "cut card" is used. The is a specially colored card that a player inserts into the deck to indicate the cut point, where the dealer then completes the cut.

After the cut, the dealer **burns** a card, and sometimes multiple cards. This means that he removes the top card(s) to the bottom of the deck in a single-deck game, or into the **discard tray** in a shoe game.

Before any cards are dealt, all bets must be placed. Each player has a betting spot on the table on which his wager is made. The dealer then deals two cards to each player. The players' cards may be dealt face up or face down. In hand-held games, facedown is more common, while in shoe games face-up is typical. Since players do not play against each other, but only against the dealer, and since the dealer must play his hand according to preset house rules regardless of what any player holds, it makes no difference for most basic strategy players if the hands are dealt face up or face down. If the cards are dealt face up, players are not allowed to touch their cards. If dealt face down, each player must pick up his two cards in order to see his hand and make his playing decisions.

Insurance

In most U.S. casinos, insurance is allowed. Prior to playing any hands, if the dealer's upcard is an ace, he will ask, "insurance?" To understand this option, you must know that if the dealer's first two cards are an ace and a ten-valued card—blackjack—he will automatically beat every player hand on the table except for another blackjack, which would push his hand.

So, when the dealer shows an ace upcard, the player hands are in danger. By offering **insurance**, the dealer gives the players a chance to make a side-bet that he has a natural, i.e., a ten-valued card in the hole. Note the specially marked area on the table layout for insurance bets. If the player is willing to bet that the dealer does, in fact, have a ten-valued card in the hole, for a blackjack, the player places an amount of money equal to up to one-half his original bet in the insurance space. So, if a player has $10 bet on the hand, he may make an insurance bet of up to $5, but no more.

After all insurance bets are placed, the dealer peeks at his hole card. If he has a natural, he immediately turns it up and proceeds to pay off insurance bets, and to collect all original wagers placed by the players. Since insurance bets are paid at the rate of 2 to 1, a player with a $10 original bet, and a $5 insurance bet, would lose his original $10, since the dealer's natural is an automatic win, but would be paid $10 (2 to 1) for his $5 insurance bet. Thus, the player breaks even.

If a player has a blackjack when the dealer has an ace up, instead of offering insurance, the dealer usually offers "even money" to this player. This means that before the dealer checks his hole card, the player may accept an even money win for his blackjack. Many players do not understand that an offer of even money is identical to an offer of insurance when a player has a blackjack.

This is because a player who takes insurance when he has a blackjack will ultimately be paid even money whether or not the dealer has a ten in the hole. Consider: with $10 bet on your blackjack hand, and a $5 insurance bet, if the dealer does not have a ten in the hole, then you'll lose your $5 insurance bet, but win $15 (1 1/2 to 1) for your $10 blackjack hand. That's a net win of $10, or even money.

On the other hand, if the dealer does have a ten in the hole, then you win $10 (2 to 1) on your $5 insurance bet, but push on your $10 blackjack hand, again for a net win of $10—even money. So, if you have a blackjack, an offer of even money is the same thing as an offer of insurance.

If the dealer doesn't have a natural, he immediately collects all insurance bets, and the play of the hands resumes, starting with the first base player and working clockwise. In some casinos, dealers do not check their hole cards or settle insurance bets until after the play of the hands.

Hitting

Assuming the player does not have a natural, which is an automatic win, the player's most common decision is whether to hit or stand. **Hitting** is taking another card; **standing** is refusing one. Example: A player holds a 5 and an 8 for a total of 13. Wanting to get closer to 21, he signals the dealer for a hit. In a face-up game (i.e., a game in which all players' cards are dealt face up, so players are not allowed to touch their cards), the player signals for a hit by scratching or tapping the tabletop with his finger. In a facedown game where the player must pick up his first two cards, the player signals for a hit by scratching or tapping on the tabletop with the edge of his cards. The dealer then deals the player another card face-up on the table. The player may not touch this or any subsequent cards dealt to him. Let's say this card is a deuce—the player may now decide to stand or hit again. The player may hit as many times as he chooses, so long as his total does not exceed 21.

Standing

A player signals he wants to stand by either waving his hand sideways, palm down in a face-up game, or, in a facedown game, by sliding his original two cards facedown beneath his wager.

Busting

In a facedown game, if a player hits his hand to a total of more than 21, he should immediately lay his original two cards face up on the table. The dealer will collect the player's wager. In a face-up game, players don't have to do anything, as the dealer will see the bust, sometimes remarking, "too many," as he collects the bet.

Doubling Down

A player may also elect to **double down** on his first two cards. This means that the player doubles the size of his bet, and receives one and only one hit card. In the face-up game players double down by placing an amount of money equal to the original bet on the table, beside the money already wagered. In the facedown game, the player places his original two cards face up on the table behind his bet, then places an amount of money equal to his original bet beside it in his betting spot. A casino may have restrictions on when a player may double down: Some allow doubling down on any two original cards; others restrict the play to hard totals of 9, 10, and 11 only, some to 10 and 11 only. There are even a few casinos that allow doubling down on more than two cards, but this rule variation is rare. Many casinos allow players to "double for less" than the original wager, but none allow players to double down for more.

Splitting Pairs

If a player holds two cards of the same value, he may **split** the pair into two separate hands. For example, let's say you're dealt two 8s. You do not have to play this as a single hand totaling 16. By placing an amount of money equal to your original bet on the table, you may play each 8 as a separate hand. Again, in the face-up game, you do not touch the cards, but simply take this option by putting your money on the table. In the facedown game, you separate each of your cards face-up on the table, and add the bet for the second hand beside one of the cards. When you split aces, most casinos do not allow more than one additional card on each ace. Likewise, most casinos allow non-ace pairs to be re-split up to four hands. If, for instance, you split a pair of 8s, and received another 8 on one of the hands, most casinos would allow you to re-split and play a third hand.

Usually, split aces may not be re-split. If you receive a ten on one of your split aces, this hand counts as 21, but is not a blackjack. You will not be paid 3 to 2. The dealer will complete his hand, and if he also totals 21, it's a push. Most casinos, though, allow you to split any ten-valued cards. For instance, you may split a jack and a king. Some casinos, however, require that only identical ten-valued cards, such as two kings, may be split. As with split aces, if you split tens and draw an ace on one of them, it is not counted as a blackjack.

Unless told otherwise, assume the standard pair-splitting rules: Any pair may be split; any pair, except aces, may be re-split; split aces receive only one card each. There are also some casinos that allow you to double down after splitting. For instance, you split a pair of 8s, and on one of the hands you're dealt a 3 for a total of 11. Some casinos will allow you to double down on this hand if you like.

Surrender

In a few casinos, the player may **surrender** his first two cards and lose only half his bet. This means that the hand will not be played out. The dealer will collect the player's cards and exactly one half the amount the player had wagered. The other half of the wager is returned to the player. Surrender is not allowed if the dealer has a natural, in which case the player loses his whole bet. When the Atlantic City casinos first opened in the late 1970s, they did allow players to surrender before the dealer checked for a natural. This rule is called **early surrender**. It is not currently available in Atlantic City, but has occasionally been offered at other casinos. (The original surrender rule is now often referred to as **late surrender**.) Some casinos in Europe and Asia allow early surrender against a ten, but not against an ace.

No Hole Card

In some casinos, the dealer does not check his hole card until after all the players complete their hands; in others, the dealer does not even deal his hole card until the players' hands are completed. This means that the dealer may ultimately get a natural and beat the table. If a player had doubled down or split a pair, he would lose only his original bet if he were playing in any U.S. or Canadian casino, but the European **no-hole-card** rule is different. In most European casinos, if the player doubles down or splits a pair, he will lose all double and/or split bets if the dealer gets a natural.

Multi-Action

Some casinos use special table layouts that allow players to place up to three simultaneous bets. In these **Multi-Action** games, the player will play his hand once, but the dealer will play out his hand three times. He will use the same upcard, but will draw a new hole card, and hit cards if necessary, against each successive player bet. In these games, all other blackjack rules and options remain the same.

The Dealer's Hand

The dealer completes his own hand only after all players have completed theirs. The dealer has no options: He is not allowed to double down or split any pair, he's not allowed to surrender, and he must hit any hand totaling less than 17 and stand on any hand of 17 or more. The only exception to this is that some casinos require the dealer to hit a soft 17 (such as A, 6). In these casinos, the dealer stands on hard 17 or over, and soft 18 or over. In no casino does the dealer have any choice about how to play his hand. He must follow house rules. If, for instance, you are playing in a face-up game and the dealer sees that you have stood on a total of 15, when his hand totals 16, he does not automatically win. He must hit his hand when his total is less than 17, and he will only win your bet if he does not bust.

That covers all of the rules of standard casino blackjack, although there are some obscure practices you may encounter that do not affect the game significantly: A few casinos offer bonuses for certain player hands, such as three sevens, or 6, 7, 8 of the same suit; some casinos offer a blackjack variation called **Double Exposure** in which both of the dealer's first two cards are dealt face up, but the dealer wins all ties. This is a relatively rare game, requiring a different strategy.

A few casinos also offer various side-bet options—Over/Under, Royal Match, and Super Sevens are among the most common. These types of options allow the player to place a separate bet, usually in a specially marked area of the table, and do not affect the play of the regular blackjack hand.

WARNING:

Many casinos today also offer games that look like blackjack, but in fact are NOT. At least they're not the traditional game that can be beaten with card counting. In some of these games, a blackjack only pays even money, or 6:5, instead of the traditional 3 to 2. Another variation, in which blackjacks pay even money, called "Super Fun 21," (Yeah, super fun for the casino that's taking your money!) is a pseudo-blackjack variation that mimics the traditional game. In some games, ten-value cards have been removed from the shoe, another sucker game to avoid. This awful game is usually called "Spanish 21." It was apparently invented during the Spanish Inquisition as a form of torture!

EARNING YOUR WHITE BELT

If you have never played blackjack in a casino, then you should spend an hour playing with a friend or just by yourself, until you feel comfortable with the game. If you have a computer, there are many excellent and inexpensive software programs available that provide realistic practice games. When practicing, whether on a computer or your kitchen table, don't worry about minor details, such as the precise method of "scratching" for a hit. You'll understand the correct signals within a few minutes of observation in a casino. If you're not quite sure of some signal or rule variations when you are playing in a casino, the dealer will be happy to explain if you ask. There is no harm in appearing clueless; casinos cater to tourists, and explaining the procedures of the games is a regular part of their job.

4

BASIC STRATEGY

Once you understand how to play blackjack, you can get into a game without losing your bankroll. If you make your decisions by playing your hunches, you will lose in the long run—there is only one correct decision for any given play, and that decision is based strictly on mathematics. Whether or not you should hit or stand, double down or split a pair, depends on what the laws of probability dictate. Mathematicians, using computers, have matched every possible hand you might hold against every possible dealer upcard—and it's their way or the highway.

> ## BASIC STRATEGY:
> Basic strategy is the best way, mathematically, to play your hands if you are not counting cards.

Depending on the rules and the number of decks in use, basic strategy will usually cut the house edge to no more than about 1/2% over the player. This makes blackjack the most advantageous game in the casino, even if you are not a card counter.

To explain why various basic strategy decisions work would require extensive mathematical proof. Unless you understand the math, and have a computer to work it out, you'll have to accept basic strategy on faith.

There is an underlying logic to basic strategy, however, which can be understood by anyone who understands the rules of blackjack.

Why Basic Strategy Works

In a 52-card deck there are 16 ten-valued cards: four tens, four jacks, four queens, and four kings. (For purposes of simplification, when I refer to a card as a "ten" or "X," it is understood to mean any 10, jack, queen, or king.) Every other denomination has only four cards, one of each suit. You are four times more likely to pull a ten out of the deck than, say, a deuce. Because of this, when the dealer's upcard is "high" — 7, 8, 9, X, or A — he has a greater likelihood of finishing with a strong total than when his upcard is "low" — 2, 3, 4, 5, or 6.

So, if the dealer's upcard is a 7, 8, 9, X, or A, and you hold a "stiff" — any hand totaling 12 through 16 — you would hit. When the dealer's hand indicates strength, you do not want to stand with a weak hand. Even though when you hit a stiff you're more likely to bust than to make a pat hand, you will lose more money in the long run if you stand on these weak hands when the dealer shows strength.

On the other hand, if the dealer's upcard is 2, 3, 4, 5, or 6, and you hold a stiff hand, you should stand. Since he must hit his stiff hands, and since stiffs bust a large percentage of the time, hitting your weak hand isn't the right play.

Similarly, if the dealer's upcard indicates he may be stiff, it's in your favor to double down or to split pairs, thereby getting more money onto the table when the dealer has a good chance of busting. You double down and split pairs less often when the dealer shows a strong upcard.

That's the basic logic of casino blackjack. There are exceptions to these oversimplified guidelines, as the actual basic strategy decision for any given hand is determined by working out all of the mathematical probabilities, but this gives you a working idea of the strategy.

GENERIC BASIC STRATEGY
FOR ANY NUMBER OF DECKS

	2	3	4	5	6	7	8	9	X	A
STAND										
17	S	S	S	S	S	S	S	S	S	S
16	S	S	S	S	S	H	H	H	H	H
15	S	S	S	S	S	H	H	H	H	H
14	S	S	S	S	S	H	H	H	H	H
13	S	S	S	S	S	H	H	H	H	H
12	H	H	S	S	S	H	H	H	H	H
A7	S	S	S	S	S	S	S	H	H	H
DOUBLE DOWN										
11	D	D	D	D	D	D	D	D	D	D
10	D	D	D	D	D	D	D	D		
9		D	D	D	D					
A7		D	D	D	D					
A6		D	D	D	D					
A5			D	D	D					
A4			D	D	D					
A3				D	D					
A2				D	D					
SURRENDER (LATE)										
16									¢	¢
15									¢	

S = Stand   H = Hit   D = Double Down   ¢ = Surrender

This generic basic strategy may be used for any game. See *Appendix* for comprehensive basic strategy according to all rule variations and the specific number of decks in play.

PAIR-SPLITS

NO DOUBLE AFTER SPLITS

	2	3	4	5	6	7	8	9	X	A
AA	$	$	$	$	$	$	$	$	$	$
99	$	$	$	$	$		$	$		
88	$	$	$	$	$	$	$	$	$	$
77	$	$	$	$	$	$				
66		$	$	$	$					
33			$	$	$	$				
22			$	$	$	$				

WITH DOUBLE AFTER SPLITS

	2	3	4	5	6	7	8	9	X	A
AA	$	$	$	$	$	$	$	$	$	$
99	$	$	$	$	$		$	$		
88	$	$	$	$	$	$	$	$	$	$
77	$	$	$	$	$	$				
66	$	$	$	$	$					
44				$	$					
33	$	$	$	$	$	$				
22	$	$	$	$	$	$				

INSURANCE

Do Not Take Insurance

$ = Split

Using the Basic Strategy Chart

Do not attempt to learn all aspects of basic strategy at once, but remember that regardless of the number of decks in play or the rule variations, basic strategy for any game is essentially the same. Since so few casinos offer early and late surrender, don't bother with these options unless you plan to specifically play those tables that include this variation, or are interested in the academic exercise. Early surrender is not included in these charts; should you find a casino that offers this option, you will find the basic strategy for it in the Complete Basic Strategy Chart section in the Appendix.

The basic strategy chart presented here is a "composite" basic strategy, good for any set of rules and any number of decks. Actually, as these conditions change, some of the basic strategy decisions also change. Usually, these apply to borderline decisions, and do not significantly change your expectation. I know a number of high stakes pros that know only one basic strategy, and ignore the fine changes caused by rule variations and the number of decks in play. In the Appendix, a complete basic strategy, including all the changes according to rule and deck variations, is presented. This is for advanced players, or for players who expect to do most of their playing under the same set of rules and conditions, and who would like to play accurately. For now, I advise learning this composite basic strategy, which may be all you will ever need.

Two pair-splitting tables are presented here. Note that I use the symbol "$" to denote a pair-split decision. The first pair-split table assumes that you are not allowed to double down after splitting, and that's the rule in many casinos, though in some, including many in the Las Vegas Strip and all of Atlantic City's, players are allowed to double down after pair-splits. If you plan to play primarily in these casinos, study the second table, and note that there are only a few differences between these tables. If you'll be playing in games with both rules, just learn the first table, then brush up on the differences prior to playing in the double-after-split (DAS) casinos.

Notice also that I use the symbol "¢" to denote a basic strategy surrender decision.

The charts are straightforward: The player's hands are listed vertically down the left side, and the dealer's up-cards are listed horizontally along the top. Thus, if you hold a hand totaling 14 against a dealer's 6, you can see the basic strategy decision is "S," or Stand. With a total of 14 against a dealer 7, the "H" indicates you would hit. Note: If your total of 14 is comprised of a pair of sevens, you must consult the pair-splitting chart first. You can see that with a pair of sevens against either a dealer 6 or 7, you would split ($) your 7s.

Order of Decisions

Use the basic strategy chart in this order:

1. If surrender is allowed, this takes priority over any other decision. If basic strategy calls for surrender, throw in the hand.

2. If you have a pair, determine whether or not basic strategy calls for a split.

3. If you have a possible double down hand, this play takes priority over hitting or standing. For instance, in Las Vegas and Atlantic City, you may double down on any two cards. So, with A7 (soft 18) against a dealer 5, your basic strategy play, as per the chart, is to double down. In Northern Nevada, where you may usually double down on 10 or 11 only, you should stand.

4. After determining that you do not want to surrender, split a pair, or double down, consult the "Stand" chart. Always hit a hard total of 11 or below. Always stand on a hard total of 17 or higher. For all **stiff** hands, hard 12 through 16, consult the basic strategy chart. Always hit soft 17 (A,6) or below. Always stand on soft 19 (A,8) or higher. With a soft 18 (A,7), consult the chart.

How to Practice Basic Strategy

Study the Charts

Any professional card counter could easily and quickly reproduce from memory a set of basic strategy charts. Study the charts one section at a time. Start with the hard Stand decisions: Look at the chart and observe the pattern of the decisions as they appear in the chart—close your eyes and visualize this pattern. Study the chart once more, then get out your pencil and paper. Reproduce the hard Stand chart. Do this for each section of the chart separately—hard Stand, soft Stand, hard Double Down, soft Double Down, Pair-splits, and Surrender. Keep doing it until you have mastered the charts.

EARNING YOUR WHITE BELT

Practice with Cards

Place an ace face up on a table to represent the dealer's upcard. Shuffle the rest of the cards, then deal two cards face up to yourself. Do not deal the dealer a downcard. Look at your two cards and the dealer's ace and make your basic strategy decision. Check the chart to see if you are correct, but do not complete your hand. If the decision is "hit," don't bother to take the hit card. After you've made and double-checked your decision, deal another two cards to yourself. Don't bother to pick up your first hand. Just drop your next, and all subsequent, cards face up on top of the last cards dealt. Go through the entire deck (25 hands), then change the dealer's upcard to a deuce, then to a 3, 4, 5, and so on. You should be able to run through a full deck of player hands for all ten dealer upcards in less than half an hour once you are able to make your decisions without consulting the charts. Once you start to get the hang of it, every decision should be instantaneous. Strive for perfection. If you have the slightest doubt about any decision, consult the chart.

To practice your pair-split decisions, which occur less frequently than other decisions, reverse the above exercise. Deal yourself a pair of aces, then run through the deck changing only the dealer's upcard. Then give yourself a pair of deuces, and all the cards that follow. Don't waste time with any exercise you don't need. Your basic strategy for splitting aces, for instance, is always to split them. You don't need to run through a whole deck of dealer up-cards every day to practice this decision. Likewise, basic strategy tells you to always split eights, and never to split fives or tens. You should concentrate mostly on learning when to split 2s, 3s, 6s, 7s, and 9s, which you'll master soon enough.

If you learn to play basic strategy without counting cards, most casinos will have only a 1/2% edge over you, meaning that in the long run, they will win about 50¢ for every $100 you bet. (In some games, the house advantage over basic strategy players amounts to slightly more or less.) If you play blackjack for high stakes, it is wise to learn basic strategy, even if you are not inclined to count cards, as using it accurately will greatly cut your losses.

Simplified Basic Strategy

If you do not intend to learn accurate basic strategy, you can cut the house edge to about 1% by playing an approximate basic strategy. Follow these rules:

1. Never take insurance.

2. If the dealer's upcard is 7, 8, 9, X, or A, hit until you get to hard 17 or more.

3. If the dealer's upcard is 2, 3, 4, 5, or 6, stand on all your stiffs, hard hands of 12 through 16.

4. Hit all soft hands of soft 17 (A6) and less.

5. Stand on soft 18 (A7) or higher.

6. Double down on 10 and 11 against any dealer upcard from 2 through 9.

7. Always split aces and 8s.

8. Never split 4s, 5s, or 10s.

9. Split all other pairs—2s, 3s, 6s, 7s, and 9s—if the dealer shows up—cards of 4, 5, or 6.

10. Surrender 16 vs. 9, X or A.

MULTI-ACTION BLACKJACK

In Multi-Action games, your basic strategy does not change. Always play every hand exactly as if it is the only hand on the table. Do not be afraid to hit your stiffs—a common Multi-Action error. The Multi-Action format does not alter the house percentage, or basic strategy, in any way.

If you intend to learn to count cards, you first have to nail down accurate basic strategy. Once you know basic strategy, your decisions will become automatic. Even when counting cards, you will still play basic strategy on 80% or more of your hands. Basic strategy is your single most powerful weapon.

5

THE RED SEVEN COUNT

Balanced vs. Unbalanced Counting Systems

In casino blackjack, high cards—tens and aces—are favorable to you, the player, and low cards—2s through 7s—are favorable to the dealer. With more tens and aces in the deck, more blackjacks will be dealt, and even though these blackjacks will be evenly distributed between you and the dealer, you get paid 3 to 2 for your blackjack, while the dealer only gets 1 to 1—the amount of your original bet. In addition, more tens and aces mean that you will have more double-down wins, and that the dealer will bust more often, since the dealer must hit all hands of 16 or less, even when you are stiff.

So, all blackjack card-counting systems keep track of the high cards versus the low cards. When more low cards have already been dealt, leaving the deck(s) rich in high cards, this is favorable for you. When more tens and aces have already come out of the deck(s), the reverse is true. Most professional-level counting systems are **balanced** point-count systems. The counter assigns plus and minus point values (usually +1 or -1) to the various cards based on their value to him. The system is said to be "balanced" when there are an equal number of plus and minus point values, so that the sum of all these values in a full deck adds up to zero.

51

As cards are dealt, the player adds the values of the cards he sees to his "running count." The **running count** is the total count since the last shuffle. If you started your count at 0, then saw five low cards dealt (valued at +1 each), and three high cards dealt (valued at -1 each), your running count would be +2, since 5 - 3 = 2.

Once learned, this aspect of card counting becomes automatic and easy. The difficulty of playing a balanced point-count system comes when you must use the count to determine how much to bet and how to play your hand. First, the running count must be converted to a "true count" (there is an in-depth explanation of true count—for those who choose to use this more advanced technique—in a later section). Second, the player must memorize, and be able to apply, the correct playing decisions based on this true count. Learning to keep a running count is not difficult for most players. Applying the count properly at the tables, however, may be such a mental strain that many either give up on card counting completely, or continue to count but extract very little value from their efforts. This is why simpler "unbalanced" systems were developed.

Unbalanced Systems

In 1969, a Berkeley math professor, using the pseudonym "Jacques Noir," wrote a book called *Casino Holiday*, which contained an "unbalanced" ten count system which required no true count conversions. Within a few years, more refined versions of Noir's running-count system were published by Stanley Roberts, and then John Archer. The power of the Noir count derives from its built-in imbalance, which makes it very simple to play. Tens are counted as -2, and all non-tens, including aces, are counted as +1.

We call this an unbalanced count because the value of the complete deck, when all point values are added together, does not equal zero. Because of the imbalance, however, no true count adjustments are necessary for many important playing decisions.

If you count down a deck using this count, any time your running count is +4, then the ratio of non-tens to tens is exactly 2 to 1, making this running count a perfect insurance indicator. This count has one major weakness—its betting efficiency: that is, the count is weak at telling you how much to bet. The ten-count has a betting correlation of only 72%. Compare this to the Hi-Lo count's 97% correlation.

Quite a few players still chose to use this unbalanced ten-count, despite its betting weakness, because they did not consider their abilities in making true-count conversions to be very accurate anyway. Both Roberts and Archer advised players to keep a side-count of aces, which could greatly improve the poor betting efficiency of the Noir count, but because it was that much more difficult to keep a side count, then use it to adjust the primary count, many Noir counters simply ignored their advice.

Why, I asked myself, was this unbalanced ten-count, which had been around for more than a decade, the only unbalanced count system ever invented? Why not an unbalanced point count system designed to indicate perfect betting by running count, rather than perfect insurance?

The Red Seven Count

Thus, in 1983, the Red Seven Count was born. When the first edition of this book was published, many blackjack authorities expressed disbelief that such a simple counting system could be so strong. Peter Griffin, whose monumental *Theory of Blackjack* (GBC, 1979) established him as the game's reigning math guru—a position he held deservedly until his untimely death in 1998—reviewed the first edition of *Blackbelt in Blackjack* in *Casino & Sports #23* (1983):

> *Arnold Snyder's latest offering will undoubtedly prove to be a mild disappointment . . . I have a developing sense that Snyder enjoys being different and provocative. This probably accounts for his advocacy of the 'Red Seven' system . . . Snyder bases his assertion of the dominance of unbalanced counts over balanced counts on the existence of a 'pivot'... What Snyder appears unaware of is that a balanced count also has a pivot, and that pivot is zero. This locates a far more useful and common point of reference...*

Given Griffin's stature in the blackjack community, and the fact that I had developed the Red Seven system almost entirely from the data in *Theory of Blackjack,* which was my bible, I was crushed. Within weeks of his review, I was being barraged with letters from those who had already purchased *Blackbelt in Blackjack,* asking me if I had revised my opinion about the strength of the Red Seven, in light of Griffin's review. Many pointed out that Joel Friedman, another prominent gambling authority at that time, in that same issue of *Casino & Sports,* also expressed disappointment, pointing out that the Red Seven was weaker than traditional counting systems.

I had claimed in that first edition that despite its running count simplicity and a playing strategy that advised only half-a-dozen changes from basic strategy, the Red Seven system would capture 80% of the profit potential of the traditional, balanced point-count systems in multiple-deck games, even when those systems used over 100+ strategy changes. This was in the pre-personal computer days of blackjack, when you couldn't just sit down and whip out a few million hands to test a system. If you weren't a programmer yourself with access to a million-dollar mainframe through some university or major corporation, simulation testing of blackjack systems was not feasible.

Despite Griffin's reputation, and his unparalleled comprehension of blackjack's mathematics, I felt certain that the Red Seven would perform as I claimed, capturing 80% of the profit potential of the more difficult true count systems.

So, I enlisted Peter Griffin's colleague at California State University, Dr. John Gwynn, Jr., to test the Red Seven Count via computer simulation. I assured Dr. Gwynn that regardless of the results he obtained, and even if they proved the Red Seven system to be far less powerful than I'd claimed, I would publish his results in *Blackjack Forum* exactly as I received them.

I asked him to simulate the Red Seven Count, exactly as I had published it, with only six strategy changes, all made by running count, in two common games (at that time), and to compare the Red Seven results with two versions of the Hi-Lo Count, as published by Stanford Wong in *Professional Blackjack,* one version utilizing all 184 indices by true count, and one using Wong's condensed -6 to +6 version (34 indices) by true count.

I published Gwynn's results in the December 1983 issue of *Blackjack Forum*. John Gwynn did not test the 184-index version of the Hi-Lo in the one-deck game, though it surely would have outperformed Wong's 34-index version, probably by a couple tenths of a %. He tested the full-blown Hi-Lo in the shoe game because I had also expressed the opinion that card counters were wasting their time memorizing 100+ index numbers for shoe games. I had published my Zen Count system in 1981 with only 25 indices, and had stated that no counting system needed more than these for multiple-deck games. Among professional players, this was another area of great controversy at that time, though today, thanks to Don Schlesinger and others, most experts embrace my simplified approach as common wisdom.

Gwynn's computer results, which substantiated my claims of the Red Seven's power, surprised many experts, and revolutionized blackjack

4 Decks, 75% Dealt, Vegas Strip Rules, 1-10 Spread

# Indices	Win Rate
Red Seven 6	*0.77%*
Hi-Lo (condensed) 34	*0.87%*
Hi-Lo (complete) 184	*0.87%*

1 Deck, 75% Dealt, Reno Rules, 1-3 Spread

# Indices	Win Rate
Red Seven 6	*0.73%*
Hi-Lo (condensed) 34	*0.89%*

system development, as many other authors have since devised unbalanced count systems. For example, Ken Uston self-published his "Uston SS Count." Uston, in fact, hired me to produce the strategy charts for him. George C. came out with his "Unbalanced Zen 11." Eddie Olsen, with assistance from Michael Dalton, presented his "TruCount" system.

More recently, Olaf Vancura and Ken Fuchs published their popular *Knock-Out Blackjack*. They presented their "knock-out" counting system, which essentially was a knock-off of the Red Seven Count; the only difference between the count values was that Vancura and Fuchs counted all the sevens, instead of just the red ones. Their system was one I had abandoned when I was devising the original Red Seven Count back in the early '80s, because the imbalance created by counting all of the sevens was too heavily skewed toward the low cards. My analysis showed that if all the sevens were counted, the system wouldn't perform as well.

I was amazed when *Knock-Out Blackjack* came out with computer simulation data that showed the knock-out count to be not only more powerful than the Red Seven Count, but more powerful than just about every other counting system on the market, including many of the "advanced" multi-level counts.

As it turned out, the authors of the system had made some major errors in their simulation methods. In the Fall 1999 issue of *Blackjack Forum* magazine, John Auston, author of the *Blackjack Risk Manager* software, provided his extensive computer simulation data that compared the win rates of the K-O count with both the Red Seven and Stanford Wong's Hi-

Lo Count in one, two, six, and eight-deck games. Auston's data agreed with my own—in most games, both the Hi-Lo and Red Seven outperform the K-O Count. I still believe that the Red Seven count is the easiest, most straightforward, and most effective system ever devised.

The Red Seven Point Values

Learn to count cards by adding and subtracting the following values as the respective cards are removed from the deck:

Ace	-1
10	-1
9	0
8	0
Black 7	0
Red 7	+1
6	+1
5	+1
4	+1
3	+1
2	+1

The one strange mechanism here suggests that you count black sevens as zero, and red sevens as +1! This device creates the exact imbalance necessary for this to work as a running count system. (Technically, it does not make any difference whether the red 7 or the black 7 is counted, so long as this precise imbalance is attained. One may even count all sevens as +1/2, or simply count every other seven seen as +1.)

How to Practice Counting

Start by buying yourself a couple dozen decks of cards. Put one in the pocket of every one of your jackets. Put one by each telephone you use regularly. One on the kitchen table. One by each TV set. One on the dashboard of your car. Always have a deck of cards at hand. As you watch TV, talk on the phone, or enjoy your morning coffee, practice keeping your running count using the chart's point values for the individual cards as you turn them over.

Start your count at 0. Turn cards one at a time face-up onto the bottom of the deck, adding each card's point value to your running count. For example:

EARNING YOUR WHITE BELT

Cards seen: 2, A, 8, 9, X, X, 5

Point values: +1, -1, 0, 0, -1, -1, +1

Running Count: +1, 0, 0, 0, -1, -2, -1

By the time you get to the end of the deck, your running count should be +2; if it isn't, then you have not counted correctly, assuming your deck contains 52 cards. If you have miscounted, turn the deck over and run through the cards again, until your final running count is +2. Then shuffle and go through the deck once more. Build up speed and accuracy.

When you are proficient at counting down a deck of cards in this manner, practice turning the cards over two at a time, and learn to count cards in pairs. It's faster and easier for most people to count that way, because many pairs cancel each other out. For instance, every time you pair a ten or ace (both -1) with a 2, 3, 4, 5, 6, or red 7 (all +1), the pair counts as zero. You will quickly learn to ignore self-canceling pairs, as well as 8s, 9s, and black 7s, since they're all valued at 0. When you're good at counting cards in pairs, start turning them over three at a time. You must be accurate in your count—speed without accuracy is worthless. It may take you weeks to master running counts, but once you learn it, it's like telling time. You'll find you can do it almost automatically.

To test yourself, after learning to count cards in pairs and groups of three, run through the cards by fanning them from one hand to the other as you count. Allow your eyes to quickly scan the exposed cards for self-canceling pairs, even when these cards are not adjacent to each other. *You should be able to count down a deck in 40 seconds or less before you ever attempt counting in a casino.* Most pros can easily count down a deck in less than 30 seconds, and professional teams usually require players to demonstrate that they can do it in 25 seconds or less, with perfect accuracy every time.

No matter how fast you can count when turning cards over yourself, you'll probably find counting at a casino blackjack table to be difficult at first. In facedown games, some cards will appear as mere flashes as players throw in their hands, and dealers scoop upcards as quickly as they're turned over. Before counting cards in a casino, spend a half-hour or so counting while watching others play. Do not sit down to play until you feel comfortable counting while watching the game.

If you expect to play in shoe games, practice counting down multiple decks of cards at home. Note that your final count should always amount to twice the number of decks you are using: With six decks, your running count at the end should always be +12; with two, it would be +4.

The Starting Count

With any balanced point count system, a count of "0" indicates that the high cards and low cards are evenly balanced in the remaining deck(s). The zero count is the "pivot" count that always tells the player that the value of the cards remaining to be dealt has returned to whatever the house edge was right off the top of the deck(s). The **pivot count** is the running count that we would have if we counted down all of the cards in the deck or decks.

With a balanced count, the pivot is always zero, and it always indicates that the cards have returned to the "normal" house edge off the top. With the Red Seven Count, because it is unbalanced, our pivot count is two times the number of decks in play, since there is an imbalance of +2 in the card point values for each deck. And, instead of indicating to us that the cards remaining have the normal house edge off the top, the Red Seven pivot indicates that the player's advantage has risen by 1% over the house edge. The Red Seven pivot is a much more useful and common point of reference for a card counter who desires to know when to raise his bet and alter his strategy. The imbalance in the count values allows us to make our most important betting and strategy decisions by running count, with no deck estimates or "true count" adjustments.

But there is a more practical way to use unbalanced counts for players who are frequently changing games, playing against various numbers of decks, and especially if using extended strategy indices. Instead of altering the pivot count according to the number of decks in play, you can alter the starting count so that the pivot will always be 0. Instead of starting your count at 0 off the top of the deck(s), subtract the pivot count from 0, and start counting at a negative number. Then, regardless of the number of decks in play, when your running count rises to 0, you raise your bet.

In 1986, when Ken Uston hired me to help him devise his unbalanced SS Count, he wanted to provide more complete strategy tables, with separate sets of charts for each number of decks. Since Uston's level-three count had an imbalance of +4 per deck, his 8-deck pivot was +32, and his index number for hitting 15 against 10 was +44. His 6-deck index for the same decision was +33, and his 4-deck index for 14 against 10 was +40. Even his 2-deck number was +22. Ken felt these numbers were unwieldy, and I agreed.

The device we decided to use for the SS Count was a "Starting Count" other than zero. Multiplying the number of decks in play by -4, the SS one-deck starting count became -4; the eight-deck starting count became -32. Thus, the SS pivot was always 0, regardless of the number of decks in play, and the strategy charts look a lot less intimidating. A few years later, when George C. developed an unbalanced version of my Zen Count, he used the same device.

With the Red Seven Count, we'll use this technique for adjusting the starting count, always multiplying -2 by the number of decks in play to get the starting count. For example, the 4-deck starting count is –8 (-2 x 4). This methodology will always make your pivot equal zero.

Red Seven Starting Counts

# Decks	Starting Count
1	-2
2	-4
3	-6
4	-8
5	-10
6	-12
7	-14
8	-16

Now, when you practice counting, always start at the appropriate starting count for the number of decks in play. Your pivot is always 0, and when you come to the end of the deck(s), you should always have a final running count of 0 as well.

The Red Seven Betting Strategy

Once you're comfortable counting, you can begin to apply the Red Seven betting strategy at the tables. When counting in a casino you always begin your count after each shuffle with the starting count that corresponds to the number of decks in play, as above. Any time your running count is 0 your advantage will have risen by about 1% over your starting advantage. This 0 pivot is a good indicator of when to raise your bet for nearly all the blackjack games available in this country; about 80% of the games have a starting advantage between -0.4% and -0.6%. So, your 0 pivot usually indicates an advantage for you of approximately 1/2%. (In a later section, you will find a method for determining the house's starting advantage more precisely, according to the exact rules and the number of decks in play.) Simply stated, the Red Seven betting strategy is to bet more when your running count is 0 or higher, and less (or nothing) when your running count is negative. Your betting spread is the amount of your smallest bet compared to the amount of your biggest bet. This may be expressed in either dollars or "units." Example: If your smallest bet is $5 and your biggest bet is $50, then your betting spread is $5-50. In units, this may be expressed as a spread of 1-10.

How much of a betting spread should you use? This depends on many factors—the rules of the game, the number of decks in play, the penetration (shuffle point), the size of your bankroll, and what you can actually get away with in that particular casino, to name a few. This concept is so important that we will discuss it in depth in several later chapters, but the general rule of thumb is to bet very little when the house has the edge, and to bet more when you do. The bigger the difference between your low bet and your high bet, the greater your advantage over the house, and the more money you can expect to make. Without enough of a difference between your low and high bets, you may not get the edge at all because your relatively few big bets must cover the cost of all those bets you place when the house has the edge. For now, the chart below will provide a guide for the most common games.

Simplified Red Seven Betting (Units to Bet)

Running Count	1 Deck	2 Decks	Shoe (4 to 8 Decks)
Negative	1	1	1 (or 0)
0	2	2	2
+2	4	2	2
+4	4	3	2
+6	4	4	3
+8	4	6	4
+12	4	6	8
+16	4	6	8

Note that the suggested bets are in units, not dollars—in the next chapter you will find guidelines on how to size your bets according to your bankroll. The above guidelines are not to be taken as strict betting advice, and should only be used as a general rule for casual players. Serious gamblers will need to use more precise betting strategies, according to their advantage, table conditions, the need to camouflage, and so on.

In many one-deck games, a 1 to 4 spread according to the count is about as much as you can practically bet without getting booted out for card counting; in some casinos, even that spread will get you backed off the table in short order. In many shoe games, a 1 to 8 spread would barely get you over the break-even point, which is why the 0-unit bet is suggested in shoe games at negative counts. It's basically impossible to only play at positive counts in shoe games, but it's often wise to leave the table if the running count does not start moving quickly in the positive direction.

The Red Seven Playing Strategy

Using the Red Seven Count, you can also increase your advantage over the house by deviating from basic strategy according to your running count. First of all, insurance is the most valuable strategy decision. In single-deck games, assuming you are using a moderate betting spread, insurance is almost as important as all other strategy decisions combined. Conveniently, you have a very nice insurance indicator with the Red Seven Count. In 1- and 2-deck games, you simply take insurance any time your running count is 0 or higher. In all shoe games, take insurance at +2.

As for other playing decisions, there are only a few to remember. Any time you are at a running count of 0 or higher (with any number of decks), stand on 16 against 10 and on 12 vs. 3. (According to basic strategy, you would hit both of these.) In single-deck games, the decision to hit or stay on 16 against 10 is the second most important choice for a card counter. After you've gotten the hang of these strategy changes, there are a couple of others you can add that will further increase your advantage. At running counts of +2 or higher, with any number of decks, stand on 12 versus 2, and on 15 versus 10; and double down on 10 against X.

By using this simple running count strategy, in multi-deck games you will be taking advantage of about 80% of all possible gains from card counting. Because you won't be sloppily attempting to adjust your running count to true count on every hand, your decisions will be made with devastating accuracy. Using the simple Red Seven Count, you have no strategy tables to memorize; you simply have a basic strategy, which you play on more than 90% of your hands, and you'll have to make so few changes according to your running count that it would be pointless to draw up a chart.

There are, to be sure, weaknesses in this vastly simplified system, but, in my opinion, most card counters would be wise to ignore more difficult strategies. Because of its combined power and simplicity, the Red Seven Count lends itself to many advanced, professional strategies for beating the game of blackjack. It's also an excellent system for teams and partners. The Red Seven Count requires the minimum amount of memory work for a professional level system, and also spares the player from having to worry about mathematics at the table, except for the simple adding and subtracting necessary to keep the running count.

If you find it very confusing to add and subtract when your running count is negative, you may totally avoid negative running counts by adding 50 to all of the recommended starting counts, which will also make your pivot 50, instead of 0, no matter how many decks are in play. For instance, adding 50 to the 1-deck starting count of -2 makes your starting count 48. Because your pivot is always 50, strategy changes that you would normally make at +2 are now made at 52. Again, I advise this only for players who have trouble dealing with negative numbers. If that's you, then the corrected starting counts you should use for 1, 2, 4, 6, and 8-deck games, are: 48, 46, 42, 38, and 34, respectively. Use these numbers when you practice counting down decks. There is no loss of power if you use this method.

The Advanced Red Seven Count

For those players who've been bitten hard by the blackjack bug, and might be considering moving on to a more advanced true count system, such as the Hi-Lo Lite, let me suggest that you first try the Advanced Red Seven. This system uses the same Red Seven count values, and continues to work as a running count system, but we expand on the strategy changes so that you can play more accurately. For dedicated players there is also a precise method of estimating your advantage, so that you can use the same proportional betting schemes as professional players.

How to Read the Strategy Charts

In the 1 & 2-Deck Strategy Chart, the heavy bold index numbers are to be used for both 1- and 2-deck games. For 2-deck games, these are all the indices you will need. The lighter numbers should be used for single-deck games only. They are not as important as the bold indices, so if you play in single-deck games, learn the ones in bold first.

The Shoe Game Chart is to be used in the second half of the shoe only. For example, in an 8-deck game, use the Advanced Red Seven indices

THE ADVANCED RED SEVEN
1 & 2-DECK STRATEGY

	2	3	4	5	6	7	8	9	X	A
16							6	2	-2	4
15							6	4	2	4
14	-4	-4							6	
13	-2	-2	-2							
12	2	0	0	-2	-2					
11								-4	-4	-2
10							-4	-2	2	2
9	0					2				

INSURANCE: 0

SURRENDER

	2	3	4	5	6	7	8	9	X	A
15								2	0	0
14									2	

BOLD = 1 & 2-Deck   Light = 1-Deck Only

ALL SHOE GAMES

	2	3	4	5	6	7	8	9	X	A
16								4	-4	
15									4	4
14										
13										
12	4	0	-4							
11										-4
10									4	4
9	-4					4				

INSURANCE: 4

SURRENDER

	2	3	4	5	6	7	8	9	X	A
15								0	-4	0
14									4	

only after the first four decks are in the discard tray. In a 6-deck game, wait until three decks have been played to start using the advanced indices. In the first half of the shoe, follow the simple Red Seven strategy, utilizing only the primary half-dozen strategy changes.

Note that the shoe game indices are quite different from the 1- and 2-deck charts. If you sometimes play in shoe games, and sometimes in hand-held games, then I would suggest learning the 1- and 2-deck chart for the hand-held games, but reverting to the simple Red Seven system for shoe games, using only the half dozen indices prescribed earlier. Naturally, if you memorize things easily, or if you are very dedicated, you could learn both of these charts. Do not try to do more than you're comfortable with; remember that it's better to do a few things well than to bungle your game by trying to do too much.

These are presented in the standard format of blackjack strategy charts, like those presented earlier. If there is no entry for a decision, then you should always use basic strategy. No pair-split indices are provided because the gains are too small to bother with. For all of the player-hand totals of 12-16 at the top of the charts, the index numbers provide the running counts at which you should stand. For example, with 12 against 4 in the Shoe Game chart, note that you should stand if your running count is -4 or higher. This means that in the second half of the shoe, you would stand on a count of -4, -3, -2, and so on, and hit on -5, -6, -7, and below.

If surrender is allowed, that takes precedence over other decisions. Since no indices are provided for surrendering on 16 against 9, 10, or A, always follow basic strategy and surrender the hand.

The easiest way to learn the index numbers is to learn them in blocks. First learn all of the 0 (pivot) indices. Then learn the +2 and +4 indices. After you have learned all of the positive indices, learn the negative ones, starting with the -2s. Many players make flash cards to drill themselves on index numbers, and there are also many excellent software programs available that allow you to input and practice card counting systems.

The Advanced Red Seven "True Edge"

There is a simple and accurate method for estimating your precise advantage at any point in the deal with the Advanced Red Seven Count. I do not recommend this method for any player who finds it confusing or difficult. Such players must resign themselves to using the betting chart shown earlier, along with the advice on bet-sizing according to your bankroll in the following chapter.

Advanced players, however, will want to bet more precisely according to their exact advantage over the house. You may do this with the same precision as users of balanced true count systems by using your running count to make a simple fraction that equates to your true edge over the house.

Many professional players have shied away from the unbalanced counting systems because without a "true count," it's impossible to follow a proportional betting scheme, where each bet is dictated by the approximate advantage on the hand about to be dealt. The true edge method described below solves that problem by directly converting the running count into the precise fractional advantage.

Make a Fraction

First of all, any time your running count is negative, assume that either the house has the advantage, or your advantage is less than 1/2%, so you do not want to bet much more than one unit regardless. Make a fraction only when your running count is positive.

Every fraction has two parts, a numerator and a denominator. The numerator is on top, and the denominator is on the bottom:

$$\frac{\text{Numerator}}{\text{Denominator}}$$

In the fraction 1/2, the numerator is 1, and the denominator is 2. To estimate your precise advantage with the Red Seven Count, your numerator, the top number, is your current running count. So if your running count is +6, the fraction becomes:

$$\frac{6}{\text{Denominator}}$$

The denominator is simply *twice the number of decks remaining to be dealt*. For example, let's say you are in an eight-deck game, and your Red Seven running count is +6. Two decks have been dealt, with six decks remaining in the shoe. Your numerator (the running count) is simply 6, and your denominator is 6 (the number of decks remaining) x 2, or 12. So your fraction is:

$$\frac{6}{12} = \frac{1}{2}$$

This means your odds have improved by exactly 1/2% above your pivot advantage. If this were a typical eight-deck Atlantic City game, where your pivot (0) indicated a 1/2% advantage, then this +6 running count with 6 decks remaining means your advantage has gone up *another* 1/2%, so that you now have a full 1% advantage over the house. Note that in order to estimate your true edge, you simply add the amount of the fraction you make with your running count to your pivot advantage.

Consider what happens to your advantage if, in this same eight-deck game, your running count is +6, but 5 decks have been dealt out, leaving only 3 undealt in the shoe. Your denominator becomes 3 x 2 = 6, and your fraction is:

$$\frac{6}{6} = 1$$

So, at this point in the shoe, your +6 running count indicates a full 1% raise in your advantage above your 1/2% pivot advantage, and your total advantage over the house is now 1 1/2%.

Another example: Assume that in this same game you have a running count of +6, but now six of the eight decks have been dealt, with only two left in the shoe. Using the true edge method, your denominator is 2 x 2 = 4, and your fraction is:

$$\frac{6}{4} = 1\ 1/2$$

This deep in the shoe, your +6 running count indicates a 1 1/2% raise above your 1/2% pivot advantage, so that your total advantage over the house is now 2%.

Note that as the shoe is dealt deeper, the same +6 running count indicates an increase from your pivot advantage of anywhere from 1/2% to 1 1/2%. In fact, if the dealer distributed all but one of the decks in the shoe, and you found yourself with a +6 running count, your advantage will have risen by:

$$\frac{6}{1 \times 2} = \frac{6}{2} = 3\%$$

Technically, we are simply applying standard true count theory in a unique way to calculate the increased advantage when the running count rises above the pivot. The advantages calculated with this method are as precise as the standard balanced true-count methods used by most pros. From the examples above, you can see why professional players have always steered away from the running count systems. If you were to always bet according to your running count, then depending on the level of penetration, you will often over or under-bet your true advantage. The true edge method solves the problem.

I have used simple examples, which resulted in simple fractions. With very little practice, however, you should have no difficulty estimating your raise in advantage, even when the numbers are not so convenient.

For instance, if you are in an eight-deck game, with a running count of +4, and 3 1/2 decks are remaining to be dealt, you'll know that since 3 1/2 x 2 = 7, your fraction becomes 4/7.

This may be a more complicated calculation, but you should be able to determine in an instant that it's just slightly more than 1/2%. Likewise, with fractions like 5/7 or 6/7, just knowing that your advantage has risen more than 1/2% but less than 1% is all you need for purposes of bet-sizing.

In using this method, always round up to the nearest half-deck when you estimate the remaining decks for your denominator. For instance, if slightly less than five decks have been dealt, and you estimate that about 3 1/4 decks remain, round up to 3 1/2, and your denominator becomes 3 1/2 x 2 = 7. This way, your denominator will always be a whole number, which is very convenient. This method also assures that you are being conservative in estimating your advantage, and therefore, safer in bet-sizing. If you have any difficulty whatsoever calculating your denominator when 1/2-deck increments are involved, then simply look at the following chart:

$$1/2 \text{ x } 2 = 1$$
$$1 \ 1/2 \text{ x } 2 = 3$$
$$2 \ 1/2 \text{ x } 2 = 5$$
$$3 \ 1/2 \text{ x } 2 = 7$$
$$4 \ 1/2 \text{ x } 2 = 9$$
$$5 \ 1/2 \text{ x } 2 = 11$$
$$6 \ 1/2 \text{ x } 2 = 13$$
$$7 \ 1/2 \text{ x } 2 = 15$$

I think most people with an average command of math can do this with little difficulty, but if you have trouble, then simply learn the chart.

Also, let me reemphasize that you should not be intimidated by "weird" fractions. If you come up with fractions like 5/13, 2/5, 5/11, or

4/9, so long as you know that these fractions are all less than 1/2—or even somewhere around 1/2—you have all the information you need to estimate your advantage. Most pros estimate their advantage to the nearest 1/2%, and it's impractical to attempt to size your bets with more accuracy than that. Likewise, 12/10, 11/8, 9/7, and 5/4 are all slightly more than 1. Knowing that your advantage is slightly more than 1% above your pivot advantage is all you need to know. You do not need to consider 9/7 as anything different from 12/10. For your betting purposes, just know that all of these fractions indicate a 1% raise above your pivot advantage.

If you use the true edge method in single-deck games, in the first half of the deck, you simply divide your running count by 2 (since your denominator is 1x2). So, a running count of +3 indicates about a 1 1/2% raise from your pivot advantage. At the half-deck level, your raise in advantage is your running count, since 1/2 x 2 = 1, and if you divide any number by 1, the answer is the same number. I.e., with a +5 running count and a half-deck dealt, your advantage has risen 5%. So, in single-deck games, don't even bother to make a fraction—in the top half of the deck, divide by 2. In the bottom half, just use the running count. Should you ever play in a really deeply dealt one-deck game, in the last quarter of the deck, you can actually multiply your running count by 2, as a +3 count means a 6% raise in advantage. Low stakes players may occasionally find games like this.

One convenient feature of the Advanced Red Seven Count is that all strategy decisions, which must be made very quickly, are still made by running count. The betting decisions, which are less rushed, can be made with all the accuracy of a true count system, simply by using the true edge method of directly converting your running count to your raise in advantage.

A mathematician and longtime correspondent, Conrad Membrino, who has written definitively about true count conversions with unbalanced counts, believes that estimating your true advantage with an unbalanced system tends to introduce less error into the calculated advantage than the traditional true count methods with balanced counting systems.

If you use the true edge method of estimating your advantage, you should also employ the same proportional betting techniques that professional players use, based on the "Kelly Criterion." You will want to read the following chapter on bankroll requirements, as well as the chapters that follow on true count and betting strategies, in order to develop the best betting strategies for your bankroll, the games you attack, and your style of play.

6

THE HI-LO LITE

The Hi-Lo Lite is a more advanced card counting strategy for blackjack players who are willing and able to devote the time and effort necessary to mastering it. It is simpler to learn and play than other true count strategies, because the strategy indices have been streamlined for maximum efficiency with minimum effort. Also, the true edge method has been incorporated into both the betting and playing strategies, so that one simple adjustment can be used for all decisions. The recommended exercises for learning how to count cards are the same for the Hi-Lo Lite as for the Red Seven Count, so these exercises will not be repeated here.

While I sincerely believe that most players should stick with the Red Seven Count, the Hi-Lo Lite is the system I most strongly recommend for dedicated single-deck players, or for shoe players who use advanced techniques, such as team play, shuffle-tracking, and so on. Balanced counting systems can lead to significantly more profits in these types of advanced play than unbalanced ones.

If you're serious enough about blackjack to consider forming or joining a team, then you should know that as counting systems go, the Hi-Lo Count is the industry standard. More professionals use the Hi-Lo Count than any other system, and many blackjack teams require that team players use the count as well.

The Hi-Lo Lite is a variation of the standard Hi-Lo Count that uses the same point values for the cards. I believe the Hi-Lo Lite is a more practical version of the traditional Hi-Lo, easier to learn, easier to play, yet just as strong. Those players who already know the traditional Hi-Lo, and who feel that they can play it easily and error-free, should probably stick with it, but if you are new to this counting system, I suggest you learn this easy version. Also, if you are training new players for a team, you may prefer to use the Hi-Lo Lite method—your players will train faster, and play with fewer errors. You should also note that the Lite indices could easily be converted to traditional count-per-deck indices (just multiply by 2). If you prefer the traditional true count method, but would rather take advantage of the Lite approach to index rounding, then simply adjust the indices for your purposes. You may do this for the purpose of easily learning dozens more indices, either for single-deck opportunities or camouflage plays.

The Hi-Lo Lite Point Values

The point values of the Hi-Lo Lite Count are:

A	-1
X	-1
9	0
8	0
7	0
6	+1
5	+1
4	+1
3	+1
2	+1

As the cards are played, you should keep a running count of all cards seen. After a shuffle, the count always starts at 0. This is a balanced counting system, so if you count down a deck, starting at 0, your final count will end at 0. Because the point values are balanced, you must adjust your running count to the true edge, as all Hi-Lo Lite betting and strategy decisions are made according to the true edge, not the running count.

Important note: If you have not read the section on the Red Seven Count, then go back now and read it, especially the pages that describe the true edge method of running count conversion. The Hi-Lo Lite uses the true edge methodology, which differs from the traditional true-count-per-deck method. The true edge method is simply a quicker and easier method of true count conversion, and just as accurate. In this chapter, I will briefly describe the minor differences between using the true edge method with the Hi-Lo Lite and the Red Seven, but you must read the material in the Red Seven section to fully understand the concept.

As with the Advanced Red Seven Count, we estimate our true edge with the Hi-Lo Lite by dividing the running count by twice the number of remaining decks. Example: you are in a 6-deck game and one deck has been played. Your running count is +15. Your true edge is:

$$\frac{+15}{5 \text{ (remaining decks)} \times 2} = \frac{15}{10} = +1\ 1/2$$

This means that the +15 running count at this point in the shoe indicates that your edge has risen about 1 1/2% above your advantage (or lack of one) off the top of the shoe.

Note that with the Hi-Lo Lite, both our starting count and our pivot are zero, so our pivot advantage is always the same as our advantage off the top. When we used the true edge method with the Red Seven Count, our pivot advantage was always positive, and about 1% higher than our starting advantage. So, the difference between using the true edge method with the Hi-Lo Lite and the Red Seven is that with the Red Seven we are usually adding the true edge to a positive pivot advantage, usually around 1/2%, and with the Hi-Lo Lite, we add our true edge to the starting advantage off the top, which is usually about –1/2%.

In the example above, if this were a 6-deck Atlantic City game, which is –1/2% off the top, then the 1 1/2% gain would indicate a total advantage of about an even 1%.

Another example: It's the same game, a few minutes later. 2 decks have been played and your running count is -4. Your true edge is:

$$-4\ /\ (4 \times 2)\ =\ -4/8\ =\ -1/2$$

The true edge method differs from the more common true count methodology used for most balanced counting systems, because it directly figures out the approximate gain or loss in the advantage as you make the true edge conversion. I have decided to use this methodology for the Hi-Lo Lite for a number of reasons: I think it's simpler and more convenient to estimate the raise in your edge directly, and since the true edge method works so easily with the Advanced Red Seven, it will also make it easier for Red Seven players to switch over to the Hi-Lo Lite.

With the Hi-Lo Lite, you will also use the true edge method for making your strategy decisions. The traditional true count says to divide your running count by the number of decks remaining; this may sound easy, but when your running count is +11, and 2 1/2 decks remain, what's your true count? Many players are stumped when they try to divide by half-decks, especially with odd-numbered running counts. When you're trying to make a decision quickly, you don't need the aggravation. With the above example and the true edge method, you come up with the fraction 11/5 in an instant, and you know that your edge has risen slightly more than 2%.

The Hi-Lo Lite Playing Strategy

Note that all of the index numbers are even numbers, making precision play easier than ever. The Hi-Lo Lite allows you to play your cards more accurately than if you just used basic strategy. The strategy changes presented here provide most of the gains available from the Hi-Lo Lite system. You may use these indices for any number of decks, and any set of rules. In shoe games, you only need the bold indices. If you play in games where the dealer hits soft 17, you will find these indices, along with many other less important ones, in the Complete Hi-Lo Lite Strategy Charts section. Use basic strategy for all decisions that aren't included in the index.

THE GENERIC HI-LO LITE
USE FOR ANY NUMBER OF DECKS
ASSUMES STAND ON SOFT 17

	2	3	4	5	6	7	8	9	X	A

STAND

	2	3	4	5	6	7	8	9	X	A
16						4	4	**2**	**0**	4
15	-2							4	**2**	
14	-2	-2	-2							
13	**0**	**0**	-2	-2	-2					
12	**2**	**0**	**0**	**0**	**0**					

DOUBLE DOWN

	2	3	4	5	6	7	8	9	X	A
11							-2	-2	-2	**0**
10						-2	-2	**0**	2	2
9	**0**	**0**	**0**	-2	-2	**2**	4			
8		4	2	2	0					

SURRENDER

	2	3	4	5	6	7	8	9	X	A
16							2	**0**	**0**	**0**
8-8								4	**0**	
15							4	2	**0**	**0**
14								4	**2**	4
7-7								2	2	2
13									4	

INSURANCE: 2

BOLD = Major indices for all games

[The light indices are important in single-and double-deck games.]

To Use The Strategy Chart:

Stand only when your true edge is equal to or greater than the number in the table. Double down only when your true edge is equal to or greater than the number in the table. Note that no soft doubling indices are provided here—there is very little value to varying from basic strategy in these situations. If you want to use these indices, you will find them in the Appendix.

Split all pairs according to basic strategy. A few of the ten splits have some dollar value, but there is very little value in varying from basic strategy on other pair-split decisions. You will find extensive pair-split indices, which may be useful camouflage, in the Appendix. Learn these if you want, but they are worth very little in dollars and cents.

Surrender only when your true edge is equal to or greater than the number in the table. Note that these are the late surrender indices. Should you discover an early surrender game, which is rare, you will find the proper indices in the Appendix.

Take insurance only when your true edge is equal to or greater than + 2.

The easiest way to learn the Hi-Lo Lite strategy indices is to start with the bold indices and learn them in blocks. Unless you play in games with surrender, you may ignore the bold indices for surrender.

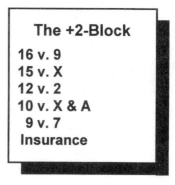

The 0-Block
16 v. X
13 v. 2 & 3
12 v. 3, 4, 5 & 6
11 v. A
10 v. 9
9 v. 2, 3 & 4

The +2-Block
16 v. 9
15 v. X
12 v. 2
10 v. X & A
9 v. 7
Insurance

The 0 Block is most important, and after that, learn the +2 Block. Shoe game players need never learn any indices other than these. If you play in hand-held games, these indices are still the most important. Learn the others in blocks, if you want to add an extra few tenths of a percent to your advantage, starting with the positive indices. The negative indices are least important.

Players who are familiar with traditional Hi-Lo strategy tables, or for that matter, with true count strategy tables for any balanced card counting system, may be surprised by the simplicity of the Hi-Lo Lite. Many experts will doubt its strength and playing accuracy. Allow me to describe the history of its development.

Early in 1991, I attempted to answer via computer simulation whether Stanford Wong's or Julian Braun's version of the Hi-Lo Count was more accurate. Both were respected programmers and blackjack authorities who had devised indices for the Hi-Lo Count that differed on dozens of decisions. Using John Imming's *Universal Blackjack Engine* software, I ran off 500-million hands of each strategy with a flat bet in single-deck games with Vegas Strip rules, using all indices between -15 and +15. At the end of the test, Wong's indices bettered Braun's result by .009% (less than one-hundredth of one percent), but the margin was within 2 standard errors, not a statistically significant result.

My simulation results led me to theorize that strategy index numbers may not be such precise indicators of when to alter basic strategy, or at least that the borderline for the coin-toss decisions may be fairly wide. I set up another test to see just how wide: I simulated a 6-deck Atlantic City game and ran off 200 million hands using Wong's *Professional Blackjack* indices. For the second simulation, I converted each of Wong's indices to -1, +1, or +4. I did this systematically—if Wong's index was -1 or -2, I made it -1. If he had an index of 0, +1, or +2, I made it +1. His +3, +4, and +5 indices all became +4. I then ran off another 200-million hands testing this simplified version of Wong's strategy. In both simulations, I used a 1 to 8 spread, and I also tested the effect of not betting on negative counts.

These were the results:

Strategy	Play All	No Neg.
Wong	+0.50%	+0.98%
Simplified	+0.51%	+0.99%

In a test of 200 million hands, the fact that the simplified version of the Hi-Lo outperformed the exact version by .01% is not mathematically significant. What is significant is that such an approximate version of the Hi-Lo strategy is equal to the standard, orthodox version.

I wondered how well this approach would work in single-deck games where playing strategy is so much more important, so I set up a Reno one-deck simulation, and used 60 indices from Wong's *Professional Blackjack*.

I ran 100 million hands, and tallied the results with both a flat bet and a 1 to 4 spread at 75% penetration. This time, in the "lite" version of the Hi-Lo, I widened the border again, converting all of Wong's indices to plus or minus 1, 5, or 10. The results:

Strategy	Flat Bet	1 to 4
Wong	-0.06%	+1.32%
Hi-Lo Lite	-0.05%	+1.33%

The fact that the Lite system outperformed Wong's by one-hundredth of one percent was, again, insignificant in a test of 100-million hands. What is important is that from the practical dollars-and-cents perspective, it doesn't matter which of these systems you use. The simulation results indicate that you may use a vastly simplified Hi-Lo strategy, and maintain full power, even in a one-deck game.

So, in 1991, I published a series of three articles in *Casino Player* magazine about this astonishing discovery. I developed the Hi-Lo Lite counting system to be a feature of the revised *Blackbelt in Blackjack,* but then, in October of 1991, the Oakland Firestorm destroyed the manuscript, so I published the Hi-Lo Lite without much fanfare in the December 1991 issue of *Blackjack Forum.* Since that time, I have been personally advising players to simplify their strategy charts with this modified approach.

John Imming later discovered the reason why the lite approach to indices works so well. In attempting to determine why his *Universal Blackjack Engine* software sometimes spat out different indices for the same counting system via simulations of hundreds of millions of hands, Imming discovered that the actual indices were not precise, but constantly wavered according to the level of penetration and other factors. Some indices went up and down by a few numbers until finally settling.

In 1997, Ken Fuchs, co-author of *Knock-Out Blackjack,* presented a paper at the 10th International Gambling Conference in which his simulation results of a slightly different lite counting system supported my findings. Then, George C. privately devised a lite version of the Zen Count, which John Auston tested against the regular Zen indices using the *Statistical Blackjack Analyzer* software. It took Auston a billion hands of each system to determine that the lite indices underperformed against the regular indices by about two-hundredths of one percent.

It was George C., incidentally, who discovered that all of the +1 and -1 lite indices could be adjusted to 0, with no notable loss of power. So, the version of Hi-Lo Lite published here has been further simplified. If you want to test the Hi-Lo Lite via computer simulations of your own, note that the true edge methodology is not the same as true-count-per-deck. If your blackjack simulation program does not allow you to enter indices as true-count-per-half-deck, then you must double the Hi-Lo Lite indices. For the most important strategy decisions, all indices are either 0 or +4. To fully adjust the complete chart, make all +2s into +4s, -4s into -8s, and so on, in order to test the system with a count-per-deck simulator.

7

TRUE COUNT

Introduction

True count is an adjusted running count that indicates the ratio of high cards to low cards. True count is, in fact, not "true" as a precise indicator of your advantage, but it does reflect the balance of the cards so that you may approximate both your advantage and your playing strategy.

Most level-one systems, like the Hi-Lo, recommend that true count be estimated as count per deck. The true edge with the Hi-Lo Lite is simply the count per half-deck. Some authors who have developed higher level counting systems, most notably Ken Uston and Lawrence Revere, have advised count-per-half-deck adjustments.

Take a full 52-card deck. Count the point value of all the tens and aces using the Hi-Lo Lite. With 16 tens and 4 aces counted as -1 each, the points add up to -20. If you now count all of the points of the low cards, 2's, 3's, 4's, 5's, and 6's, at +1 each, you'll find that these add up to +20. The deck is perfectly balanced between plus-valued cards and minus-valued cards.

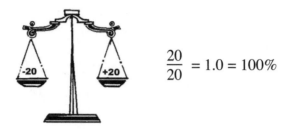

$$\frac{20}{20} = 1.0 = 100\%$$

Now, let's remove 8 tens and 2 aces from the deck. Adding up the point values of the high cards remaining in the deck, we now get -10. Our balance looks like this:

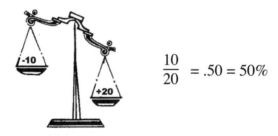

$$\frac{10}{20} = .50 = 50\%$$

The deck is heavy in low cards and light in high cards. There are, in fact, exactly half as many high card points as low card points in the remaining deck.

If this situation occurred at a blackjack table, that is, if 8 tens and 2 aces had been played in the first round of hands, and no low cards came out of the deck, the running count would be -10.

But consider what the balance would look like if this situation occurred while playing a 6-deck shoe game. To start with, six full decks contain 96 tens and 24 aces, or 120 total high cards, and there are also 120 total low cards. The high card points balanced against the low card points look like this:

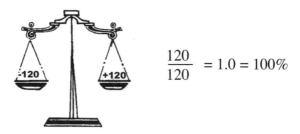

$$\frac{120}{120} = 1.0 = 100\%$$

Now, if we remove 8 tens and 2 aces, our balance looks like this:

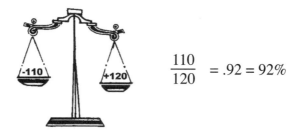

$$\frac{110}{120} = .92 = 92\%$$

The balance is only slightly tipped because there were so many more points to start with. Although the same cards as in our single-deck example have been removed, we still have nearly as many high card points as low card points in the shoe (92%, to be precise). What this means to card counters is that although the running count may be -10 in both situations, the advantage, and playing strategy, would differ. The running count must be adjusted to reflect the true balance of high cards to low cards.

True Count by Division

The most common method of determining true count is to divide the running count by the number of remaining decks (or half-decks). The chief difficulty of this method is that it often involves dividing by fractions. The true edge methods I propose solve this problem, and other methods may be used as well.

The "True Index" Method

For strategy variations, instead of adjusting your running count, you may find it easier to adjust your index number to the true index at which you would alter your basic strategy. This method works well for players who are not comfortable working with fractions.

With the Hi-Lo Lite you simply multiply the index number of the decision in question by the number of remaining half-decks, then compare this number to the running count. For instance, let's say you're trying to decide whether or not to take insurance in a 6-deck game with a running count of +9. Four decks have been played, so 2 remain. Since your Hi-Lo insurance index number is +2, you compute your true index by multiplying +2 by the 4 remaining half-decks, ending up with +8. And you would take insurance here because your running count of +9 is higher than the true index.

This method may be used for all strategy decisions, but to do it quickly, you must instantly know the number of half-decks remaining.

The "True Shoe" Method

To use this method of true count adjustment, you simply divide your running count (which is always a whole number) by the index number of the decision you are considering (also always a whole number), and the answer is the number of half-decks or fewer that must be remaining for you to make the play. For example, your Hi-Lo running count is +10 and you want to know whether you should stand on your hard total of 12 against the dealer's 2. Your standing index number for this decision is +2. Simply divide the running count of +10 by 2, which of course equals 5, and if less than 5 half-decks (2 1/2 decks) remain, you would stand. In order to justify this strategy deviation, with this running count, your true shoe size must be 2 1/2 decks or fewer. Otherwise, follow basic strategy and hit.

The easiest way to use the true shoe method, with any counting system, would be to first convert all strategy indices to count per deck. This way your running count divided by your index always results in the true number of decks remaining, instead of half or quarter-decks, where the decision changes.

NOTE:

If your running count is negative and your index number is positive, or vice versa, don't bother to make any true count adjustment using any method. Follow basic strategy.

Estimating the Remaining Decks

One art you will have to perfect, regardless of your method of true count adjustment, is estimating the number of remaining decks. You cannot do this without practice.

Buy yourself a few dozen decks of standard playing cards. Use casino-quality cards, preferably used ones from a casino, so that the thickness of the decks is the same as you will encounter when it counts. Many casinos sell their used decks in their gift shops. Make up stacks of cards containing 8 decks, 7 1/2 decks, 7, 6 1/2, 5 1/2, 5, 4 1/2, 4, 3 1/2, 3, 2 1/2, 2, 1 1/2, 1 and 1/2. (You will need to purchase 62 decks of cards to make up all of these stacks. Believe me, pros do it.) Familiarize yourself with exactly what each sized stack looks like.

In casinos, you won't see such precise stacks of discards very often, but your eyes will estimate to the nearest sized stack you can recognize so that you may make your adjustments effortlessly.

Never waste a moment in this estimation process. If it appears 2 1/4 decks are remaining, call it 2 1/2. Always round up—this way you'll play more conservatively. Call it 2 only when it's definitely below 2 1/4.

Also, when you eyeball one of your practice stacks, remember that you are looking at the *discards*. Therefore, if you assume that you're in a 6-deck game, and you look at a stack of 4 decks, you will make your true count adjustment based on 2 decks—the *remaining* decks. Be sure you practice this way.

True count adjustment is one of the most difficult aspects of card counting to master. Most counters are poorly trained in this area and should stick with the running count systems. If you ever try to join a professional blackjack team, don't be surprised if you are tested rigorously on true-count adjustments. The team captain will likely show you various-sized stacks of discards and give you hypothetical strategy decisions. He will expect you to respond with the proper plays immediately, based on your system. After each response, you'll have to explain in detail the method you used to make your decision.

I'm always surprised to hear sloppy, slow, and badly trained players profess that they would win a fortune if they just had the big bankroll behind them. They often complain about cheating dealers, poor conditions, negative fluctuations, and the like. But they use systems beyond their abilities and can't make accurate decisions to save their lives. These players—and the majority of card counters fall into this group—are the meat and potatoes of the casino industry.

8

THE ZEN COUNT

The Zen Count is a balanced card-counting strategy for counters with above average skill. If you can use the Zen Count accurately, it will add about 0.1% to your advantage in shoe games, and about 0.2% in single-deck games, compared to what you would expect with the Hi-Lo Lite. The recommended drills for learning how to count cards are the same for the Zen Count as for the Red Seven Count or the Hi-Lo Lite, so these exercises will not be repeated here.

The Zen Count Point Values

The point values of the Zen Count are:

A	-1
X	-2
9	0
8	0
7	+1
6	+2
5	+2
4	+2
3	+1
2	+1

As the cards are played, keep a running count of all cards seen. After a shuffle, the count starts again at 0. Like the Hi-Lo Lite, this is a balanced counting system, so if you count down a complete deck, starting at 0, your final count will also be 0. Because the point values are balanced, you also have to adjust your running count to the true edge. All Zen Count betting and playing strategy decisions must be made according to the true edge, not the running count.

Because the Zen Count has more complex point values than the Hi-Lo Lite, it is more accurate. With the Zen Count, you must estimate the true edge by dividing your running count by the number of remaining decks, multiplied by 4 (instead of 2). Otherwise, you use the same make-a-fraction method, in which the running count is the numerator, and the denominator is the number of remaining decks multiplied by 4. In order to do this quickly at the tables, you must memorize the following chart:

Decks Remaining	Denominator
8	32
7	28
6	24
5	20
4	16
3	12
2	8
1	4
1/2	2

I think most players who remember their multiplication tables from third grade could reproduce this chart with no memory work whatsoever. It is important that you are able to immediately insert this denominator into your fraction so that your true edge does not require you to make calculations at the table. If your running count is +7 with 3 decks remaining to be dealt, you should immediately know that your true edge has risen by 7/12, or slightly more than 1/2%.

With a running count of +19, and 2 decks remaining, the true edge is 19/8, or almost a 2 1/2% raise from the starting advantage. If you have any trouble with fractions like these—for instance, if you do not know fairly quickly that 19/8 is about 2 1/2—then you should not use the Zen Count. I would suggest that you stick with the simple Red Seven, and play according to running count. In my opinion, the true edge method is the easiest way to adjust a running count to estimate your advantage precisely, but not all players are comfortable with the math.

In the first half of the shoe, you can just as accurately estimate the remaining decks to the nearest whole deck by always rounding up. For example, if your running count is +10, and 5 1/2 decks remain to be dealt, round up to 6 decks, and then make the fraction 11/24, which is easy and accurate enough for bet-sizing. It is clear that your advantage has risen slightly less than 1/2%. Technically, with 5 1/2 decks remaining, it would be more accurate to use the denominator 22, halfway between 5 and 6 decks remaining. The true edge is more precisely 11/22, or exactly a 1/2% raise. The real difference between 11/24 and 11/22, however, is so small that it is unlikely to have any effect on the bet size.

Deeper in the shoe, however, as the denominators get smaller, the effect of rounding the remaining decks up to the nearest full deck will have more of an effect. In the previous example, with a running count of +19 and 2 decks remaining, we came up with the fraction 19/8, or just under 2 1/2. If there was actually only one deck remaining (which we rounded up to 2), our actual fraction should have been 19/6, which is slightly better than 3%.

Again, this is more important when there are fewer than 4 decks remaining. By rounding up from 1 1/2 to 2 decks, you should tend to bet more conservatively, which is better than rounding down and overbetting. Some players may want to make a chart of denominators in half-deck increments, but I doubt that it's necessary. If you know that your 4-deck denominator is 16, and your 3-deck denominator is 12, it would probably not take more than an instant for you to come up with a denominator of 14 if you estimated that 3 1/2 decks remain in the shoe.

In single-deck games (or in any multiple-deck game that's played down into the last deck), the most accurate method of true edge adjustment is to break the deck into four distinct quarters. In the first quarter, your true edge is your running count divided by 4; in the second quarter, it's divided by 3; in the third quarter, divided by 2. And in the bottom quarter, your true edge is simply your running count, as a running count of +6 with a quarter deck or less remaining to be dealt would indicate a 6% raise in your advantage.

I think it is very practical to know your advantage quickly while you play, and the Zen true edge method is simply a count-per-quarter-deck adjustment, which will always provide you with your true edge when you use the make-a-fraction technique. You might also note that the Zen true edge playing strategy chart is much simpler than the old count-per-deck chart. In fact, it is very similar to the Hi-Lo Lite chart.

The Zen Count Playing Strategy

The strategy changes here provide most of the gains available from the Zen Count system. You may use these indices for any number of decks, and any set of rules. In shoe games, you only need the bold indices. If you play in games where the dealer hits soft 17, you will find these indices, along with many others, in the Appendix. Use basic strategy for all decisions for which no index number is provided.

TO USE THE CHART:

Stand only when your true edge is equal to or greater than the number in the table.

Double down only when your true edge is equal to or greater than the number in the table. Note that no soft doubling indices are provided here, as there is very little value to varying from basic strategy on soft doubling decisions. (If you want to use these indices, you will find them in the Appendix.)

Split all pairs according to basic strategy. A few of the ten splits have some dollar value, but it's not a great play for most card counters because it draws so much heat. There is little dollar value to varying from basic strategy on other pair-split decisions. You will find extensive pair-split indices in the Appendix. Learn these if you want, but they are worth very little in dollars and cents.

Surrender only when your true edge is equal to or greater than the number in the table. Note that these are the late surrender indices; should you discover an early surrender game, you will find the proper indices in the Appendix.

Take insurance only when your true edge is equal to or greater than the +1.

THE GENERIC ZEN STRATEGY FOR ANY NUMBER OF DECKS ASSUMES STAND ON SOFT 17

	2	3	4	5	6	7	8	9	X	A

STAND

	2	3	4	5	6	7	8	9	X	A
16							4	**2**	**0**	3
15	-2							4	**1**	4
14	-1	-2	-2						3	
13	**0**	**-1**	-1	-2	-2					
12	**1**	**1**	**0**	**-1**	**0**					

DOUBLE DOWN

	2	3	4	5	6	7	8	9	X	A
11								-2	-2	**0**
10							-2	-1	**1**	**1**
9	**0**	**0**	-1	-2		**2**	4			
8		4	3	2	1					

SURRENDER

	2	3	4	5	6	7	8	9	X	A
16							2	**0**	-2	-1
8-8								4	**0**	
15							3	**1**	0	1
14							4	2	1	2
7-7									1	
13									3	

INSURANCE: 1

BOLD = Major indices for all games

[The light indices are important in single-and double-deck games.]

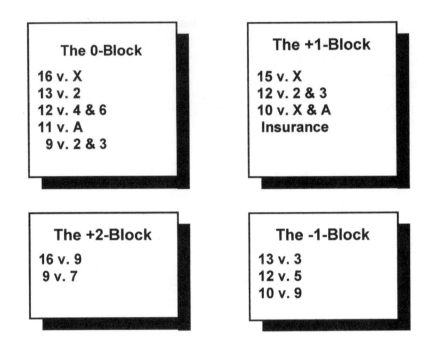

The easiest way to learn the Zen strategy indices is to start with the bold indices and learn them in blocks. Unless you play in games that include it, you may also ignore the bold indices for surrender.

The 0 Block is most important. After you learn that, learn the +1 Block, then the +2 Block, and finally, the -1 Block. Shoe game players don't have to bother with any indices other than these. If you play in hand-held games, these indices are still the most important. Learn the others in blocks, if you want to add an extra few tenths of a percent to your advantage, starting with the positive indices. The negative indices are least important.

If you want to test the Zen Count system using computer simulations, and your blackjack program does not allow you to enter indices as true-count-per-quarter-deck, then you must multiply all of the Zen indices by 4, in order to use a traditional count-per-deck adjustment. The -1, +1, and +2 indices become -4, +4, and +8, respectively.

9

PHONY SYSTEMS

If you ever read any of the slick gambling magazines that you find in casino gift shops and hotel rooms, you've probably noticed ads telling you that you can haul in mucho bucks anytime you want, that you won't have to work for a living any more, and, in fact, you can even buy your own private jet and an island in the South Pacific if you just buy one of the advertised systems, which are so easy to use that some of the lower primates could probably learn them. It's a good thing casinos don't pay off in bananas.

Ads like this remind me of the comic book ads that used to catch my attention when I was a kid. I was a *Superman* addict, and every issue had a few pages of ads for mail order products that indulged my fantasies of becoming the "Man of Steel." Of course, there was the familiar "I-was-a-97-pound weakling" pitch for turning my puny 12-year-old excuse for a body into something that looked like King Kong on steroids. According to the ad, with only 15 minutes per day of easy exercise, I'd be huge in a month. Or, for only a buck, I could get a secret ancient chart of the body's "pressure points," which would immediately transform me into an invincible Master of the Asian Fighting Arts. Muggers, thugs, and linebackers would gasp and tremble when I entered the room.

My favorite, however, had to be the ad for the "X-Ray Specs." Here was a 59¢ pair of glasses that purported to give me Superman's incredible x-ray vision—and with it the ability to see through doors, walls, and most importantly, clothing. This ad always had a cartoon illustration of some dodo wearing the specs with his tongue falling out of his mouth while he's gawking at a fully clothed dish striking a come-up-and-see-me-sometime pose.

For years, I read this ad and relished the possibilities. Even at that age, however, my inborn cynicism told me the specs probably wouldn't work. And 59¢ was too much to gamble to find out.

I'll never forget that hot day in August, however, when my friend Ralph announced he had broken down and sent away for a pair of X-Ray Specs. Word spread through our neighborhood like wildfire. Every pubescent kid on the east side of Detroit had been fantasizing about owning a pair of these goggles since they'd first laid eyes on a Superman comic. Now Ralph was going to realize our fantasies.

It must have been 10 weeks before the specs came in the mail. To us it seemed like an eternity of asking Ralph day after day, "Did they come yet?" We all had big plans for those wonder glasses. As soon as we saw that Ralph's worked, we would all get some. We'd wear 'em to school. The nuns would never suspect what we were up to. We'd go watch the girls play softball. The women of Detroit were about to become unwitting exhibitionists for a gang of horny 12-year-old Catholic schoolboys in funny glasses.

To make a long story short, the X-Ray Specs didn't x-ray anything. They were ridiculous-looking cardboard and plastic gizmos that made the person wearing them look like a jerk. As Ralph described the phenomenal X-Ray power of the lenses when he slowly and reverently placed them on his eyes for the first time, "Well...um...they just make everything look...um...blurry."

Alas, the women of Detroit were safe.

I haven't read a *Superman* comic in quite a few years, but it wouldn't surprise me one bit if X-Ray Specs are still being hawked to 12-year-old thrill seekers. Meanwhile, *Gambling Fool* magazine is publishing adult variations of this comic book advertising ("Win a Million Bucks a Day Even if you're Stupid!"). I find it amusing how these ads for "incredible and amazing" gambling systems insist that it doesn't take much effort to get rich. That's exactly who's going to fall for this nonsense—people who don't put much mental effort into anything.

If Ralph reads this ad, he'll break down and have a check in the mail before his next mortgage payment is due. Six months later, when the bank is foreclosing on his house, if you ask him how his mail order blackjack system is working, he'll say, "Well...um...you see...um..."

Alas, the casinos of Vegas are safe too.

The Martingale: Progression To Depression

I used to write a blackjack Q & A column for *Card Player* magazine. This was one of the questions that came in:

> I lost a substantial amount of my savings playing blackjack at in Atlantic City—almost $30,000. I admit that I was using a progressive betting system—a "straight martingale," and I know that won't give me any advantage—but even so, I feel pretty certain that I was cheated. I was winning steadily for quite a few hours using this system (a simple double-up after a loss), then in a short series of hands that lasted only about 30 minutes— they totally cleaned me out. I was playing perfect basic strategy.
>
> I have enclosed a chart that shows the series of bets I made, and the win/loss results that eventually bankrupted me. I would like to know your expert opinion on whether or not this could have happened in an honest game. Can I take any kind of legal action against the casino if this series of hands [indicates] cheating? I have a friend who witnessed the debacle who can attest to the truth of what happened.

The "martingale" is the granddaddy of all "betting progression" type systems. It is essentially a system whereby you progressively increase your bet to make up for prior losses. The theory sounds reasonable, since no one will lose forever. A single win will wipe out all prior losses, so the system seems foolproof. So, how did this guy lose $30,000? He sent me a partial record of what had happened.

Here's how I answered his letter:

> I have studied your results, and although anyone would acknowledge that you suffered an unusually unlucky series of hands—and an especially devastatingly unlucky series for any martingale player—the series of hands in and of itself would not be indicative of cheating.

I highly doubt you were cheated.

The straight martingale is one of the riskiest betting systems any gambler could use. Any gambler who ever has used it with any regularity could tell you his own hair-raising "impossibly unlucky" tale of why he gave it up for more conservative methods. Here is what happened to you:

1. You bet $10, and lost.
2. You bet $20, and lost.
3. You bet $40, and lost.
4. You bet $80, and lost.
5. You bet $160, and doubled down on your 11 vs. the dealer 8, and you lost.
6. This double loss required you to place a next bet of $480, which you then lost.
7. You placed a bet of $960, and split your 8s vs. a dealer 10, and you lost both hands.
8. This double loss required you to place a bet of $2,880, which was higher than the $2,000 table max. So you bet the max, and lost.
9. On your next hand, you bet the max again, and insured your 20 vs. the dealer ace. You lost both the insurance bet, and your hand when the dealer hit to 21. This put you behind by a total of $7,880.
10. You then bet the max, and pushed.
11. You then bet the max and won!

You say that the above series of results took about 10 minutes, and that you do not recall the exact series of wins and losses in the approximately two-dozen hands that you played over the next 20 minutes. You note there were a few wins interspersed with the losses, but you had to have had 12 more max bet losses than wins (perhaps 18 losses and 6 wins?), as you left the table a $29,980 loser.

How "impossible" is this?

Unfortunately, not very.

You must realize that you were required to start placing max bets after only seven consecutive losses.

Once you are actually placing $2,000 bets, a loss of $30,000 is not at all unusual. This would be equivalent to a $5 bettor losing $75—which any experienced $5 bettor could tell you would not be uncommon. If you count your double loss on your split pair as two hands, you actually began your unfortunate series of losses by losing 10 hands in a row. How unusual is this?

If I was flipping a coin, with heads being a win, and tails a loss, the odds against me coming up tails 10 times in a row would be about 1,000 to 1. That's pretty unlikely, though far from impossible.

Blackjack, however, is less advantageous than a coin flip. In 100 hands, a basic strategy player will experience, on average, 43 wins, 48 losses and 9 pushes. Since a martingale bettor ignores pushes and lets his bet ride, we can ignore them in our analysis. For every 100 win/loss decisions, a basic strategy player will see about 53 losses and 47 wins.

With these win/loss proportions, the odds against losing 10 consecutive decisions are only about 500 to 1. Now 500 to 1 may seem nearly impossible to many people, but realistically, at any given time, a series of losses equivalent to yours happens to dozens of players in Atlantic City, and to hundreds of people every day of the year in U.S. casinos. It's happening right now to one out of every 500 people who are playing. How many tens of thousands of people are playing blackjack right now in U.S. casinos?

You must realize that if you had been flat-betting $10, instead of "doubling-up" to try to recapture your previous losses, you would only have lost $110 (and this includes both your pair-split and your double down loss!), instead of being behind by $7,880 at the end of that first unfortunate string of losses. And your total loss at the end of the debacle would only have been $230, not $29,980.

The martingale is a systematic method of chasing your losses. There's no other way to describe it. This is about the most foolish way to gamble. You violated the single most important rule for gamblers: "If you can't afford to lose it, don't bet it."

Shuffle-Bored, Anyone?

Ever since players learned that there was a real method of beating the casino blackjack tables based on "tracking" the shuffles, the "nonrandom shuffle" gurus started making the rounds with systems that seemed to be based on related theories. Every few years for the past two decades, some self-proclaimed genius starts hustling a blackjack system based on the fact that casino shuffles do not distribute the cards randomly. For a few hundred bucks, one of these brilliant system developers will sell you the inside scoop on how to play blackjack by following the "trends," "clumps," and "biases."

Many variations have hit the scene, but the theory and playing methodology never really change much. Here's how Swami Nonrandomi's logic goes:

First, it's necessary to acknowledge that casino-style shuffles are less than perfect, and that the cards are not randomly distributed by these shuffles. No problem, since anyone who has played any length of time at casino blackjack tables can see that sloppy shuffles are easy to find. When new decks are brought in, it's not unusual to see occasional cards being dealt in consecutive new-deck order. So we know the shuffles are imperfect.

Next, you must accept the fact that these nonrandom shuffles affect the decisions on the hands dealt. No problem again. If you happen to see a dealer hit his fourteen with a six of spades, right after you doubled down on your eleven against his four up—and you caught the spade five—then you will be a believer. Yes! Yes! Those nonrandom clumps are killing me!

Now, what if you had a system designed to play those clumpy games? A system that made rational assumptions about hitting and standing based on the severity of the clumps? Yes! Yes!

Finally, a blackjack system that takes into account the kinds of weird stuff we actually see in the casinos. It's not a system based on some mathematician's analysis of some computer programmer's simulated billion hands of play. This is a reality-based system, and that's the only kind of system that works in the real world.

Card counters are out there talking about advantages of 1%, and they don't even realize that the casinos sometimes have a 10% advantage over them, based on the nonrandom shuffles. What's worse is that the same counters don't realize that they can get a 10% advantage over the casinos, courtesy of the same lousy shuffles.

Et cetera, et cetera, et cetera…

A lot of players buy this baloney, and to be honest, it sounds very legit. There's only one thing I don't like about Swami Nonrandomi's "logic," and that is that it cannot be proven by computer simulation.

John Imming's *Real World Casino* (RWC) software was the first software available to players that allowed programmable, nonrandom, casino-style shuffles. (The RWC software is no longer on the market.) The deck(s) begin in regulation new deck order, and the shuffle routines simulate actual riffles, strips, cuts, and washes, as fine or as clumpy as you decide, even utilizing casino-style breaks into multiple shuffling segments if you so desire.

Here's what I found with the RWC software:

The biggest effect on the player's expectation that I could find comes from no shuffling whatsoever. Ironically, this is a player advantage, not a house advantage. I've tried Imming's software with 1, 2, 4, 6, and 8 deck games, with both lay & pay and pick & pay dealing styles, and the player advantage rises by .70%-.75% if playing one-on-one with the dealer, regardless of the number of decks in play or the pick up style. Somehow, the play of the hands puts the cards into an order that favors the player.

Both Stanford Wong and John Gwynn had independently discovered this years earlier. Wong, in fact, ran a computer analysis to determine how the play of the hands ordered the discards, and he discovered that in the discard pile high cards do tend to clump with high cards, and vice versa. We don't know why this favors the player, but it does.

As multiple players are added to the table, this no-shuffle player advantage diminishes. For some reason, the first base side of the table retains the advantage, but the third base side loses it and then some.

Once you start adding any type of shuffle at all to the game, however, the player advantages decrease, until the real world shuffle results are indistinguishable from the outcome of random-number-generated shuffles. The biggest effect I could find in a simulated casino game, utilizing what I figured to be the sloppiest shuffle you might realistically expect to find, was a couple tenths of a percent more or less than the normal basic strategy expectation.

My attempts at creating a sloppy shuffle that would have a greater effect than this were unsuccessful, even though the RWC software allows unlimited variations on lousy, inadequate shuffles.

So, where is this monstrous effect that Swami Nonrandomi promises? I just don't buy the explanation that it happens in a casino, but not in a computer. Why not? New deck order is new deck order, and nonrandom sloppiness is nonrandom sloppiness. There's nothing magical about a lousy, lopsided riffle that a computer can't simulate.

But there is one factor all the nonrandom shuffle gurus have in common. They all say: "Oh, by the way, you can't simulate this effect on a computer." Yet they spout all kinds of precise percentages, based on their "personal studies."

I say, "Baloney." Computers may not be able simulate everything under the sun, but card games are one of the things computers are very good at simulating, especially if what you're looking to calculate is a player's expectation against a fixed house strategy. So take a hike, Swami. I don't believe in gambling systems based on faith. If you can't do the math, hit the path.

The "No Need To Count" System

Various books and systems purport to contain workable "non-counting" systems for blackjack. Most of these systems are based on some form of betting progression—and there are hundreds of variations on both the martingale and other types of progressions and regressions.

Some systems, however, take a "situational betting" approach. These types of systems are a radical departure from normal card counting systems, and also from the standard "betting progression" systems. The system sellers who propose these types of systems claim that computer simulations show that without counting cards, per se, certain playing situations will indicate that the house advantage will be higher or lower on the next hand to be dealt.

In fact, there is a truth to this claim. As far back as 1978, Dr. John Gwynn and Professor Armand Seri (both of California State University in Sacramento) published a paper that first described valid situational betting techniques—and Gwynn and Seri based their findings on extensive computer simulations.

What Gwynn and Seri determined beyond any doubt were three facts:

1. If a player loses a hand, he will be more likely to win the next one—i.e., losing one hand is a positive indicator that the player has a better expectation on the next.
2. If a player wins a hand, he will be more likely to lose the next one—i.e., winning one hand is an indicator that the player's expectation on

the next has dropped.

3. If a player pushes a hand with the dealer, it is an even stronger indicator that the player's expectation on the next hand has dropped.

For a number of years following the Gwynn/Seri situational discoveries, blackjack betting systems began appearing that advanced situational betting theory beyond the win/loss/push indicators. Other proven situational advantage indicators are:

4. Following a non-ace pair-split, the player's expectation rises.

5. Following an ace split, the player's expectation drops.

6. Following a hard double down, the player's expectation rises.

7. Following any hand (player or dealer) that requires 4 or more cards, the player's expectation rises.

8. Following any hand in which both the player and the dealer use 4 or more cards, the player's expectation rises more dramatically.

9. Following any blackjack (player or dealer), the player's expectation drops.

10. Following any hand in which neither the player nor the dealer has taken any hits, the player's expectation drops.

All of this can be proven by computer simulation. A player who always raises his bet after positive indicators, and lowers it after negative indicators, will have an expectation greater than a player who puts the same amount of money into action flat betting. (We're assuming that both players are playing basic strategy.)

Now, wouldn't it be much easier than employing a card counting system for a player to just memorize the 5 positive indicators and the 5 negative indicators and to raise and lower his bets accordingly?

Absolutely!

So, why aren't blackjack experts singing the praises of the situational systems?

The problem with utilizing this type of strategy is that none of the advantage indicators are very strong. In most games, they would simply indicate that the house had less of an advantage over the player, not that the advantage is with the player. In deeply dealt one-deck games, with good (Las Vegas Strip) rules, all of these indicators combined might provide a player making small bets of $5 and high bets of $100 (1-20 spread) with an expectation of about $1-$2 per hour. In other words, no individual situational indicator is worth more than a few hundredths of a percent, and all of them combined are not worth much more than a few tenths of a percent, in a deeply dealt one-deck game with a big betting spread.

I have nothing against any player making $1-$2 per hour, especially if he would otherwise be breaking even (or worse) just using basic strategy, so why don't I advise players who are not up to the task of card counting to use this easy situational approach? Because this non-counting method looks more like card counting to the game protection personnel than real card counting! Using a system like this is the fastest way to get barred as a card counter! All you have to do is consider the situations that are used as positive/negative indicators. In every case, the positive indicators coincide with a probability that more low cards than high cards have just come out of the deck. The negative indicators come into play when the opposite is true.

For example, Indicator #3 is that a push indicates a drop in player advantage. Why would this be true? It's not that every push indicates this; but the most common push is a player 20 (two tens) against a dealer 20 (two tens), so that pushes taken as a group more often indicate that high cards have been removed from the deck.

Gwynn's and Seri's studies also showed that, more often than not, a player win was slightly more likely with high cards coming out of the deck, and vice versa. Technically, it's not the win, loss, or push that really indicates the more probable result of the next hand, but the removal of high or low cards from the deck.

In fact, this type of situational play—despite the fact that you are not technically assigning count values to the cards—really is just a very weak card counting system. It's not strong enough to win you any money, but it will be recognizable enough to casino personnel to get you kicked out of the game (assuming you can find a deeply dealt one-decker with Strip rules, so that you can even test your 1-20 betting spread).

So, situational play is just an interesting theory, not a practical moneymaking system.

The "Overdue" Systems

Here's another question sent to me by a player:

> What do you think of the "Triplet" system, which I recently purchased by mail order. The system is made for playing craps, but I think the theory behind it would be useful for blackjack also, or any other games of chance. The author even says you can use it for roulette, and

100

describes how on the last page. The system costs $100, but I only had to send $25 to get it. I'm supposed to send the other $75 after I win it from the casinos. It seems to me the publisher is pretty confident that I'll win, since he sent me the complete system below wholesale.

My answer:

"You purchased four photocopied pages for $25. The total cost to 'manufacture' this system to the author/publisher/seller was realistically about 25¢. Add to this the cost of an envelope and a 37¢ postage stamp, and the seller's overhead expenses on this sale come to about 65¢. So, even though you were shrewd enough to buy this system 'below wholesale,' I don't think the seller is sweating that $75 you still owe him. I suspect most 'shrewd' purchasers of this system never send the remaining $75 owed for one simple reason: This system isn't worth the paper it's printed on. My heart goes out to the tree that died for this nonsense.

"I agree with you that the 'theory' behind this craps system would apply equally to all even money bets in any game of chance, assuming the theory was valid for the game of craps in the first place. But it's not. Ironically, it's slightly more valid for blackjack than it is for other casino games—but not valid enough to be profitable.

"To simplify the author's brainstorm, he is proposing that because it is unlikely to have three consecutive same results, you will make money if you wait until two consecutive same results have already occurred, then bet against the third occurrence. For example, if the pass line wins twice in a row, bet 'no pass' rather than pass. At roulette, if red comes up twice in a row, bet black, etc. The system also combines this ploy with a martingale double-up betting strategy to be applied when you are losing.

"At any given time in the past twenty years you would have been able to find dozens of craps, roulette, and blackjack systems on the mail order market espousing this same faulty theory. When I read your letter, and examined the 'Triplet' system you enclosed, I almost tossed it in the circular file as just more garbage. I wanted to write you a short personal note telling you the system was worthless, but you failed to include your address on your letter. Then, it struck me that this type of system is one of the most common types of phony baloney systems on the market that seem to be based on 'logic.' So, let's debunk this theory once and for all.

"It makes sense to many people that it is unlikely (or, at least, less than a 50/50 chance) that three consecutive same results would occur. If the crap table had an even money payout bet on the layout that three consecutive pass or don't pass results would occur, and you could take either side of this wager—call it 'triplet' or 'don't triplet'—we could all get rich by betting 'don't triplet.' This, in fact, is the analogy the author of the Triplet system uses in describing the 'logic' behind his method.

"The error the author makes is in assuming that the "don't triplet" bet is just as strong after two of the three 'don't' results have already occurred, when all you're betting against is the occurrence of the third result.

"WRONG!

"The reason the 'don't triplet' bet would be so profitable if it were on the layout with an even money payout is precisely because there are three chances for the triplet to fail. Using a simple coin flip example, we all know that with an honest coin there is a 50/50 (even money) chance that heads will come up.

"For two consecutive heads results, however, the odds are 3 to 1 against it. This is easy to see if we consider all possible results of two flips:

1. H,H

2. H,T

3. T,H

4. T,T

"We only win once, but lose three times, with the four possible outcomes. For three consecutive heads to come up, the odds are 7 to 1 against it:

1. H,H,H

2. H,H,T

3. H,T,H

4. T,H,H

5. H,T,T

6. T,H,T

7. T,T,H

8. T,T,T

"Out of these eight possible outcomes of three consecutive flips, there are seven losses and one win, if we're betting on three consecutive heads.

"But, as soon as I stipulate that two consecutive heads have already occurred, the odds against the third occurrence are no longer 7 to 1. What

I'm looking at is 'H, H,' where only that third result figures into the bet, and we're back to a 50/50 chance of it being either heads or tails. If I pulled out an honest quarter, and offered you an even money bet that I could flip three heads in a row, you'd be very smart to take the bet, since the odds against me doing it are 7 to 1. In fact, you could give me 6 to 1 odds and still make money on this bet in the long run. But if I said, 'Wait until I flip two consecutive heads, then I'll bet you that I can flip a third head,' you'd be foolish to give me anything other than even money, because it's back to being a 50/50 proposition. At a crap table, or roulette table, you are giving the house odds on that third bet, because unlike our coin flip example, the house has a 1.41% advantage over you on the pass line, and a 5.26% advantage over you on the even money bets with a double-0 wheel. The Triplet system does nothing to change the house edge.

"Any time you see a system that tells you to consider the likelihood or unlikelihood of occurrence of some result, based on results that have already occurred, don't waste your time or money with it. I call these 'overdue' systems, because the sellers often claim that when there has been a preponderance of reds, black is 'overdue.'

"The reason I said that this 'Triplet' system is slightly more valid if applied to blackjack than to other casino games is that computer simulations have shown that in blackjack, wins are slightly more likely to follow losses, and losses to follow wins, as explained in our discussion of 'situational' betting systems. Unlike dice or roulette, the cards do have 'memory.' That is, cards that have already been played are out of the game until the next shuffle.

"But, as also explained, you can't expect to get rich applying the 'Triplet' system to blackjack. The total change in your win/loss expectation based on previous wins or losses at a blackjack table is measurable in thousandths of a percent, not enough to overcome the house advantage."

Big Secrets

Another player's question:

> I purchased a blackjack system through the mail about six months ago. It was very expensive, and in order to obtain it I had to sign a contract stating that I would never disclose the system to anyone else, and that I would never show the materials I received to any other blackjack system seller. The advertising materials made a big issue of the fact that some other system seller might try to steal

this system, and that the author would prosecute any purchaser who revealed his secrets to competitors. After six months of losing with this system, I feel I've been had. I would like to get a professional opinion on whether or not this system has any value, but how can I get an opinion if I can't even show this system to anyone else?

My answer:

"You've been had, in my opinion. Over the years I've seen photocopies of about a dozen different systems sold with some kind of binding contract stating that the purchaser would never reveal the system to anyone else, and in every case so far, my opinion has been that the system was worthless. My cynical opinion of the secrecy contract is that its sole purpose is to keep you from obtaining a professional opinion, not to keep unscrupulous peddlers from stealing the system.

"There are very few blackjack books or systems that have been published in the past decade that I haven't had a chance to examine. Most authors send me their books for review. Those systems that aren't sent to me by the authors or publishers are usually sent to me by players who want to know my professional opinion. Secrecy contract or not, I think just about everything published on blackjack crosses my desk eventually.

"Some system-sellers write long treatises on how you will be violating international copyright laws if you photocopy their material; you'll be investigated by the FBI, the CIA, the Federal Trade Commission…and it's all nonsense.

"The copyright laws are written to protect authors and publishers from losing income. If you photocopy something for the purpose of obtaining a professional opinion from an expert in that field, you haven't violated copyright laws. You're not selling the photocopies for any personal gain, nor are you in any way affecting the copyright owner's income from the sale of his work.

"Signing a contract not to disclose information is something else again. I'm no attorney, and I'm not going to get into my understanding of the validity of inane contracts. My advice to anyone who is required to sign a secrecy contract in order to purchase a gambling system is simple. Don't do it. The system is probably worthless. The system seller is probably trying to keep you from obtaining honest expert opinions. The system seller probably doesn't care if the secrecy contract you signed is valid, so long as the check you signed is."

Psychic Gamblers

One more real question sent to me by a player:

> Has there ever been a test of psychic abilities with regards to making gambling decisions? How would the casinos protect themselves against psychic gamblers?

> I am not psychic myself but I have seen some pretty impressive demonstrations by psychics, especially one very gifted individual with whom I have discussed this idea at some length. I am considering forming a team with this gentleman to take on the casinos of the world, starting in Atlantic City. Would the A.C. casinos be allowed to prohibit us from playing for exhibiting psychic abilities under the current regulations?

My response:

"Is this a put on? Every few years it seems I get a letter asking about the use of mental telepathy, or astrology, or numerology, or some other less-than-scientific approach to beating the gaming tables. Though I make no personal claim to psychic talents, I prefer to take these queries at face value, give the questioner the benefit of the doubt, and assume the question is sincere.

"The good news is that the Atlantic City casinos are not allowed to bar players for displays of psychic power! In fact, if it's the possibility of being barred that most distresses you in this proposed venture, then you and your psychic sidekick should just stay put in A.C., and forget the rest of the world.

"Casinos in Nevada, and everywhere else that I know of except New Jersey, may bar players from their games pretty much at whim. In New Jersey, the Casino Control Commission requires casinos to allow all players who are playing according to the rules and regulations—provided they are not drunk and disorderly or otherwise a public nuisance—to gamble. The official rules and regulations do not define psychic decision-making as a gaming violation.

"You can thank the late Ken Uston for making AC's gaming tables safe for psychics—though I'm sure he never intended that.

"I have a couple questions for you, however:

"One, why would any real psychic want to team up with you, since you admit you possess no such skills? Any player who could predict just the blackjack dealer's hole card, or the next card to be dealt from the shoe, could quickly bankrupt any table he sat down at. Likewise, if he could predict the next roll of the dice, or where the roulette ball would fall…A psychic doesn't need a team. Donald Trump is no match for an honest-to-goodness psychic.

"Two, don't you find it just a little bit curious that no casino in the world has provisions for dealing with psychic threats to their coffers? Especially when you consider that no casino could survive if even a small handful of psychics were roaming the pits looking for action?

"Wait…I know…your job in this 'psychic team' deal is to supply the money, right? Am I right? (Am I psychic, or what?)

"Quite frankly, if there is some self-styled psychic trying to convince you to 'invest' in this get-rich-quick scam, wise up. And why didn't this psychic wonder inform you in advance of my opinion on this matter?"

10

PROBLEM GAMBLING

It may seem peculiar for a book on card counting to address compulsive gambling, but I've gotten too many letters through the years from players who have lost their life savings trying to beat the tables. I've been asked many times if I thought a compulsive gambler could learn to play blackjack professionally.

This used to strike me as a weird question; now I know that it's a question that is seriously pondered by compulsive gamblers. I have no way of knowing how many compulsive gamblers will read this book, but I suspect more than a handful.

If I were considered to be an expert on fine wines by those who appreciate fine wines, would I be asked: "Do you think an alcoholic could learn to be an expert on wine so that he could make his living by drinking?"

I suppose a compulsive gambler could learn to play blackjack at a professional level, to the same extent that an alcoholic might be able to make a successful career out of drinking. This is a bizarre world we live in, so anything is possible. I'm sure a sex addict could find work in porno films, and a psychopathic killer could get a job as an executioner.

Generally speaking, however, most addicts do best in life by learning to stay away from activities and environments that fuel their addictions. One problem that a compulsive gambler faces is that he is competing with professional gamblers (in most cases, casinos), who do not share his compulsion, and his competition will likely take advantage of his weakness, which means that he will have more than his share of losing streaks...and if you lose more than you win, are you still a professional?

Let's define the players:

A professional gambler is a player who's willing to risk money on the outcome of the game, and who, by selecting only advantageous bets, wins more than he loses in the long run. In poker games, for instance, the professionals make a living by taking money from the amateurs. At the racetrack, the pari-mutuel betting system assures the track of making a profit, while the professional horse bettors beat the public. Likewise, a bookie, or any casino sports book, takes it's vigorish from both sides of the line, while the pro sports bettors beat the public at large. In all of these arenas, bettors primarily compete against each other, while the house rakes a percentage from everybody. In all of these types of games, compulsive gamblers contribute mightily to the share taken home by the pros. In a game like casino blackjack, however, the bettor competes with the casino directly. The casinos are themselves the largest class of blackjack professionals, as they *always* make money at this game, though there are a few professional players (mostly card counters) who beat the casinos.

But whether we're talking about individual players, teams, or casinos, any professional gambler will immediately put his money away the moment it becomes apparent to him that he no longer has the best of it. This is not an emotional decision to a professional gambler, any more than it is an emotional decision to a professional stock investor to pull capital out of one investment, and stick it in another, based on factors of estimated risk and expected return on investment.

A pro has one goal: to maximize the return on his investment. He's in it for the money. A compulsive gambler has a different goal: to keep his money in action. He's in it for the action. It's a different motivation, that's all.

This is what it boils down to: A pro sees gambling as a means to money; a compulsive sees money as a means to gambling. That's the difference between the two.

Compulsive gamblers pose big problems to the professionals, like, "should we eat them for breakfast, lunch, or dinner?" This is true in all forms of gambling, including the stock market, real estate, commodities, and just about any activity that could fall under the general headings of "business" or "investing." If any risk of capital is involved, it's gambling, and the pros will beat the amateurs and the compulsives.

So, although I believe it's possible that a compulsive gambler could become a professional blackjack or poker player; the problem is that he'll operate in the red a lot. If he is an otherwise intelligent person who has access to money from some other source, he will provide bread and butter for the noncompulsive professionals, who much prefer to operate in the black.

This could be the best way to tell the compulsives from the noncompulsives. Operate in red: compulsive; operate in black: non-compulsive. Unfortunately, it's not easy to gather data on this, because both compulsive gamblers and professional gamblers tend to lie about their finances.

So the real answer to the question is: *No.*

In the same way that the liquor industry thrives on alcoholics, the gambling industry thrives on gambling addicts. Despite the Gamblers Anonymous brochures most casinos display near their cashiers' cages, usually in compliance with state gaming regulations, the industry knows that addicts are their best customers, just like your local bartender knows that the neighborhood drunks pay a good portion of his rent every month.

One of the main dangers of gambling addiction, compared to other self-destructive addictions, is that—unlike drinking or eating or taking drugs—gambling really is a profession for some people. So any gambler can convince himself that he is "investing" his money in his chosen occupation, since every gambler does sometimes see a return on his investment. Casinos understand the compulsive gambler's perspective, and they target their marketing specifically at players who possess the one psychological trait found in virtually every gambling addict—an inordinate desire to get something for nothing. Casinos offer more freebies to their customers than any other business, and these misnamed "complimentaries," or "comps," are NEVER really complimentary. They are always based on a player's volume of action at the casino's games, and that action has a real cost in dollars and cents.

If you think that card counting is an easy road to riches, you're deluding yourself. The pro gamblers I know work harder for their money than most people who hold regular jobs. They don't even begin to think they're getting "something for nothing." They know that every penny they make comes from long hours of work, study, sweat, and guts.

And don't think that just because the state requires a casino to post the 800-number for Gamblers Anonymous that the state has any concern whatsoever for gambling addicts. They care as much about gambling addicts as they do about drunks. Every state makes bundles of money from casinos, and politicians in states where gambling is legal get their palms greased regularly by the industry powers that be. The state will be just as happy to take money from you as any casino, poker player, or racetrack.

I live in Nevada now, but up until a few years ago, I lived in California, and the Golden State provided me with an invaluable education in the perfidious tactics of pushers who supply gambling addicts with an excuse for indulging in their drug of choice. Shortly after California instituted its usurious state lottery some years back (50% house edge, like most state lotteries), a front-page article in the *San Francisco Chronicle* revealed that nearly half of the lottery tickets sold in the state were being purchased by the same small percentage of buyers, who happened to reside in the depressed big city ghettos, with little education, and poverty-level incomes. An official spokesperson for the lottery commission stated that these high volume ticket buyers fell into two classifications—"compulsive gamblers" and "professional gamblers."

I like that. Professional lottery players. A spokesperson for the state declares on the front page of the daily papers that certain individuals whom demographics would lead us to categorize as poor and uneducated, are in fact a new breed of urban professional. Perhaps, it won't be long before California's universities begin offering classes like Big Spin 101, so that some of the more educated citizens of the state, who don't currently buy lottery tickets, can obtain a Bachelor of Lotto degree.

If you are a compulsive gambler, my advice is: *Don't gamble.* And don't try to convince yourself that counting cards is an "investment." Throw this book away—and stay away from the casinos.

11

TABLE CONDITIONS

Counting Is Not Enough

Many card counters believe that as long as a game is called "blackjack," and is being offered by a legitimate casino, they can win by applying their counting systems. But the fact is that while some games can be beaten by card counting strategies many can't, and table conditions make the difference. I've written two books on this subject already, my first two books, *The Blackjack Formula*, and *Blackjack for Profit*, plus five technical reports: "Beat the 1-Deck Game," "Beat the 2-Deck Game," "Beat the 4-Deck Game," "Beat the 6-Deck Game," and "Beat the 8-Deck Game." The first two books are now out of print, but the reports have been recently updated and are available (See the reference section in the back of this book).

In this chapter, I will attempt to update and condense some of the most important information from these books and reports so that you may choose your games wisely. There are simple guidelines you can follow that will help to keep you from throwing your money away in unbeatable games.

First, let's define table conditions. There are four distinct conditions of any blackjack game that directly affect the profit potential for card counters:

1. The number of decks in play: In U.S. casinos, this may range from one to eight.
2. Rules: There are about a dozen common rule variations, and dozens more uncommon variations in U.S. casinos.
3. Crowd conditions: You may be the only player at the table, or one of as many as seven.
4. Depth of deal, or deck penetration, between shuffles: Anywhere from 2% to 90% of the cards may be dealt out.

Let's go through these conditions one at a time.

The Number of Decks in Play

First consider the effect of the number of decks shuffled together. All other conditions being equal, single-deck games would be the most profitable for card counters. The more decks being used, the less profitable the game becomes, not only for card counters, but for basic strategy players as well. A single-deck Vegas Strip game (blackjack pays 3 to 2, double down on any two cards, and dealer stands on soft 17), is pretty close to being a break even proposition for a basic strategy player. With four or more decks in play, and the same set of rules, the house has about a 1/2% edge. Use this chart to estimate your basic strategy (dis)advantage due to the number of decks in play:

# Decks	Advantage
1	+0.02%
2	-0.31%
3	-0.43%
4	-0.48%
5	-0.52%
6	-0.54%
7	-0.55%
8	-0.57%

The Rules

The second condition you must consider is the set of rules used in the game. Some rules, notably those that offer more options, favor the player, assuming he applies the correct strategy. Among those options are surrender, doubling after splitting allowed, and re-splitting aces allowed.

Those rules that limit the player's options, such as doubling down on 10-11 only, or no re-splits, are disadvantageous to the player.

Some rules neither limit nor offer options to the player, but alter the dealer's procedure. An example of one such rule would be dealer hits soft seventeen. That's disadvantageous to the player. An advantageous dealer rule, used occasionally in short-term special promotions, would be "blackjack pays 2 to 1."

Another set of rules that work in the player's favor are the "bonus" rules, such as "dealer pays $XXX bonus to player hand of 6, 7, 8 same suit." Most bonuses, due to the rarity of bonus hands, have very small dollar value to the player.

Earlier, most of the common rules were explained. In this chapter, we'll look at the approximate effect of each rule on your basic strategy expectation. By adding the effect of the number of decks in play to the effects of the rule variations, you will know the house advantage against basic strategy players. Card counters call this the "starting advantage," or the advantage off the top.

Most rules, to be sure, affect card counters differently than they affect basic strategy players. The house edge off the top, however, is always an important consideration, as that's what you're working to overcome. For instance, insurance has no value to a basic strategy player, since correct basic strategy is to never take insurance. If a casino disallows insurance, however, this hurts card counters, since they profit from their selective insurance bets. Likewise, the surrender option has little value to basic strategy players—less than one-tenth of 1% increase in expectation. For a card counter, however, surrender is, like insurance, very valuable.

In order to figure out the starting advantage of a game, you should begin by defining a benchmark game—i.e., a set of standard rules, which you can then add to or subtract from. Most authors define this benchmark game as Vegas Strip rules:

1. Dealer stands on soft 17.

2. You may double down on any 2 original cards.

3. You may not double down after splitting a pair.

4. You may split any pair.

5. You may re-split any pair except aces.

6. Split aces receive only one card each.

7. No surrender.

8. Dealer either receives a hole card, or the player's original bet only is lost if the player doubles down or splits a pair and the dealer gets a blackjack (and the extra amount bet is returned to the player).

9. Insurance is allowed up to one-half the player's bet, and pays 2 to 1.

10. Player blackjack is paid 3 to 2.

The effect of any other rules must be accounted for in determining your starting advantage. The chart below shows how these rules affect the game.

Most of these rule effects have been calculated by using data from Peter Griffin's *Theory of Blackjack*. Note that the last five rules show effects of 00.00% for basic strategy players. Also, when it comes to the "bonus" rules, such as 6,7,8 suited or 7,7,7 pays 2 to 1, the general rule is to never change your basic strategy to try for a bonus payout.

In some cases, when a specific dollar amount is awarded for the bonus hand, the value is dependent on the player's bet size. For instance, if 6,7,8 suited pays a $100 bonus, then the percentage will be quite different for a player who has a $2 bet and a player who has a $200 bet. The first player would receive a 50 to 1 payout on his hand, while the second player would receive only an extra half-bet. The $2 bettor would likely be right to hit his hand against any dealer upcard, if his hand contained two of the needed suited cards. The $200 bettor would usually be in error if he hit the hand in violation of his basic/count strategy.

The best source book for determining the value of weird bonuses, and how to adjust your strategy when appropriate, is Stanford Wong's *Basic Blackjack*. All players who travel frequently to foreign countries, where some of the more unusual rules are in play, should have this book in their libraries; it defines the esoteric rules at work around the world, and provides the strategies for playing them.

Returning to the chart, note the huge negative effect of "BJ Pays 6 to 5," a rule now common in many Las Vegas single-deck games. This rule is a killer, and it's worse yet when BJ pays *1 to 1* (even money), as is standard in all "Super Fun 21" games. All those other "good" rules that the "Super Fun" game allows do not make up for this single punitive one. Serious card counters should stick with the traditional "BJ Pays 3 to 2" games.

114

	Effects in Percent		
Common Rules	**1-Deck**	**2-Deck**	**Multi-Deck**
Double on 10-11 only:	-0.26	-0.21	-0.18
Double on 9-10-11 only:	-0.13	-0.11	-0.09
Hits Soft 17:	-0.19	-0.20	-0.21
No Re-splits:	-0.02	-0.03	-0.04
Double After Splits:	+0.14	+0.14	+0.14
Re-split Aces:	+0.03	+0.05	+0.07
Draw to Split Aces:	+0.14	+0.14	+0.14
Late Surrender:	+0.02	+0.05	+0.08
Late Surrender (H soft17):	+0.03	+0.06	+0.09
Less Common Rules			
Double on 8-9-10-11 only:	-0.13	-0.11	-0.09
Double on 11 only:	-0.78	-0.69	-0.64
Double after Ace splits:	+0.10	+0.10	+0.10
Double on 3+ cards:	+0.24	+0.23	+0.23
No Ace Splits:	-0.16	-0.17	-0.18
Early Surrender:	+0.62	+0.62	+0.63
Early Surrender (H soft17):	+0.70	+0.71	+0.72
Early Surrender v. 10 only:	+0.19	+0.21	+0.24
BJ Pays 6 to 5:	-1.40	-1.37	-1.36
BJ Pays 1 to 1:	-2.32	-2.28	-2.26
BJ Pays 2 to 1:	+2.32	+2.28	+2.26
Suited BJ Pays 2 to 1:	+0.58	+0.57	+0.56
21 Pushes Dlr. 10-up BJ:	+0.20	+0.20	+0.20
No Hole Card (European):	-0.10	-0.11	-0.11
5-card 21 Pays 2 to 1:	+0.20	+0.20	+0.20
6-card 21 Pays 2 to 1:	+0.10	+0.10	+0.10
Suited 678 Pays 2 to 1:	+0.01	+0.01	+0.01
7-7-7 Pays 3 to 2:	+0.01	+0.01	+0.01
6 Cards Un-busted Wins:	+0.10	+0.10	+0.10
No Insurance:	00.00	00.00	00.00
Multi-Action:	00.00	00.00	00.00
Over/Under:	00.00	00.00	00.00
Royal Match	00.00	00.00	00.00
Super 7s:	00.00	00.00	00.00

Let's walk through the "off the top" expectations in a more typical blackjack game. Consider a standard Atlantic City 8-deck game, which allows double after splits, but no re-splits. The basic strategy expectation is derived by adding together the effects of both the number of decks in play, and the rules being used (from the multi-deck column):

8 Decks:	-0.57
Double After Splits:	+0.14
No Re-splits:	-0.04
House Advantage:	**-0.47%**

The Number of Players at the Table

The third condition you must take into account is the number of players at the table. The more hands you play per-hour, assuming you have an advantage, the *faster* your win rate. If crowded tables keep you from seeing and counting all the cards played, which is a common problem in facedown hand-held games, the effect of this is the same as the effect of an inadequate depth of deal ("bad penetration").

Consider, for instance, a single-deck game where there are seven players at the table. Two rounds will consume about 83% of the cards, which makes this game appear attractive. Who can complain about 83% penetration? Isn't that as good as it gets? But remember that your second (and last) bet before the shuffle will be made after having seen only about 42% of the cards, assuming you are able to see and count all cards from the first round. If you are at a table where players are hiding their hands, this cuts further into the amount of usable information you can actually process.

Let's also consider the effect the number of players at the table has on the speed of the game.

# Players	Hands/Hour
1	200
2	160
3	140
4	120
5	100
6	80
7	65

So, assuming all other factors are equal, including the advantage you gain over the house from card counting, and the average amount you bet per hand, you may expect to win three times as much money per hour if you are going head-to-head with the dealer than if you are playing at a full table.

I'm not saying you should always play head-to-head—there are many other factors that must enter into this decision. Some team strategies only work well in crowded casinos, and most big-money counters find it useful to play with other players around, since blending into a crowd is always good camouflage. There is also the simple fact that it's all too often impossible to find heads-up games in most casinos, as they tend to open new tables on an as-needed basis. Analyzing your expected hourly return, however, you must take into account the amount of action you are putting on the tables. This is always strongly affected by the crowd conditions.

The Depth of the Deal (Penetration)

The final table condition you must consider is the depth of the deal prior to reshuffling. This factor makes no difference whatsoever to basic strategy players, but for card counters, penetration is hugely important. It is usually the major factor in determining whether a game is beatable via card counting or a waste of time. The deeper the penetration, the more profit potential for the counter.

When I published my first book, *The Blackjack Formula,* in 1980, many players were skeptical of the weight I gave to the effect of deck penetration. I received numerous letters from players who simply could not believe that there's any great difference in profitability between a single-deck Reno game with 55% penetration and one with 65% penetration. "10% is only five cards!" one player wrote to me. "Yet your formula shows the advantage almost doubling with the same 1 to 4 spread. That's impossible!" Other card counters, who were playing 4-deck downtown Vegas games with 70% penetration and 1 to 4 spreads, were incredulous of my claim that such a small spread, with such poor penetration, left them with barely a tenth of a percent advantage over the house.

These days, any decent book on card counting will tell you that penetration is the name of the game, but before 1980 no one knew! None of the books on card counting had ever mentioned the importance of deck penetration before.

The general rule is this: The shallower the penetration, the larger the betting spread you must use to beat the game. With a bad set of rules and poor penetration, you may not be able to beat the game with any spread.

In most single-deck games, you can't win big unless more than 50% of the cards are dealt out between shuffles—with Reno rules (double 10/11 only and dealer hits soft 17), make that more than 60%. There are two main reasons for this: One, most single-deck games have poor rule sets; two, you generally can't get away with a very big spread in single-deck games. With 2-deck games, you'll want at least 65% dealt out. (But don't even bother with a 2-decker when playing Reno rules.) With 4 or more decks, a bare minimum of 70% of the cards should be dealt out. Most shoe games, in fact, are best attacked by "table-hopping," i.e., leaving the game entirely on negative counts. Regardless of the number of decks in play, a 10% difference in penetration will make a huge difference in your profit potential: A 6-deck game with 85% penetration (about 5 decks dealt) is vastly superior to a 6-deck game with only 75% penetration (about 4 1/2 decks dealt).

As a basic guideline, I rate penetration as being either good, bad, or unexceptional. Regardless of the number of decks in play, *bad* is less than 67% dealt, *unexceptional* is 67-75% dealt, and *good* is 76+% dealt. This may be overly simplistic, but even if that's all you know, you still know a lot more than many guys who think they know blackjack cold. The ability to choose a good game, based on profit potential, is the most powerful weapon of the professional card counter.

The Snyder Profit Index

In 1981, I self-published 1,000 copies of a little book titled *Blackjack For Profit,* and when I say "a little book," I mean *little.* The size was approximately four inches by five inches, and its 96 pages could easily fit into any man's shirt pocket with less bulge than a pack of cigarettes. *Blackjack for Profit* was actually my second book—my first, *The Blackjack Formula*, was also 96 pages and self-published, but I charged $100 per copy for that one.

Those two books, now out of print, initially made my reputation as a blackjack expert. What I revealed in *The Blackjack Formula* in 1980, which serious players were paying so dearly for, was the fact that the counting system in use was of less importance than the table conditions—the number of decks in play, the penetration (shuffle point), rule variations, and so forth. This was a radical idea back in 1980: system developers had been devising more and more complex card counting systems for almost two decades in an attempt to eke a few extra bucks out of the games, but none of them paid much attention to the games themselves, which were pretty much assumed to be equal.

The real eye-opener back then was the importance I placed on penetration, a game factor that had been ignored by virtually all of the best-known authors. I discovered its importance while reading a technical paper that had been published by the late Peter Griffin in 1975 titled, *The Use of Bivariate Normal Approximations to Evaluate Single Parameter Card Counting Systems at Blackjack*, which later became the core of Griffin's masterwork: *The Theory of Blackjack* (1979).

After I published *The Blackjack Formula*, which provided an algebraic method for estimating the expectation from playing any game with any counting system, I learned that bootleg copies of my formula were circulating in Las Vegas and Reno. Some players just didn't want to pay $100 for a 96-page book! So, I wrote an easier version of the book, which I titled *Blackjack For Profit,* which excluded most of the mathematics, but contained an even simpler method that virtually anyone could use to evaluate a blackjack game — "The Snyder Profit Index" — and I priced this book at a more reasonable $9.95.

I reprinted *Blackjack for Profit* numerous times over the next decade as I worked on a revised and updated version. In 1991, the infamous Oakland Firestorm destroyed my computer and all my backups of the work I had been doing (along with my house). In 1993, when I sold the last copies of the last printing of the book, I never reprinted it. Since then, the book has been out of print and unavailable at any price.

I've learned, however, from various blackjack players that bootleg copies of "Chapter Seven: The Snyder Profit Index," taken from that book, were circulating in Las Vegas and elsewhere, just like the *Blackjack Formula*, because the book was simply impossible to find, and many card counters still found the Snyder Profit Index, or SPI, to be a quick and convenient game evaluator.

Many pros today have computer software for evaluating game expectations with pinpoint accuracy, but for average players who find themselves faced with myriad table conditions, the SPI will almost always point you in the right direction. The SPI, which works by adding and subtracting points for favorable and unfavorable conditions, should be viewed as an approximate gauge rather than a precise evaluation, as there is no simple way to analyze a blackjack game precisely. The SPI will do for practical purposes, however, as it classifies games as either winners, time wasters, or losers. (In the SPI Chart below, I have revised a few of the values for better accuracy.)

To use the SPI, start by finding the column for the number of decks being shuffled together, then add and subtract points according to the crowd conditions, the shuffle-point, the rules, and the betting spread you intend to use. In estimating shuffle-points, the SPI offers four choices—50% penetration, 67% penetration, 75% penetration, and 80% penetration. Be conservative in your estimates; don't use the 80% value unless the shuffle point truly is quite a bit deeper than 75%. Remember, it's your money on the line, so proceed cautiously. In rating a game, use this barometer:

Above 50	**a winner**
0 - 50	**table-hop only**
Below 0	**a time waster**

Seek the game with the highest point value. If a game scores 50 or above, it will almost certainly provide a long-run profit for a card counter. In most cases, the SPI will accurately gauge the right game. In creating the SPI, my goal was to try and come up with an easy scoring system that would inform a player that his counting strategy in a particular game would yield at least a 1% advantage over the house, with enough hands per hour to make the game worthwhile. But do not attempt to use the SPI to discover your precise advantage as a "percentage;" the Index won't tell you that, as the crowd conditions automatically adjust the SPI for the increased hands per hour. If a game scores below 50 on the SPI, then you will probably not find it profitable to sit down and play. If you're going to play these games, you must table-hop to avoid negative counts.

THE SNYDER PROFIT INDEX

NUMBER OF DECKS

	1	2	3, 4	5, 6	7, 8
Heads-Up	+85	+50	+37	+30	+27
2-4 Players	+55	+31	+21	+18	+16
5-7 Players	+25	+13	+7	+4	+3
80% Dealt	+35	+20	+18	+16	+14
75% Dealt	+20	+11	+10	+9	+8
67% Dealt	0	0	0	0	0
50% Dealt	-32	-20	-15	-13	-11
Early Surrender	+55	+33	+26	+23	+21
Double After Splits	+10	+8	+6	+5	+4
Late Surrender	+12	+9	+7	+6	+5
No Re-Splits	-1	-1	-1	-1	-1
Stands Soft 17	0	0	0	0	0
Hits Soft 17	-15	-12	-10	-9	-8
Double Any Two	0	0	0	0	0
Double 10/11 Only	-20	-16	-14	-12	-11
No Insurance	-50	-34	-24	-20	-18
No Hole Card (European)	-9	-7	-5	-4	-3
1-2 Spread	+20	+12	+8	+6	+5
1-4 Spread	+30	+19	+14	+11	+9
1-8 Spread	+40	+26	+20	+16	+13
1-12 Spread	+50	+33	+26	+21	+17

Let's use the SPI now to evaluate a sample game: Let's say you've just walked into a downtown Las Vegas casino. The tables are about half-full (with 2 to 4 players at most tables), and the games are being dealt from 6-deck shoes. After observing for a few minutes, you note that the dealers tend to cut off about one and a half decks, so about 3/4 of the cards are being dealt out between shuffles. The standard downtown Vegas rules are in force, so dealer hits soft 17, double on any two cards. Stepping into the coffee shop, you check the Index. Under 6 decks, with 2-4 players, you get 18 points. With 75% of the cards dealt, you add 9 points to this, for a total of 27. Since the dealer hits soft 17, you subtract 9 points, bringing you back to 18 points. With a 1 to 8 betting spread—16 points—the SPI would total 34 points, and even with a 1 to 12 betting spread, the SPI would only get to 39 points. You might also note that if you could play heads-up with the dealer in this game, the SPI would go up to 49 points, bordering on playable.

The Snyder Profit Index does not evaluate profit potential for those players whose cultivated "acts" allow them to use betting spreads of greater than 1 to 12 units. As for games that rate between 35 and 50, they will almost always turn a long run profit—but due to either the slight advantage or crowded conditions, earnings will be very slow. High stakes players may find games that rate in the upper thirties and forties profitable enough for their purposes.

Now let's use the SPI to analyze some commonly available games in this country. Single- and double-deck games are analyzed at shuffle-points of 50%, 67%, and 75%, and at betting spreads of 1-2, 1-4, and 1-8 units. The six- and eight-deck games are analyzed at shuffle-points of 67%, 75%, and 80%, and at betting spreads of 1-4, 1-8, and 1-12 units. Each entry has three numbers separated by slashes—for instance, the first entry (1-2 spread) for the 50% dealt, single-deck, Downtown Vegas (H17) game reads -2/28/58. This means that with a full table, the SPI is -2 points; half-full, the SPI is 28 points; and heads-up the SPI is 58 points. So, unless you can play head-to-head with the dealer, and get away with using a 1-2 betting spread with a positive count, the game is a waste of time. You'll need deeper penetration or a bigger spread to make money in this game.

VEGAS DOWNTOWN (H17) ONE-DECK

	50% DEALT	67% DEALT	75% DEALT
1-2 SPREAD	-2/28/58	30/60/90	50/80/110
1-4 SPREAD	8/38/68	40/70/100	60/90/120
1-8 SPREAD	18/48/68	50/80/110	70/100/130

RENO (H17, D10/11) ONE-DECK

	50% DEALT	67% DEALT	75% DEALT
1-2 SPREAD	-22/8/38	10/40/70	30/60/90
1-4 SPREAD	-12/18/48	20/50/80	40/70/100
1-8 SPREAD	-2/28/58	30/60/90	50/80/110

VEGAS DOWNTOWN (H17) TWO-DECK

	50% DEALT	67% DEALT	75% DEALT
1-2 SPREAD	-7/11/30	13/31/50	24/42/61
1-4 SPREAD	0/18/37	20/38/57	31/49/68
1-8 SPREAD	6/24/43	26/44/63	37/55/74

RENO (H17, D10/11) TWO-DECK

	50% DEALT	67% DEALT	75% DEALT
1-2 SPREAD	-23/-5/16	-3/15/36	7/25/47
1-4 SPREAD	-16/2/21	4/22/41	14/32/53
1-8 SPREAD	-10/8/27	10/28/47	21/39/58

VEGAS DOWNTOWN (H17) SIX-DECK

	67% DEALT	75% DEALT	80% DEALT
1-4 SPREAD	7/21/33	16/30/42	23/37/49
1-8 SPREAD	11/25/37	20/34/46	27/41/53
1-12 SPREAD	16/30/42	25/39/51	32/46/58

VEGAS STRIP (S-17, DAS) SIX-DECK

	67% DEALT	75% DEALT	80% DEALT
1-4 SPREAD	21/35/47	30/44/56	37/51/63
1-8 SPREAD	25/39/51	34/48/61	41/55/68
1-12 SPREAD	30/44/56	39/53/66	46/60/73

ATLANTIC CITY (S-17, DAS) EIGHT-DECK

	67% DEALT	75% DEALT	80% DEALT
1-4 SPREAD	16/29/40	24/37/48	30/43/54
1-8 SPREAD	20/33/44	28/41/52	34/47/58
1-12 SPREAD	24/37/48	32/45/56	38/51/62

For the common games above, you don't have to add or subtract yourself—just look up the game in the chart and find the SPI value according to the conditions. Games not covered in these tables can easily be analyzed using the SPI chart. It should take you only a couple minutes to draw up a complete table for any common game. One word of caution: don't forget fluctuation. Even a game that rates 200 points may be a big loser in the short run. (That's the topic of the next chapter!)

Pseudo-Blackjack Games

You may note that the SPI Chart includes no entries for the new rule variations found in some of today's games. In the past few years, many casinos in Las Vegas have begun offering single-deck blackjack where naturals pay 6 to 5 instead of the traditional 3 to 2. I'll call these games "BJ Pays 6 to 5." This rule is so bad that there is little use devising an SPI value for it. The negative value would simply negate the possibility of any such game providing a card counter with a profit opportunity. Super Fun 21 is even worse than BJ Pays 6 to 5, and the host of rules favoring players are not strong enough to counter the negative effect.

Technically, both BJ Pays 6 to 5 and Super Fun 21 can be beaten with card counting strategies. The problem is that you need deeper penetration than most casinos provide, and you would also have to use a much bigger betting spread than you would need for a traditional BJ Pays 3 to 2 game. So, my advice is to avoid these pseudo-blackjack games altogether.

Likewise, some casinos now use continuous shuffle machines, or CSMs, on some tables. These machines effectively cut penetration to 0%, making card counting a complete waste of time since there's nothing to count! Stay away from tables that use CSMs.

Another disturbing development in Nevada in the past few years has been the introduction of "fake" one- and two-deck games. At these tables, a machine is used to shuffle six to eight decks, and then the dealer removes only one or two decks from the machine, dealing what appears to be a hand-held one or two-deck game. In fact, what you have is a six- or eight-deck game with extremely poor penetration. Counting cards in a game like this is a waste of time. So watch out for the fake blackjack that casinos keep introducing. All of them are sucker games.

A Fisheye View of Game Selection

In Ed Thorp's *Beat the Dealer* we were introduced to a character who was known in the Puerto Rican casinos as the "Salmon." The nickname was pinned on him by one of the casino pit bosses, as a reference to his "swimming upstream." He was winning steadily, which was going against the current in this boss's view. The pit boss also believed that this current, the house edge, was so strong that it would inevitably pull even the Salmon downstream.

This analogy to beating the house has always appealed to me. The current is so strong in most casinos that if you really spend much time at any of the games, you inevitably see player after player just floating down that mighty river...

From the perspective of a card counter, you *are* a salmon. You can and do swim upstream, watching all the other little fishies going the opposite direction. It's fun to fight a mighty river and win, but you have to pick a current you personally can overcome—not one that just looks good on paper, or may be right for some other salmon, maybe one with bigger fins than yours. Most importantly, since salmon are always in season in the casinos, you've got to watch out for bait.

I've seen dozens of players' casino rating systems over the years. Some players use standard "report card" ratings, with grades running from "A" to "F." I've seen "star" systems, kind of like movie ratings. Four stars: Don't miss it! One star: Don't even rent the video.

Many card counters today are penetration fanatics; they rate games according to the percentage of the cards dealt. They can drive down the Strip, pointing at the casinos as they go: "70%, 60%, 67%, 55% yuck, 79.8%—Hmm...valet parking's full..." It's not a bad way to rate casinos, but there's more to it than that.

High rollers rate casinos according to the action tolerated. Sawdust joints. Carpet joints. Most amateurs, on the other hand, are rule freaks. They see everything in terms of being able to split up to four hands, re-split aces, double after splits, double any two and surrender. (Sounds okay to me...) But the point is that after you analyze the table conditions, you've got to analyze the casino itself.

The rarest type of casino is one where you hardly feel the current at all. The games are just so delectable you forget you're even in the river. You look around—good rules, deep penetration. There's a lot of money on the felt, but nobody in the pit seems to be guzzling Maalox. It's not a river; it's fish heaven. All the worms you can eat, and no hooks! Or, at least, you don't see them—provided you don't try to take the entire can of worms back home with you on any one visit, you can nibble away at the feast indefinitely. Places like this pop up now and then, but they don't often last long.

More commonly, when you think you're in fish heaven, there are unseen hooks, nets, and harpoons aimed right at you. You walk in, you see these unbelievable table conditions, you notice that the dealer has dealt out almost the entire two decks, and he's still not starting the shuffle. You decide to make small talk with the dealer, test his friendliness. "So, how long have you been offering this two-deck game with double after splits and surrender? Whoops! You ran out of cards!"

Unfortunately, if you sit down at the table, you'll often get that ominous tap on the shoulder just after you make that first black chip bet on a high count, or maybe a few minutes later, after they've got a good close-up photo of your mug. By the time you hit the street, your picture is already being faxed to casinos you've never heard of.

Of course, it's possible that you misjudged this casino in the first place. It only *looked like* fish heaven. In actuality, it was, first and foremost, a fish bowl. Some salmon may be a bit large for your average fish bowl, and big fish won't last in a small bowl.

Many casinos in Las Vegas, even big casinos that can take table limit action, offer one or two hand-held games that really are nothing more than counter bait. These juicy tables are always under extra surveillance from the sky, and the casinos use these games simply to identify and weed out counters. So, if you see that a casino has 25 six-deck shoe games with mediocre penetration, and one hand-held two-decker with great rules and good penetration, you're probably best off to leave that two-decker alone.

To further confuse matters, even if the conditions look great on every table, you may have to leave the casino entirely if your bet level attracts too much attention. Look around—how much are the other players in this joint betting? Many casino table-limit signs are mislabeled; the signs may say $1,000 or even $5000, but *that's just what the signs say*. Nobody in the pit takes those things seriously. Ignore the signs. If all you see are tourists betting a red chip or two, and if a couple of black chip bets lead to a suit convention in the pit, then those limit signs are just for show.

East Meets West

Counting cards in Nevada is not the same as counting cards in Atlantic City. East Coast counters who visit Nevada for the first time are often amazed at the tremendous variety of blackjack games available, while Nevada counters in AC for the first time are likewise in for some culture shock. If you have pretty much limited your play to either Nevada or New Jersey, and you are now considering a trek across the country to test new waters, here is a brief guide to what to expect.

For AC counters heading to NV:

Yes, you will find hand-held one and two-deck offerings—but that doesn't mean you actually want to play them! Most big money players would tell you the single-deckers are unplayable. The penetration sucks—if you raise your bet, they shuffle up, and do it a few times and you'll be nailed as a counter. Unlike in AC, they can throw you out for counting It's not illegal to think in Nevada per se; it's just against Gaming Control Board regulations for smart players to think while they're in the casinos.

Advice: Look for a decent six-deck shoe.

For NV counters heading to AC:

The preponderance of eight-deck tables will be depressing, especially when you see signs all over that say "No Mid-Shoe Entry," and the penetration is not that great to begin with. It's not against CCC regulations for smart players to think while they're in the casinos; it's just against house policies in the AC casinos to give players anything to think about. How do you beat these games?

Advice: Look for a decent six-deck shoe.

For AC counters heading to NV:

So you just walked up to a hot six-deck table, dropped some chunky black action on the felt, and nobody's even looking! This is incredible! Or so it seems... Unlike in AC, surveillance in the big Vegas stores is usually done from the eye. Assume you're being watched, and with black action, it's a good bet that you are—especially if they don't know you. The first tap on your shoulder is likely to be a smiling host, asking if you need a room for the night. Meanwhile, the surveillance goons upstairs will count down your shoes, entering your plays into their counter-identification software, and searching their photo files for your mug.

Advice: Don't drop your camouflage.

For NV counters heading to AC:

So you just walked up to a $100-minimum six-deck table in the VIP pit, converted a few thousand dollars into black chips, and suddenly, you've got three suits staring at you—and they don't look friendly. What's going on? Do you have a new photo spread in the card-counter mug books you were unaware of? Probably not. In AC, the pit attitude toward new big players is always one of suspicion, and they don't hide it. Since they can't bar counters, they go for intimidation. They'll hawk your game until they feel you're safe, and that could be a long time. And don't expect a casino host to come running to greet you just because you started pumping a little black action onto the felt. There are black chip players in AC who have been playing there for years who don't even know what a host is. Comps don't come so easily in AC; you've got to prove yourself to be a real idiot before the pit warms up to you. Losing a bundle helps.

Advice: Don't drop your camouflage.

For AC counters heading to NV:

The true count just hit +4 and suddenly a pair of college kids are splashing black action on your table, eating the tens and aces you worked so hard to get to. Welcome to the world of mid-shoe entry. They may or may not be counters, though you can probably determine this in the next few minutes by the way they play their hands, and especially if they leave the table as soon as the count nose-dives.

Advice: If you don't start table-hopping yourself, you will come to hate many Nevada counters.

For NV counters heading to AC:

The true count just hit +4 and suddenly the pair of college kids sitting beside you start discussing the number of aces left in the shoe and the proper index for standing on 15 vs. 10, *right out loud.* You leave quickly when one of them asks you what system you're using. Are they imbeciles? Shills? House dicks? No, they're college kids. Since casinos can't bar counters, many amateurs and wannabes discuss count strategies right at the table. Although the AC casinos can restrict them to a flat bet, this countermeasure simply gives them bragging rights. If they're half-shoed or bet-restricted, nothing can stop them from getting up and walking over to a table in the next pit, where they are again free to spread their bets until they're caught again.

Advice: If you are trying to make money at the tables and not just brag to your friends about being labeled a pro, you will come to hate many AC counters.

For AC counters heading to NV:

The game has great rules, deep penetration, and no heat. Unfortunately, although you're currently stuck about eight thousand due to bad cards, the "friendly" pit boss just told you to take a hike and don't come back. At least, not to the blackjack tables—ever. Can he do that?

Advice: Yes. Go back to AC where the games are better.

For NV counters heading to AC:

You're stuck eight thousand bucks and the boss just told you you're being restricted to a $100 flat bet. How are you going to dig out? Should you sneak over to the next pit where those college kids are playing? Can the boss do that?

Advice: Yes. Go back to Nevada where the games are better.

In other words, your assessment of table conditions in any individual casino depends on many factors, not just the game itself. One counter's dream game may be another counter's nightmare. This will become even clearer to you in the upcoming chapters, as we discuss the all-important money issues. How much money do you need? How much should you bet? We'll also touch on casino surveillance, countermeasures, legal issues, and so on.

Blackjack may be just a card game, but you'd better take it as seriously as the casinos do if you expect to beat them. And believe me, they are dead serious about beating you.

12

HOW MUCH MONEY DO I NEED?

Whole books have been written for gamblers in an attempt to answer this question. Whole lives have been dedicated to research on it. Still, in my opinion, the greatest failing of most books on card counting—even some of the best ones—is that they do not adequately provide players with a clear picture of how much to bet, based on the various factors, such as bankroll size, game conditions, betting spread, and counting system, to name a few. There is no simple answer, and no "right" answer either. But most books either oversimplify the answers—which leaves players wondering why their system doesn't seem to be working when they hit a perfectly normal downswing—or they overcomplicate the answers, providing perplexing formulas and tables of numbers carried out to four decimal places that are fine for academic discussions by mathematicians, but unwieldy, intimidating, and unnecessary for real players.

I suspect the reason that many authors provide either middling advice or overcomplicated data is that none of the answers are pleasant or comforting. Nobody wants to hear that the fluctuations are wild, that there's no way around the flux, and that you must not only learn to cope with it, but understand it. I will give you the facts as clearly as I can, though, and in such a way that you can make informed betting decisions, with no unpleasant surprises later.

Inevitably, every serious blackjack player ends up learning more about

131

math than he ever thought he wanted to. Any pro can discuss esoteric statistical concepts like standard deviation, risk of ruin, the Kelly Criterion, bet-to-bank ratios, and, by the time you finish studying this book, you should have a pretty good working knowledge of these terms. This is not to say that you must take a course in statistics in order to figure out how much to bet on a hand of blackjack—like everything else in this game, most players can find answers in a few simple charts and an understanding of what they're up against. Most high-stakes pros, in fact, would tell you that they do not use or pay any attention whatsoever to the massive amount of technical data available on every aspect of win rate, risk, variance, and covariance. It is simply unnecessary for real-world play.

But even if you have no intention of going pro, you should understand the basic concepts of normal fluctuation, and exactly what is meant by "win rate." Stick with me; these concepts are not too difficult to comprehend.

Many card counters would like to believe that mastering a counting system gives them the keys to the vault. They'd like to think that since they have the edge over the house, they can't lose. One of the most common complaints I've heard from players goes something like this: "The table conditions were great, I know I was playing my system well, but I lost my shirt! What happened?"

Why is it that so many smart players believe that negative fluctuations are something that only happens to the other guys?

Forget the math for now. Let's look at a practical example of what can happen. In order to demonstrate what you might have to deal with—in the short run, in a very profitable game, even when you're using your system perfectly—I ran 100 consecutive computer simulations of 1,000 hands of blackjack each. Each simulation represents about 10 hours of play in a truly great game: single-deck, Vegas Strip rules, with double after splits, and 80% dealt out. The player is using the Zen Count with all published indices, and spreading his bets from $25 to $100. His long run advantage in this game is 2.1%, which translates to about $105 per hour. Before I ran the 100 simulations of 1,000 hands each, I ran a 10-million-hand simulation to come up with the 2.1% win rate. Since you probably won't play any 10-million-hand sessions, let's look at what happens in your real world 10-hour sessions. Let's say that you, a dedicated card counter, actually went out on 100 consecutive weekends, and played ten hours of blackjack every weekend for almost two years, in this same game. What happened?

Of these 100 10-hour sessions, you won at least some money on 76 of them, but lost on 24 of them. That sounds great—you lost on less than one out of four 10-hour playing sessions. However, these wins and losses were not evenly distributed. The longest series of consecutive winning sessions not interrupted by a single losing session of any amount, was 18. During this simulated 180 consecutive hours of real-time play, you won an average of $198.50 per hour, almost twice your actual expectation! In dollars and cents, after 180 hours of play in this game, you would expect to be ahead by $18,900. Due to this fluctuation, however, in this 18-session run you were ahead by $35,640. In your single best playing session, during which you had an expectation of $1,050 after 10 hours of play, you actually won $6,200, which translates to a win rate of 11.76%! Not bad for ten hours of play where you never raised your bet higher than $100...

Hey, if you won an average of 200 bucks an hour, for 180 consecutive hours of play, you'd probably figure it was time to quit your day job! What a marvelous game! Ain't counting wonderful?

But wait a minute. If your wins were fluctuating and clumping so wildly, doesn't that mean your losses did too? You'd better believe it. On your worst losing session, instead of winning your expected $1,050, you lost an even $4,000. And on your worst two consecutive losing sessions, instead of winning your expected $2,100, you lost $7,675. Your worst 10 consecutive sessions contained seven losing sessions and three winning sessions. At the end of this simulated 100 consecutive hours of play, you would expect to be ahead by $10,500; instead, you were behind by $8,175.

And what was the longest series of consecutive sessions in which you still failed to show a net win at the end? Nineteen.

One hundred and ninety hours of consecutive play.

The series contained 11 losing and 8 winning sessions. Your expectation after 190 hours at this game is to be ahead by $19,950. Instead, you were still behind by an even $2,000. This is a negative fluctuation of almost $22,000 below your expectation!

Mercifully, on a game as great as this, there wasn't a series of 20 consecutive sessions in which you did not show at least some small win. So, in this game, if we define "long run" to mean approximately how long you must play before you're more or less assured of being ahead, the answer is about 200 consecutive hours.

And, how much bankroll was needed to place bets on one hand from $25 to $100, based on your count? You were never behind by more than about $10,000, so we might say that you would have been safe in this game with a total bankroll of $10,000. But, here's what you must consider…

If you were behind by $9,500 dollars, would you still feel safe making bets of $100? I doubt it. Nor would it be wise to do so if this $10,000 starting bankroll represented your life savings. There is no magic mathematical formula that says that you cannot possibly lose more than $10,000 at this betting level when you have a better than two% edge over the house. That's just what occurred in this particular computer simulation. Different computer simulations using the same criteria would have similar numbers, sometimes with greater fluctuations, sometimes milder, on both the positive and negative sides. This simulation just gives us a ballpark estimate of what to expect at this betting level in this game.

If this was the start of your card counting career, the first ten weekends of your big money play, you'd probably pack it in and figure that whoever devised the system you'd spent so long to learn was a con artist and crook just selling dreams to the gullible public. But you must realize that normal fluctuation is what makes and breaks most card counters. You can't get away from it. No system, no betting method, no "money management" strategy, no "stop loss" limit will have any effect whatsoever on normal fluctuations.

In the unrealistically marvelous game described, in which you ultimately won 76 out of 100 playing sessions, and in which you ultimately won a total of $101,400 (within 0.1% of your actual expectation), look what you had to go through to get there! Had you played eight hours per day, five days per week, you would have had to withstand one series of playing sessions of almost five consecutive weeks still showing a net loss!

Look at the numbers on the next page and let them sink in. This is the kind of normal fluctuation that card counters must understand, and live with.

Really look at those numbers that show how badly you can lose in a truly great game, where your overall result after 100 sessions is close to your actual expectation. Even more sobering is the thought that you will never find a game this great that lasts this long! Most professional counters are happy to play at half of this 2.1% win rate. So, most counters can expect to experience fluctuations more drastic than those in this simulation.

With a 1% advantage, you'll win on only about 60 of 100 ten-hour sessions. Sometimes you can expect to show a net loss after 30 to 35 consecutive ten-hour sessions, up to two-plus months of full time play!

Player advantage:	2.1%
Total sessions played:	100
Hands per session:	1,000 (@ 10 hours)
Betting level:	$25 to $100 per hand
Total win:	$101,400
Avg. Hourly win:	$105
# winning sessions:	76
# losing sessions:	24
Biggest session win:	$6,200
Best winning streak:	18 consecutive sessions
$ won in this winning streak:	$35,640
Biggest losing session:	-$4,000
Worst result in 10 consecutive sessions (at 100 hours play):	-$8,175
Longest streak showing net loss:	19 sessions (at 190 hours with 11 losses, 8 wins)
Amount lost in this 19-session streak:	-$2,000

I would guess that I have some two-dozen letters from players in my slush pile right now lamenting just this kind of result. Many of these queries are from players who won for a while, but recently switched systems, tried a new game, or played in some casino they hadn't visited before. They want to know if their new counting system is no good, or if the dealers cheated, or if the shuffling routine is designed to foil card counters. (Incidentally, I used a random shuffle in all of my computer simulations above.) I also have some letters that say: "I've won nine out of 10 sessions for the past six months. Do you think it's because of my new system or money management technique, or the house shuffle?"

The fact is that you can't judge a game or a system on the basis of a weekend, a week, or even a month of full-time play. Even in an entire year of play, many pros have experienced a net loss. If you're playing for high stakes, you've got to have a large enough bankroll to withstand incredible negative fluctuations, and cover your living expenses. The long run takes a long time, but it does come around.

Card counters have used many different methods, borrowed from various mathematical formulas employed by statisticians, to calculate their ideal bet size. You do not need to be a mathematician to understand these concepts, but it's very important that you grasp them if you intend to make money gambling. Let's look at the two most important concepts serious players use to figure out how much to bet, based on the size of their bankrolls, and we'll describe these concepts in plain terms, with no formulas or difficult. I want you to understand the logic and practical considerations of *risk of ruin* and *Kelly betting*.

Risk of Ruin

Years ago, a mathematician determined that it was possible to figure out the likelihood of a gambler either doubling his bankroll or going broke trying to do so. The formula is just a simple algebraic equation that takes into account the size of the gambler's bankroll in units, the size of his bets, and the advantage or disadvantage in the specific game being played. This concept has traditionally been called the Gambler's Ruin Formula.

Professional card counters more commonly call a variation of this formula specifically devised for blackjack games the "risk of ruin" (or RoR); it was discussed by Ed Thorp in *Beat the Dealer*, Allan Wilson wrote about it in his 1965 *Casino Gambler's Guide*, and it was further described by Ken Uston in *Million Dollar Blackjack*. Since then, the concept of risk has been analyzed to the nth degree by many of the major authors.

Personally, I'm not crazy about the idea of individual players determining their bet sizes solely based on Risk of Ruin. Uston discussed how some of the teams he was involved in based their bets on a 5% element of ruin. This sounds pretty good to most players; if you double your bank 95% of the time (19 out of 20 banks double) that's a huge win-expectation in the long run.

But Uston was involved in big teams of players, with multiple investors, and if the team went broke on a play, the investors could simply put together another bank and do it again. That's not an option easily available to a solo player. If you have a bank of $10,000, and you lose the whole bank on your first play, can you simply put together another $10,000 and do it again? You might argue that it's unlikely that you'll lose your bank on your first attempt to double it, but consider it from my perspective as an author whose advice is being followed by thousands of individual players: For every ten thousand players who go out and plays to a 5% RoR, *500 of them will go broke!* How many of these players can quickly put together another bank? How many have lost their life savings? How many will write nasty letters to me blaming me for their new poverty?

Basing your bet sizes on a 5% (or any!) risk of ruin should be left to those who can afford to put together another bank easily if the first one fails. This is for big teams supported by investors, and solo players who have the capability of forming another playing bank through easily accessible outside sources of funding. A better method for bet-sizing for most players is…

Kelly Betting

It's very important that you understand the logic of what statisticians call the *Kelly Criterion*, another mathematical concept discussed to death in many other blackjack texts. With Kelly betting, you cannot lose your entire bankroll. *Never.* Or, at least, that's how it works in theory. The basic premise is that you always bet a percentage of your bankroll based on your percentage advantage over the house. Though somewhat oversimplified, a good example would be that if I have a 2% advantage on a blackjack hand based on my count, then I bet 2% of my bankroll. If I had a $10,000 bankroll, then I would make a $200 bet. The reason I would never go broke is because I can never place a final bet in which I put more than a small percentage of my bankroll at risk. If my bankroll gets smaller due to negative fluctuations, my bets will likewise get smaller in proportion. If I lose $5,000 of my original $10,000, then my Kelly bet with a 2% advantage becomes $100 instead of $200.

The theory behind Kelly betting is that not only does it prevent me from ever losing my whole bank, but since I increase my bets as my bankroll grows, I also maximize its growth by betting more when I can afford more risk. For instance, if my bankroll grows to $15,000, I can bet $300 with a 2% advantage over the house.

This description of Kelly betting is oversimplified in order to clearly show its logic. But I do want you to understand the pitfalls of Kelly betting in a game like casino blackjack. First, consider what your ideal Kelly bet is on hands where the house has the edge…*it's zero*. You shouldn't bet at all on hands where the house has the edge over you or you violate the Kelly betting system—even in a game like the single-deck version in our example that would simply be impossible. In virtually all casino blackjack games, the house has the edge more than 50% of the time over card counters.

Second, the Kelly betting system is based on a theoretical fact that you can never go broke, since you always bet only a percentage of your current bankroll. But what if my $10,000 bankroll fluctuates downward to $100?

And what if the table minimum bet allowed is $5? That means I have to have a 5% advantage over the house, based on my count, before I can even place a single table-minimum $5 bet! This may sound extreme, but the fact is that betting full out according to the Kelly Criterion causes *huge* fluctuations. There's wisdom in raising and lowering bets based on current bankroll, but betting full-Kelly is too risky in a game like blackjack.

How do the pros handle bet-sizing? Most employ some form of fractional Kelly betting. After determining the size of their bank—that is the total amount they have available to risk at playing blackjack they devise a chart of bet sizes based on one-third, one-quarter, or even smaller fractions of the ideal Kelly bets. By doing this, they hope to reduce fluctuations to a tolerable level, compensate for the increased fluctuations caused by placing bets when the house has the edge, bets placed for purposes of camouflage, and occasional errors in the application of their playing and betting strategies. (Many other methods used by professional players to limit fluctuations will be discussed in Chapter Fourteen.)

However, for a solo card counter, starting out on a limited bankroll, it's often all but impossible to stick to fractional Kelly betting. If you've got a total playing bankroll of $2,000, and you want to bet at the one-quarter Kelly level, with a 1% advantage you would place a bet of only $5, and at a 2% advantage your bet would be only $10. With the rare 3% advantages that occur in shoe games, you could place $15 bets, and these would be your high bets! If you could actually find a game that allowed minimum bets of $1, then you could use a betting spread of 1 to 15, and beat these games handily. Unfortunately, $1 minimum tables are pretty much a thing of the past. If you can find a $5 minimum table, you'd have to bet from $5 to $75 to employ this 1-15 unit betting spread, but you'd need a bankroll of $10,000 to afford it if you were determined to minimize your risk by betting at the one-quarter Kelly level.

All of this may sound very discouraging if your hopes and dreams have been centered on making a living by playing blackjack, and you're currently looking at a total playing bank of only a few thousand dollars. But stick with me...

Most pros that I know started small, and if you are cut out for it, you can do it too. By the same token, card counting still has a lot to offer players who are not cut out to be pros. If you always play with an edge over the house, at a level that you can afford, in the long run you will come out ahead—which puts you way ahead of the rest of the gambling public who are all a bunch of sure losers. If you follow the advice provided in this chapter, you should be able to keep yourself from getting in over your head, and you should be able to beat the casinos over time so that you can pay for your vacations at the table, maybe even bank a few thousand bucks per year, and have a lot of fun doing it.

For those of you crazy enough to still entertain notions of playing this game professionally, or with any serious amount of money, there is one simple mathematical formula you should learn, which I call the Profit Formula. You may use this formula to get a handle on what your expectation from the blackjack tables might be, based on your average bet size.

The Profit Formula

Average Bet x Advantage x Hands Per Hour = Hourly Profit

The formula is simple, yet it provides a good approximation of what a card counter might expect to win per hour in the long run. Say that you are making average bets of $10 with a 1% advantage over the house from card counting. You estimate you're playing about 80 hands per hour. To calculate your expected hourly win:

$10 x .01 x 80 = $8 per hour

(Note that your 1% advantage is expressed decimally as .01, for use in the formula. A 2% advantage would be .02, etc. How about 2 1/2%? That would be .025, while 1 3/4% would be .0175. You might find it helpful to follow this math with a pocket calculator, and you must familiarize yourself with expressing percentages as decimals if you are at all serious about making money from gambling, as most books on gambling use this notation.)

Let's also say that you want to increase your expectation above $8 per hour. That's simple enough to do, keeping the Profit Formula in mind. Simply raise the value of one or more of the three vital factors in the formula.

Start with the first: average bet. Obviously, if you made an average bet of $25, assuming the same 1% advantage over the house, and the same 80 hands per hour, your expectation would immediately rise to $20 per hour:

$25 x .01 x 80 = $20 per hour

It's a simple solution, but it's problematic if you have a limited bankroll, as increasing your bet size leads to greater fluctuation. Although your long-run win rate may rise to $20 per hour, you may never see the long run. Do you have a big enough bankroll to increase your average bet size to this level? Don't guess! Instead, keep reading…

The next variable in the Profit Formula is advantage. It's simple enough to see how to raise your expectation to $20 per hour by altering this factor; just raise your advantage to 2 1/2%. Thus:

$$\$10 \times .025 \times 80 = \$20 \text{ per hour}$$

This is the tactic most card counters employ—they start using an "advanced," higher-level, system, and keep side counts of aces, and sometimes fives or sevens, and memorize more extensive strategy tables.

Unfortunately, this tactic does not pay as well as most counters would like. Even the most advanced counting system will rarely raise your advantage by more than 1/4% to 1/2% over your advantage with a simpler system, and that's only if you can deploy the more complicated system without errors.

If you're playing with black ($100) chips, a 1/4% increase in your win rate may be worth the trouble, if you can play an advanced strategy with speed and accuracy. If not, you may be wasting your time, or even lowering your win rate.

Consider a game that would net the Red Seven Count about 1%, and would net a more advanced system, like the Zen Count, about 1 1/4%. Whereas the Red Seven Count would win at a rate of $8 per hour, the advanced system would win only about $10 per hour, even if you played with equal speed and accuracy.

$$\$10 \times .0125 \times 80 = \$10 \text{ per hour}$$

So, if it's $20 per hour you're shooting for, the advanced techniques alone won't accomplish your goal. By all means, go for the greater win if you can, but don't delude yourself if you're struggling with decisions at the table. Your mental efforts are unlikely to pay off in dollars and cents.

For the average card counter, there is little to gain from an advanced counting strategy. Most players would either slow down so dramatically, or play so inaccurately, that they would gain nothing. Many would actually decrease their win rates.

The last factor in the Profit Formula is hands per hour. Most blackjack authors estimate that a player gets about 75 to 100 hands per hour. Full tables may cut this down to 60 hands per hour, or even fewer if the other players act slowly. Head-on play, when you can find it, will get you about 200 hands per hour. Many players do not believe they can find head-on games, and when they can, they do not believe they can play that fast. Actually, this is a pretty normal rate of play in a head-on game—if you don't waste time making your decisions.

Playing faster is more challenging, and is also excellent cover. Dealers and pit bosses expect card counters to play slowly and thoughtfully. Also, in hand-held games, dealers will sometimes deal deeper into the deck for fast players, which is another advantage. After all, the faster you play, the more often the dealer must shuffle. If you're accomplished enough as a counter to carry on some semblance of small talk while playing your hands at a good clip, you will more likely be judged as no threat to the house.

To find head-on games (also often called heads-up, or head-to-head), especially at low stakes, you must play at off hours. Mornings and early afternoons on weekdays are often excellent times to go hunting for dealers who are standing behind empty tables twiddling their thumbs. The best times are often different for different casinos; scout and you'll find out. There are, to be sure, other arguments—pro and con—with regards to playing under various crowd conditions for purposes of camouflage, team/partner attacks, and the like. I will attempt to cover all of these considerations later. For now, it's important that you understand the basic math of how a card counter estimates his win rate in dollars and cents.

In a game where 80 hands per hour nets you $10 per hour, 200 hands per hour, assuming the same average bet size, and the same % advantage from your card counting efforts, will raise your expectation to:

$$\$10 \times .01 \times 200 = \$20 \text{ per hour}$$

One question that many new counters ask is, "How much money can I make?" The answer, as you can see, is not so cut and dried. Every one of the factors in the Profit Formula is a variable, and every one has a big effect on the answer.

Stem-sellers who claim that using their blackjack system will net you $XXX per hour, per day, per week, or per year, are generally hawking nonsense. Unless they fill in all the variables of the Profit Formula—which will differ for every player, and change according to the table conditions you face—any such claim is pure speculation. In the meantime, to best apply the Red Seven Count, or any other card counting system, you'll need to learn much more about table conditions, betting strategies, camouflage, toking, and every other aspect of casino blackjack that is important to a professional player.

But how do you figure out your average bet size? You don't just pick a number out of thin air and decide to bet that much per hand. Any pro will tell you that the most important factor in bet-sizing is the size of your playing bankroll, and even if you don't see yourself as a pro player, you must take into account the same factors that professionals do when sizing your bets.

Allowing for Normal Fluctuation

So, let's look at some of the practical considerations of bankrolling your play. Essentially, what you are up against is what mathematicians call normal fluctuation.

As shown by our computer simulation results, even when you have a strong advantage over the house, you'll still sometimes lose, because in the short run, anything can happen. This is true even for the casinos—although the house enjoys a large edge on their slot machines, on any given day some slot players will win more than they lose, which is why people return to the slots. If all slot players lost every time they played, no one would play. All casino games are designed to allow players to go home winners fairly regularly—just not often enough to compensate for their long run losses.

Let's stick with blackjack, though. Assume you learn to play basic strategy, so that you nearly eliminate the house edge. How much can you win or lose due to normal fluctuation?

To answer that, start by imagining that all of your bets are of equal size. Rather than assigning some dollar value, let's say instead that you bet one unit on each hand. We will assume you are in a traditional single-deck Las Vegas Strip game, playing perfect basic strategy, so that for all intents and purposes, the game is dead even. Over the long run, you'd expect to win nothing and lose nothing. It's like flipping a coin.

Of course, if you try flipping a coin a thousand times, and recording the results, you'd be highly unlikely to come up with exactly 500 wins and 500 losses. There are precise mathematical formulas for predicting the limits of normal fluctuation, and with an introductory course in probability and statistics, you would know how to make such estimations. But for now, let's develop some practical guidelines describing the best and worst you might expect due to normal fluctuation.

Statisticians use the term *standard deviation* to explain variations from the expected result. For instance, if you flip an honest coin 10 times, your expected result is five heads and five tails. If, however, you came up with 7 heads and 3 tails, this would not be indicative that the coin was dishonest. It would be considered a normal fluctuation. However, if you flipped a coin ten thousand times, and it came up 7,000 heads and only 3,000 tails, it would be very unlikely that this was an honest coin. Even though the ratio of heads to tails has remained 7 to 3, the large number of tosses makes the result highly unlikely.

Standard deviation is the square root of the number of trials, divided by 2. It's not difficult to figure out on any pocket calculator that has a square root key. The square root of 100 is 10, so the standard deviation on 100 trials is 10/2 = 5. The square root of 1,000 is approximately 31.6, so the standard deviation on 1,000 trials is 31.6/2, or approximately 15.8.

Once you understand what the square root of a number means to a statistician, you will understand why it is perfectly normal for you to come up with 7 heads on 10 flips of a coin, but nearly impossible for you to come up with 7,000 heads out of 10,000 flips of the same coin.

The standard deviation of 10 = 3.16/2 = 1.58.

The standard deviation of 10,000 = 100/2 = 50.

So, to come up with heads seven times in ten flips, is to be 2 away from the expectation of 5, and well within two standard deviations (3.16).

But to come up with heads on 7,000 of 10,000 flips, is to be 2,000 heads over the expectation of 5,000. And since one standard deviation on 10,000 flips is only 50, this result is 40 standard deviations away from what's expected. Statistically, this is nearly impossible.

Just how impossible is it? Statistically, we expect to be within one standard deviation 68% of the time, within two standard deviations 95% of the time, and within three standard deviations 99.7% of the time. Suffice it to say that if we get a result that is 40 standard deviations away from our expectation, either the coin or the flipper is crooked. You have a much better chance of winning your state lottery than you do of flipping 7,000 heads in 10,000 tries with an honest coin.

All blackjack players must be concerned with normal fluctuations, as they are a crucial factor in the size of the bets you can afford to make. The following guidelines are based upon statistical realities that should be more than enough for most casual players.

In an hour of play, or about one hundred hands, in a dead even game, you generally will not be ahead or behind by more than 20 units. On rare occasions, however, in a single hour of play, you may expect to be ahead or behind as many as 35-40 units.

If you play off and on over a period of a few days—say, ten hours of play, or about a thousand hands—you probably won't be ahead or behind by more than 75 units, but on rare occasions, you might be ahead or behind by 120 units in a one-thousand-hand period. These estimates of fluctuation assume you always bet only one unit on each hand, and that neither you nor the house has any significant long-term advantage.

Your Bankroll

So, how big should your playing bankroll be? If you are a recreational player, playing a few times a year, ask yourself, "How much can I afford to lose this weekend, painlessly?" That's the size of your bankroll for the weekend. How big of a unit can you afford to play with? Divide your weekend bankroll by 120—that's your safe betting unit. If you intend to play longer than one weekend, and especially if you are serious about card counting for profit, you must use more sophisticated methods of bet-sizing. But even if you do not go on to become a serious card counter, you should understand the basics of normal fluctuation if you ever gamble in casino games, even for fun.

When you first start to play blackjack in a casino, regardless of whether you are playing basic strategy only or attempting to count cards, your first sessions must be viewed as practice. There are a number of betting guidelines you can follow when initially practicing in casinos that will prepare you for the more difficult techniques of bet-sizing once you start counting cards and playing seriously. These guidelines do not comprise a winning system, but merely amount to a practice exercise that will train you to size your bets in proportion to your bankroll. Later, when you count cards, you will use these same techniques in conjunction with other methods.

Your bankroll, in units, must be able to withstand the short run fluctuations. If you have a total of about $500 "play money," you would be courting disaster if you started making $25 bets. $500 would represent only 20 units of $25 each, and you could easily lose your whole stake in less than an hour. Making $10 bets would be safer, since you would have 50 units to play with, but this could also be lost in a relatively short run of hands just due to fluctuation. With $5 bets, or 100 units, you'd be unlikely to lose your whole bankroll in a single weekend of play, although it's certainly not unheard of.

The first step to proportional bet-sizing is to constantly reassess the size of your bankroll and to systematically change the size of your betting unit. Here's how to do it:

Bet-Sizing for a Weekend (1,000) Hands

First, divide your total bankroll into one hundred units. Let's assume you have $1,000, so you have one hundred $10 units. Here's how to handle a losing streak:

If you lose twenty units, or $200, quit play and reassess your bankroll. Since you now have only $800, divide that into one hundred units, and your new unit becomes $8. Play at this level until your bankroll either goes back up to $1,000, or spirals downward to $600. Whichever direction it goes, continue to reassess the size of your bankroll, and resize your bets accordingly so that you never bet much more than 1% of your total bankroll on any given hand.

None of this will have any effect on the fact that over the long run, your expectation will be to break even, assuming you're playing in an even game. In a slightly negative expectation game, the house will slowly grind you down the longer you play. The purpose of this betting method, then, is primarily to train you to constantly monitor your bankroll size, and to keep you in the game longer when you hit a losing streak. It will not give you any long run advantage—in fact, if you are not playing with an advantage, as we assume here, you may expect that you may eventually lose your entire $1,000 bankroll to normal fluctuations. This is especially true if you practice in casinos where the table minimums are $5, so that you cannot reduce your bet any more if your bankroll dips below $500.

On the other hand, you may occasionally double your $1,000 starting bank in a weekend's play. Every gambler who plays in games where the house has only a small edge, such as blackjack, baccarat, or craps (pass or don't pass), will on occasion win or lose 100 betting units. Most players call this "luck;" mathematicians call it normal fluctuation.

If you practice in a casino where you must place $5 minimum bets, and your starting bankroll is $1,000, you would be wise to start out with a $5 betting unit and never waver, unless you came ahead a few hundred dollars. If your starting bankroll is less than $1,000, or if $1,000 represents a significant amount of money to you, play only table minimum bets when practicing. Be aware that you must view the cash as "play money," as you could conceivably lose it all due to normal fluctuation.

If the house has a slight edge (1/2% is typical in most traditional blackjack games), you may still use these guidelines for sizing your bets, but be aware that when the house has an edge, your bankroll will inevitably be depleted over the long run. Nevertheless, in the short run, anything can happen.

For card counters, and especially for high-stakes card counters, bet-sizing is more complex than the simple guidelines presented here, which are meant for beginners to use when practicing at low stakes. If you have a $50,000 bankroll, you would be ill-advised to follow the guidelines in this chapter, dividing your bankroll into 100 units of $500 each, in a break-even (or negative-edge) game, just so you could practice basic strategy. Why chance losing twenty-thousand-dollars in a short period of play just for practice? Practice at low stakes, and then use your big money to bankroll your play when you know what you're doing.

My bet-sizing advice here is pretty conservative. If you're purely a recreational player who typically goes to Las Vegas with $1,000, and can easily live with a total loss on your trips, then feel free to bet at whatever level of risk you feel comfortable with—my advice is primarily for players who want to learn to manage their money the way the pros do, minimizing the possibility of ruin.

If you have a computer, then by all means acquire one of the excellent software programs on the market that allow you to practice counting cards. Save your casino practice until you are an accomplished card counter, as practicing in a casino will always be more expensive than practicing at home. Get your basic skills down with as little expense as possible.

Bet-Sizing for a Month (10,000 Hands)

Let's say you are planning an extended session of blackjack during a 3- or 4-week trip, and you expect to play for a total of about 100 hours, or roughly 10,000 hands. After playing this many hands, you would not usually be ahead or behind by more than 250 units, but on rare occasions, you might find yourself off by as many as 400 units, due to normal fluctuation.

So, if your total bankroll is only a few thousand dollars or less, you could conceivably lose it all, even if you become an expert card counter. You could also ultimately be a victim of the table minimum bets, if, as your losing streak continued, you were not allowed to cut back to smaller bets to keep you from losing all your money. Frankly, if your bankroll is insufficient, you should not be making any bets at all.

Most players, of course, will not immediately have to fight through inordinate losing streaks, and some will even have the pleasure of improbable winning streaks. But fluctuation remains the leading deterrent to card counting: Most beginning counters overbet their bankrolls; those with negative fluctuations give up; those with positive fluctuations usually increase the size of their bets proportionately, continuing to over-bet their bankrolls, until their first big negative swing wipes them out.

Bet-sizing for a 3- or 4-week period (10,000 hands), works exactly the same as bet-sizing for a weekend. The only difference is that you should start by dividing your bankroll by 250, instead of 100, in order to determine your betting unit. In other words, to make $10 bets, you should have a bankroll of $2,500. Cut back to an $8 betting unit if your bankroll goes down to $2,000; $6 units if it falls to $1,500, and so on.

As you can see, the more hands you will play, the larger your bankroll must be to ensure your continuance in the game—even when the game is a break even proposition. In fact, the only way to get around this is to *get the edge in your favor*. If you can get the edge, via card counting, then your long run edge assures that your expected winnings will be greater than the possible negative fluctuations (assuming you also have the fortitude to continue hammering away at the tables through all the ups and downs).

To last in this game, you must have the money, you must size your bets in proportion to your bankroll, and you must reassess your bankroll frequently. You must never chase losses by increasing your bets to win back the money you've lost. If you follow these guidelines, you will have staying power at the tables. If you persevere and acquire skill as a counter, you're on your way to winning.

So, How Much Money Do You Need?

We still haven't answered the question that is the title of this chapter. Most players would consider it a waste of time to make $10 bets when they arrive at a casino with $2,500 to play with. In fact, very few players would do this—if you're going to gamble with that amount of money, you generally want to see a meaningful result. My ultra-conservative betting advice above, though, assumes that you have a *fixed* bankroll of funds that are not easily replenishable. For most players, that's not the case.

A *replenishable* bankroll has no fixed dollar amount, and most players, in fact, play on replenishable bankrolls. There are various common types of replenishable bankrolls, the most common being a job. If you are currently earning an income from some non-gambling source, and some portion of this income is expendable, in the sense that it is money you would normally spend on recreational pursuits, hobbies, entertainment—your disposable income money—then so long as you stay employed, that's your replenishable bank. If you deliver pizza for a living, then this bankroll may be less than $100 per month, if you're a dentist, it may be quite a few thousand dollars more. Much depends on your lifestyle and obligations—if you are a married dentist with five kids and you're paying off a mortgage, the pizza delivery boy may actually have a larger replenishable bankroll than you do.

I will leave it to you to figure out exactly how much of a replenishable bankroll you have, but here is the important distinction between a fixed bankroll and a replenishable one: A *replenishable bankroll* is a specified number of dollars that replenishes itself over a given time period. For instance: $300 per month, or $1,000 per week, or $52,000 per year. It does *not* include your life savings, or some amount of money you can borrow against your credit cards.

Compared to a fixed bankroll, a replenishable bankroll is an absolute joy for a card counter. With the replenishable variety, you can never go broke from negative flux. You may be put out of commission for the rest of the week, but come next month and a couple more paychecks, you're back in business.

If you're working a job that pays $40K per year after taxes, and you figure your real living expenses to be about $30K per year, then you've got a replenishable bankroll of about $10K per year. It may only be $833 per month, but in fact, you can play as if you've got $10,000 behind you, provided you strictly adhere to never losing more than your monthly replenishable amount. This means that in many months you will be put out of commission at the tables very quickly due to negative but entirely normal fluctuations. But you'll compensate for that when you win inordinate amounts, wins that never would have been possible on an $833 bankroll.

Just about every book on card counting addresses the bet-sizing question from the perspective of the player who is on a fixed bankroll, even though most players, including many semi-pros and serious high-stakes players, operate from replenishable funds. If you have an annual replenishable bankroll of $10,000, you will never make it as a card counter if you always play as if you have a total bankroll of $833, since that is the actual amount in your pocket. If you're going to make it as a counter at a serious level of play, then you will have to have the *guts* to bang out some bets that could easily break you on that trip if the flux go against you, and you will have to have the *discipline* to quit, on that trip, when that occurs.

My advice for a player on a replenishable bankroll is very simple. Always play as if your total bankroll is the annual replenishable amount, and play at the one-quarter-Kelly level. This boils down to a fairly simple chart: The percentage of your replenishable bank that you bet is always one-quarter of your % advantage (or true edge). Whether you use the Red Seven Count, the Hi-Lo, or the Zen Count, it looks like this:

Annual Replenishable Bankroll

True Edge	$2,000	$5,000	$10,000	$20,000
1%	$5	$12	$25	$50
2%	$10	$25	$50	$100
3%	$15	$35	$75	$150
4%	$20	$50	$100	$200

This means that if you've got that $10K replenishable bankroll, you can actually bet from $25 to $100 on your high counts, even though you may not be going into the actual game with much more than $800 bucks in your pocket. When you've only got $800+, bets of $100 are close to suicidal. What if you have to double down? What if you have to split, and re-split, and then double after you split? You can lose half or more of your trip bankroll on a single round of play! Mitigating this risk is the fact that 4% advantages very rarely occur. You won't often place $100 bets in today's blackjack games. But when these strong advantages do occur, then bite the bullet and bang it out. This is no time to be chicken; these are the types of opportunities that you're looking for as a card counter. If you lose your trip bank, so it goes. If you've got enough hours at the tables, maybe the casino will comp you to dinner. There's always next month, and in the long run, you'll get them more than they'll get you on these advantage plays. You either have the heart for this game or you don't.

A few final comments on playing on a replenishable bankroll: If you want to take one month's win—after a successful trip—and add it to the amount you can afford to lose the following month, this will give you a lot more flexibility, to say nothing of total playing hours. In fact, I recommend that you do this if you are serious about making money from the casinos. But never, *never*, borrow against next month's replenishable funds—that's a *very* bad habit to get into. In fact, about the only time I would recommend it would be when you need the extra funds to double down or split on a current hand in play. You always want to maximize your win potential in these types of situations, but if you lose those "borrowed" funds, then you must seriously consider whether or not you can play next month on your full replenishable amount. If the amount you go over your trip bank is negligible, forget about it. But if you lose half of next month's playing bank due to some incredible double/split opportunity that doesn't go your way, then seriously consider playing the following month on half of your normal allotment, or even waiting until you can add that allotment to the following month's playing bankroll, so you can play with more flexibility then.

Regardless of how big or small your annual replenishable bankroll is, you should be able to draw up a bet-sizing schedule using the chart above as a guideline. Do not waste your time studying complicated Kelly betting strategies or risk of ruin charts, or any of the complex methods that pros on fixed bankrolls use, or teams of pro players seeking investors must master. With a replenishable bankroll, you're well on your way to making money at this game. But if you quit your job, move to Vegas, and start playing full time on the fixed amount of capital you arrived with, you've got some serious considerations ahead of you.

Fixed Bankroll Strategies

Let's assume that you have a fixed bankroll, which is not replenishable because you either have no income, or every penny of your income goes to paying bills and supporting your lifestyle, with no regular expendable funds. Unless you've got a bunch of money at your disposal, engaging in a high-risk pursuit like card counting may not be a great idea. You could lose quite a bit, or even see all your cash disappear. But only you can decide how much risk you want to assume with your own money, so let me spell out the facts as best I can so that you're able to decide for yourself.

There is one concept in place in every betting strategy for card counters: bet more when you have the edge, and less when the house has it. However, a number of factors complicate this point. First, you must know how much more to bet when you have the edge, and second, you must raise your bet in a way that does not attract unwanted attention. Third, you have to have a big enough bankroll to withstand the fluctuations.

Players who use the simple Red Seven Count, or for that matter any unbalanced card counting system that does not include a true edge adjustment, must bet more conservatively than players who use an accurate method of estimating their advantage as they play.

Single-Deck Betting on a Fixed Bank

In single-deck games, your high bet with the simple Red Seven should be your total bankroll divided by 100—given a $10,000 bankroll, your high bet should be $100. This assumes that you use the simplified betting chart on page 60 with a 1 to 8 spread. With a smaller bank, you may find it impractical or even impossible to spread 1 to 8 with a 1% maximum bet, due to high table minimums, so you'll be stuck with a 1 to 4 spread. In this case, you do not want to place your maximum bet until your count justifies the 8-unit bet according to the betting chart. Otherwise, you will place far too many bets max when you do not have the advantage to justify them.

Players who use the True Edge adjustments that more accurately gauge their precise advantage will find more aggressive betting advice in Chapter 14, "Professional Betting Strategies." The conservative betting advice here is geared to keep casual players from getting into trouble.

You must constantly reassess the size of your bankroll as you play, and alter the size of your bets accordingly. This doesn't have to be a complicated procedure: You know the size of your bankroll prior to the beginning of play, so just keep track of how much money you pull out of your pocket as you play.

Always buy chips in small amounts. If you're playing with nickels ($5 chips), don't buy in for more than $100. If you're playing with quarters ($25 chips), you shouldn't buy in for more than $500. If you need more chips, you can always pull more money out of your pocket. Pit bosses, meanwhile, are sometimes wary of players who buy in for large amounts, then start betting small. Casino floormen like to see players digging into their pockets for more money since that means they're losing. By keeping track of how much money you pull from your pocket, you'll always know your bankroll position—the difference is right in front of your eyes. When there is a significant change in your bankroll, divide your new current bank by 100 to re-determine the size of your high bet. Most of the time, you will have to approximate this figure. For instance, with a $3,150 bankroll, your optimal high bet would be: $3,150 / 100 = $31.50

So, practically, your high bet would be $30. Remember that you will see wild swings, both positive and negative. On occasion, you may have to reassess your bankroll after only 10 minutes of play. If you fail to reassess your bankroll often enough, it could be devastating to you in a few hours. You must cut back when you lose, and you must do it quickly. Try to reassess after winning or losing ten high bets, so with a high bet of $25, you should stop and reassess after winning or losing about $250. Again, if you keep track of how much cash you've pulled out of your pocket, the process is automatic.

The betting spread you need to beat a game depends on the rules and what percentage of the cards you are able to see and count. One of the best guides for choosing a single-deck game was created by a *Blackjack Forum* contributor who called himself "Brother William." He noted that many casinos instructed their dealers to deal a specified number of rounds between shuffles, based on the number of players at the table. In order to get a one percent advantage over the house, using the simple Red Seven, and based on the number of rounds between shuffles and the number of players at the table, the following chart shows the required betting spreads.

In each row, the top spread is for Reno rules, where dealers hit soft 17, and you may double down on 10 and 11 only. The spreads on the following page, in italics, are for downtown Vegas rules, where the dealers hit soft 17, and you may double on any two cards.

Assuming there are only two players at the table, and you are playing Reno rules, if the dealer is dealing only four rounds between shuffles, then you will need a 1-8 spread in order to get a 1% advantage. Note that if there were three players at the table, and four rounds, you could get this 1% advantage with only a 1-4 spread.

Red Seven players should use this chart as a guide to choosing single-deck games. If you cannot get a 1% advantage because the dealer is dealing too few rounds, don't play, but rather find a better game. Note that the five-player game is extremely poor—with Reno rules, you can't beat it (unless you spread bigger than 1 to 8!). Five players with two rounds is very poor, and no dealer will attempt to deal a third round with five players at the table. The best games are three rounds to four players, or four rounds to three players.

Rounds	Number of Players						
	1	2	3	4	5	6	7
One	-	-	-	-	-	-	-
	-	-	-	-	-	-	-
Two	-	-	-	-	-	1-8	1-6
	-	-	-	-	*1-8*	*1-5*	*1-4*
Three	-	-	1-6	1-4			
	-	-	*1-4*	*1-3*			
Four	-	1-8	1-4				
	-	*1-6*	*1-3*				
Five	1-8	1-4					
	1-6	*1-3*					
Six	1-5						
	1-4						
Seven	1-4						
	1-3						
Eight	1-3						
	1-2						

If you use the full set of indices provided for the Hi-Lo Lite, you may spread two units less than the spreads recommended in the chart. Strategy plays have great value in single-deck games.

If you use the Red Seven Count, you raise your bet from the minimum at the pivot (0). If you use the Hi-Lo Lite, raise your bet when the edge has turned in your favor by at least 1/2% (see prior sections). Unless you're a good actor, you should stick with the lowest recommended betting spreads in single-deck games. A wider spread will increase your win rate, but it will also increase your chance of being identified as a card counter.

Players who make bets above $50 might be wise to avoid single-deck games altogether, or at least until you have a better feel for casino play, and how to get away with card counting. At low stakes (all bets below $50), many casinos ignore spreads of 1 to 4 or even 1 to 8, but don't take unnecessary chances. Some casinos will tolerate no counters at all at their tables. If you sense heat, leave and play elsewhere. Return another day, or on another shift.

Two-Deck Games on a Fixed Bank

Two-deck games are common in Nevada. When playing them, calculate your high bet for 2-deck games by dividing your bankroll by 120. With Reno rules, play in one-deck games only, which are commonly available—do not play two-deckers with Reno rules. You can beat these games if there is 75% penetration, and you use a 1 to 8 spread, but much better single-deck games are available in Northern Nevada. In Las Vegas, play in 2-deck games only if at least 60% of the cards are dealt out between shuffles. You must use at least a 1 to 5 spread to get a 1% edge at these games. With more favorable rules, and a deeper shuffle point, you can get a stronger advantage, or use a smaller spread.

Four+ Decks on a Fixed Bank

For all shoe games, determine your high bet by dividing your bankroll by 150. When you play against four or more decks, frequent table-hopping is generally a good idea, as you want to leave the table on negative counts. This technique is often called "Wonging" by card counters, after blackjack author Stanford Wong, who popularized this playing style. Wonging means simply refusing to play against negative situations. When your count indicates that the house has any significant edge, you leave the table to find a better game. On the first couple of rounds after a shuffle, you may tolerate a low negative running-count, but after the first half-deck or so is in the discard tray, stay only if the count is neutral or positive. If you are in a large casino and there are many open tables, do not play against any negative running count.

Your best approach to table-hopping is to keep your eyes open as you walk through the blackjack pits. Look for dealers who are shuffling, finishing a shuffle, or just beginning a new deal (with very few cards in the discard tray). When you spot a crowded table with an open betting spot or two, and the felt gets covered with low (plus) cards, get as accurate a count as you can, and get a bet onto any open spaces. If you are using the Red Seven Count, seek tables with running counts at, or close to, your pivot. In 6 and 8-deck games, you will rarely hit your pivot in one round of play, but if the count goes beyond the halfway point, either watch the next round, or get a small waiting bet on the table. The Red Seven Count is particularly powerful for this playing style—its betting efficiency is high, and all of its variations from basic strategy are plus-count variations. If you use a true edge adjustment, you should seek out tables where your true count indicates that you have the advantage. This will depend on the number of decks, rules, and so on.

When table-hopping, you will sometimes walk for long periods without placing a bet, sometimes playing only one hand before the count goes down again. For this reason, it's best to cover two (or more) betting spots when you find the right situation.

Your table-hopping must also appear natural or you will be recognized as a card counter. You cannot stand behind a table and count round after round, jumping in only when the count goes up—it's too obvious. You must appear casual. Table-hopping is probably easiest to pull off when you are with a companion of the opposite sex. While searching for good tables, you can act like you're more interested in each other, wandering around like lovers at a carnival.

In Atlantic City, many casinos prevent table-hopping by prohibiting mid-shoe entry, and others may restrict bets to the table minimum for any player who enters a game after the first round from a shuffle. These rules are specifically designed to foil Wonging. In casinos where such rules are enforced, the only way to table-hop is to enter games right after the shuffle, stay if the count goes up, and leave if it goes down, in search of another newly shuffled shoe. No card counting strategy can significantly beat a six- or eight-deck game if less than 65% of the cards are dealt out, unless you are allowed to hop. Even with table-hopping, less than 65% penetration will provide little profit potential for card counters.

When table-hopping, you may either use a betting spread or flat bet. Flat-betting will work only if you wait until you have a decided edge before entering a game. Otherwise, you must spread your bets, at least 1 to 4 units, and often higher. For camouflage, you may want to only raise your bet after a win, by parlaying. If you attempt to raise after a loss, you must appear to be chasing your losses, as a compulsive gambler might. To pull this off, you may have to make comments about "feeling a winning streak coming up," or "ending a losing streak." Many of the most successful card counters are those who can convince the casinos that they are die-hard gamblers. Some of these players even use phenomenal betting spreads, sometimes 1 to 40 units and more.

If you use a true edge adjustment, remember when adjusting your running count that the new calculation is based on unseen cards. If you enter a 6-deck game in progress after counting only one round, you must keep aware of the fact that you have seen and counted very few cards. There may be half a deck or more already in the discard pile, but do not make your true edge adjustments by estimating that you have seen all the discards unless you have actually seen them.

The rules are very important to card counters in shoe games. Surrender is worth about a quarter of a percent to a counter who is using a large spread, and double after splits is worth just a bit less. With both of these rules in place, your count strategy will be worth almost half a percent more, and that's a huge difference.

A card counter recently asked me if he could beat shoe games without table-hopping if he used a 1 to 12 spread. This may sound like a simple question, but the answer is quite complicated. How many decks? What's the penetration? What are the rules? Let's look at the player advantages (in percentage) from John Auston's "World's Greatest Blackjack Simulation" report for the Red Seven Count, using a 1 to 12 spread in both 6 and 8-deck games, with three different (but common) levels of penetration, and three different rule sets: dealer hits soft 17 (**H17**); dealer stands on soft 17 (**S-17**); and dealer stands on soft 17 plus late surrender (**S-17-LS**).

	H17	S-17	S-17-LS
6 Decks, 67% Penetration	0.39	0.71	0.99
6 Decks, 75% Penetration	0.79	1.16	1.53
6 Decks, 83% Penetration	1.31	1.68	2.07
8 Decks, 69% Penetration	-0.04	0.27	0.50
8 Decks, 75% Penetration	0.18	0.49	0.76
8 Decks, 81% Penetration	0.44	0.77	1.10

So, despite the fact that in all cases the player is using the same 1 to 12 betting spread in all of these games, with the same counting system, his expectation ranges from -0.04% (8 decks, with 5 1/2 decks dealt) to 2.07% (6 decks, with 5 decks dealt)! Notice how important all three variables—number of decks, penetration, and rules—are to the expectation. This is why many pros use computer simulation software themselves to test games and betting approaches. If you don't have a computer to run your own simulations, there are now books available (such as Auston's) that contain nothing but hundreds of charts of simulation data, comparing different games and table conditions. (In Chapter Fourteen, I will display some of the data from reports I have written.) If you intend to put any *serious* amount of money into this game, you have to invest a bit in your education.

Multi-deck games also restrict profitable playing opportunities for players with limited bankrolls. For example, suppose you find a 6-deck Vegas Strip game with 4 decks dealt (a 67% shuffle-point). Note in the chart that with a 1 to 12 spread, your expectation is 0.71%, and if you want a full 1% advantage in this game, you'll have to spread 1 to 16. Since the table minimum bet is $2, you must spread your bets from $2 to $32. Since, in 6-deck games, your best high bet is your bankroll divided by 150, you would have to have at least $4,800 ($32 x 150) in order to make this high bet. So, if you don't have $5,000 to play with, you can't beat this game because you can't afford a $2 betting unit! (And the reality is that it's hard to find 6-deck games these days with less than a $5 minimum bet. To use a 1 to 16 spread ($5-$80) in this $5 minimum game, the fixed bankroll requirement goes up to $10,000.)

The only way to compensate is to play less frequently under unfavorable circumstances; in other words, *table-hop, table-hop, table-hop*. Of course, the best solution is to find a better game — six decks with only four decks dealt sucks! The difficulty with table-hopping a game like this is that you may not find enough betting situations to justify the time spent looking.

In Conclusion

The real question is not how much money you need, but how much money you have, and how much of that you really want to devote to this endeavor. Hopefully, you have already found in this chapter the information you need to answer the question for yourself. In Chapter Fourteen, we're going to look at a lot more technical information that will primarily interest professionals and those hoping to join their ranks. Even if you don't fit into either category, do yourself a favor and read the chapter anyway. It is not too technical for average players to follow, and you just might find some information of value, even if you're learning to count cards more to have fun than to make money. One thing about money…it's always fun to win it.

13

SPECIAL RULES

In this chapter we're going to look at two distinct types of special rules. First, we'll look at traditional blackjack games that have unusual rules or side-bets added to them. Then we'll investigate variations on the traditional game that are so different that they must actually be considered different games entirely. Though many, if not most, of the special rules can be beaten with card counting systems, I won't provide any deep mathematical analyses that will help you do so. In the case of most side bets, the dollar-values obtainable are so negligible that it's a waste of time to bother exploiting them.

Side Bets

Some casinos offer side bets that can be beaten, but not with traditional blackjack card counting strategies. Generally speaking, if you see a new rule or option on a blackjack table, it's probably not going to work in your favor, and almost certainly won't if you are guessing at the value and the proper strategy. Casinos often introduce options in order to seduce players into making bad decisions. All of the options described in this chapter were introduced for that purpose, but some have proven to have some value to smart players.

From my perspective, the primary value of these side bets is camouflage. The casinos generally regard these as sucker bets, because the house edge off the top is much higher than that on the traditional blackjack game, and most of these gimmicks appeal primarily to tourists. For instance, the house edge on the Royal Match side bet is 3.8%. This means that a $5 bet on the Royal Match option costs you 19¢. If you place ten RM bets per hour, the total cost is $1.90 on average. In fact, you may lose more than this, or even win, as the expected result varies significantly. But even if you lose all ten of the RM bets you place, the maximum cost to you is $50 with $5 bets. Players who bet on the Royal Match option always look foolish to casino personnel, so, if you're trying to get away with a count game, occasional RM bets may help disguise your intentions.

Likewise, the Super Sevens bet has a house edge of about 11%, which is huge. But the maximum bet allowed on the Super Sevens option is $1, so the total cost per bet is only about 11¢. You could place 50 of these bets per hour, and the average cost to you won't be much more than $5.50.

If the maximum bet you place on your regular blackjack hand is only $25 or less, then I wouldn't bother making camo side-bets. Why give anything back to the house when your expected dollar return is so low from the traditional game? But if you're betting up to $50 or $100 or more, then occasional camouflage bets on the weird options will help to disguise you as a typical gambler at fairly low cost.

Over/Under

One of the more popular options (unfortunately not popular enough!) is the over/under bet. This is an optional side bet (actually two separate bets) that your first two cards will total either over or under 13. There is a special area on the table for you to make these bets. Aces always count as 1 for this bet, and a total of 13 always loses. If you win on an over/under bet, you are paid 2 to 1.

This rule is most often offered on 6 and 8-deck games, and it has little value with a traditional card counting system. Using the Hi-Lo Lite, you would need a true edge of +2 1/2 to just break even on the over bet, or -3 on the under. These advantages will not occur very often in shoe games, unless the penetration is quite deep.

A better counting system for this option is to count the ten-valued cards as -1 and Aces, 2s, 3s, and 4s as +1. Using this counting system, you would make an over bet at a true edge of +1 1/2 or greater, and an under bet at -2 or lower. This greatly increases the value of the option. If you know the Hi-Lo Lite indices, you may use the Hi-Lo strategy changes with the over/under count for strategy plays on your blackjack hand. In a 6-deck game, with 75% penetration, you could get close to a 1% advantage by using a 1 to 4 spread with proper over/under bets. With deeper penetration, the value skyrockets.

In some European casinos, there is an over/under variation in which a pair of aces pays a 7 to 1 bonus on under bets. This payout almost doubles the value of the over/under option. Unfortunately, there are very few over/under games anymore, and the casinos know that card counters attack them.

Most casinos that offer the over/under bet limit the amount that can be bet on this option. In many cases, this bet limitation, in conjunction with generally poor penetration, makes the over/under bet pretty worthless.

By the way, do not place over/under bets without using a card counting system. The house advantage is 6 1/2% on the over bet, and more than 10% on the under, if you're just guessing.

Royal Match

This side bet offered in some single-deck games allows you to wager on whether you will be dealt two cards of the same suit. If so, you will be paid 3 to 1; if you are dealt a king and queen of the same suit, you will be paid 10 to 1.

A card counter developed a system for beating this rule a few years ago, which he sold privately for a few months, then took off the market. I examined the system, and also had the theory tested via computer simulation, and it worked! Unfortunately, it was not an easy card counting system, as you had to keep four separate counts of the cards remaining in each suit. Most casinos that offer the Royal Match option restrict the maximum bet, usually to $25. This limitation makes it difficult to make much money with this option, except for camouflage as player advantages do not occur very frequently. Since any Royal Match counting system would prove worthless for all normal playing and betting decisions, it will rarely be worth a player's time or effort to attempt to exploit it. And do not bet on this option, except for camouflage, unless you are using a valid suit-counting system, as the house edge is 3.8%.

Some casinos also offer a multiple-deck version of the Royal Match bet where any first two suited cards pay 2 1/2 to 1, and a suited K-Q pays 25 to 1. This is far worse for the player than the single-deck version—with these multi-deck payouts, the house edge goes up to 6.7%, and no suit-counting system will beat it.

Super Sevens

This side bet was invented by the same man who invented the over/under bet; essentially, you place a one-dollar side-bet that you will be dealt one, two, or three sevens, with various payouts depending on whether the sevens are suited or unsuited. Technically, card counters can beat this option if they learn to keep a count of the sevens, and the perfect counting system for this option is to count all sevens as -12, and everything else as +1.

The house edge on the Super Sevens option is about 10.8%. This qualifies it as a true sucker bet, one of the worst bets available on a table game, similar to the house edge on the hardways bets at craps, or the tie bet at baccarat.

I no longer remember the true count at which it makes sense to place a Super Sevens bet, but it does occur occasionally. Even so, I wouldn't waste my time trying to figure it out. The problem is that the option is not worth more than a few cents per hour to a seven-counter, due to that $1 maximum bet restriction. And since the counting system has virtually no value whatsoever to your regular blackjack hand, why spend even a moment learning it? Without the seven-count, the house has about an 11% advantage over you on this bet, so it's yet another side-bet with no value to anyone. (Well, actually, it has some value to the casinos that offer it, since they keep eleven cents for every buck wagered!)

NOTE:

Some casinos offer special bonus payouts for player hands that contain three 7s, most commonly a 3 to 2 payout if the hand wins. This is not the same thing as the Super Sevens option, which requires the player to make a separate side-bet. The values of bonus hands, such as 777 pays 3 to 2, or 678 suited pays 2 to 1, are listed in the chart of rule effects in Chapter Eleven.

Lucky Ladies

Similar to Royal Match and Super Sevens, in which you bet on the appearance of specific cards (in this case, the queens and/or ten-valued cards), the Lucky Ladies option can also be beaten with card counting. Like over/under, you can use your normal card counting system to find betting opportunities, since hands totaling 20 also have value. But a count system developed specifically for the Lucky Ladies option (with a side-count of queens) would be better.

Again, I am not thrilled by the profit opportunities from any of these side bets. I think most card counters have enough trouble just keeping a simple count and playing their regular blackjack hands correctly. But more than that, any option that has a payout of greater than even money (as just about all side-bet options do), will have real-world results that vary tremendously. This means that exploiting the option by card counting would require a much larger bankroll than would be required for a regular blackjack game.

"Bonus" Blackjack Variations

Some casinos in Nevada offer a side-bet that either the player, the dealer, or both will be dealt a blackjack, with a payout of 15 to 1. Since the odds against being dealt a blackjack are about 20 to 1, this is a very bad bet. What makes the bet more attractive, in some casinos, however, is that there is a progressive jackpot that can be won if both the player and dealer are dealt a blackjack. Often, this jackpot also requires that one of the blackjacks be suited, or of a specific suit. Another version of this progressive jackpot side-bet allows the player to press a button that will cause a bonus, usually from $5 to $1,000, to appear on an LED screen above the table.

If we knew in what proportion each bonus amount would appear, we could figure out the house edge. But we don't, and somehow, I have the distinct feeling that there is a house edge on this bet, and that you're wasting your time if you think you can get an edge by counting cards.

The Pseudo-Blackjack Variations

There are many casino games that look very similar to traditional blackjack, but they are so different that they are technically not the same game. In most cases, these blackjack variations were invented for the purpose of foiling card counters. Let's look at some of the most popular "fake" blackjack games.

Double Exposure

This is a variation of blackjack in which both of the dealer's first two cards are exposed. Sounds great, but there are some bad rules that go along with it. Blackjacks only pay even money, but worse than that, the dealer wins ties (except for blackjacks). This means that if you and the dealer both have 19, you have to hit, and pray for an ace or deuce.

Most double exposure games have poor rules, and are primarily gimmicks for tourists. Although card counters can beat these games, double exposure strategies are quite complex, and I personally do not believe there are enough double exposure games of value to make it worthwhile for most players to study them.

SuperFun 21

This is becoming a common variety of single-deck blackjack in Nevada. The game offers a whole slew of great rules, especially with regards to splitting pairs, doubling down and surrendering. But there is one exceptionally bad rule, and that is that players' blackjacks pay even money. If you look at the rule effects in Chapter Eleven, you'll see that this even money payout costs you dearly—too dearly to make these games "super fun." As with many of the blackjack variations, there are ways to beat these games with card counting, but the strategies are more complex, and the returns are skimpier. Another problem that all of these newer gimmick games have is that the casinos are not accustomed to seeing big money on the tables at these games. Even if you do study and learn a strategy for this type of game, you cannot expect to put very large bets on the tables if you're trying to blend into the crowd.

Spanish 21

Similar to SuperFun 21, Spanish 21 has lots of great rules and options. Plus, blackjacks pay 3 to 2 just like in the traditional game. So where does the house get its edge? This game is not dealt from "honest" 52-card decks. There are eight 48-card decks in the shoe, and from each deck, 4 tens have been removed. That is, all of the jacks, queens and kings are there, but none of the tens are in play.

Let's use our card counting logic to estimate the effect of these bastardized decks. Using the Hi-Lo count, if I remove 32 tens from the top of the shoe, my running count would be -32. With approximately 15 half decks remaining to be dealt, I quickly surmise that the true edge is about -32/15, or -2.1%. Yuck!

Are all of those great rules enough to make up for this house edge of +2% caused by those missing tens? No. The game stinks. You can beat it with card counting, but only at a fraction of the rate that you can beat traditional blackjack. So forget it.

No-Bust Blackjack

There are numerous variations of "no-bust" blackjack, a game invented in California some years ago to skirt state laws prohibiting traditional casino blackjack. In many of these games, the player shoots for a total of 22, instead of 21. The no-bust feature is accomplished by allowing the hand that is "closest" to 22 to win. That is, a player 23 would beat a dealer 20. As you might imagine, strategies for beating these games are nothing like strategies for traditional blackjack.

Player-Banked Blackjack

In most cases, the no-bust games described above also require the player to pay a per-hand fee to play. The fee (or commission) is based on the size of your bet. For instance, with a $5 bet, you might have to pay 25 cents. With a $25 bet, the fee might go up to 50 cents, and so on. Even in a traditional blackjack game, this type of fee-to-play structure makes playing very expensive, and winning—even if you have a valid card counting strategy for such a game—near impossible.

Consider this: If you pay 25 cents to play a $5 hand, you're giving up 5% just to play! No card counting system will ever overcome a 5% vigorish, so don't even think about trying to beat this game. And although a 50-cent commission to play a $25 hand is only a 2% charge, it's still way too much. Most card counters are trying to get an edge of about 1% over the house, so how can you buck 2% off the top? Plus, this commission does not even take into account what the additional house edge might be. Commission games are almost never worth the trouble.

> ## BLACKJACK PAYS 6:5
> These games, which have become the standard single-deck game in Las Vegas, are traditional H17 games with a reduced payment on blackjacks. That reduced payout adds 1.4% to the house edge, making these games impossible to beat without a huge betting spread. Don't waste your time with them.

Summary

The general rule is to stay away from all of the pseudo-blackjack variations. Although most can be beaten with card counting, the profit opportunities are much slimmer, and the strategies are often more complex. It's all right to use the side-bets for occasional camouflage, but don't waste your time trying to make money from these options.

The only side bet that has a truly exceptional value for card counters is the over/under bet. Most of the casinos that offer this bet are on cruise ships or outside of the U.S., and the description provided above should help you to take advantage of this option if you run into it in your travels. If you have regular access to games with this rule option, then I'll advise you to get a copy of my "Over/Under Report" (see the back pages of this book), which explains the option in detail, along with a complete card counting system for exploiting it.

SECTION TWO

EARNING YOUR GREEN BELT

14

PROFESSIONAL BETTING STRATEGIES

All of the concepts described in Chapter Twelve regarding risk of ruin, fluctuations, Kelly betting, etc., apply to both casual card counters and full-time pros. But if you make your living at this game, or are otherwise betting at a level where the wins and losses make a substantial difference to you, then you should be even more aware of the dangers of losing streaks, which are inevitable. In this chapter, we're going to expand on these topics as they apply to pros. But first...

Starting from Scratch

Of the many pro players I've known through the years who were playing on small banks (say $15,000 or less), most either went broke or were scraping the bottom so often that they ended up getting jobs. Some lived in their cars, borrowed money from friends, bummed nights in friends' apartments. None had an easy life at the start.

Of those who went on to make it in blackjack, there were various reasons for their success. Some just experienced a period of unusually great luck right off the bat that gave them the bank they needed to continue. Many formed partnerships with other good players, entering into informal agreements to work together and share games and results. But most found various ways to exploit casinos without card counting. They continued to count cards, but they opened their eyes to other opportunities around them. They hustled casino coupons, comps and fun books. They knew every 99¢ meal in town. If there was a free hot dog at some casino sports book on Tuesday nights, they were there to eat it. They learned how to extract maximum value from slot clubs. They got on casino mailing lists to get every freebie possible. They kept their ears open for any promotions that gave the player an edge on any game. Some cashed in on currency exchange deals. Some were lucky enough to find investors, or teams, that allowed them to play at higher levels than their own meager bankrolls permitted.

The smartest ones discovered exceptionally high edges on games that no other players had even noticed. Others were particularly good at finding and exploiting casino "mistakes," such as a valuable new rule on a blackjack game, or a different payout on a crap table. These were usually just temporary opportunities, but these players made the most of them for a few days, sometimes for a few weeks, before other players—and finally, the casino itself—caught on. I know players who won thousands of dollars playing video blackjack machines that had incorrect slot-club cash-back bonuses. I know a player who won two cars from the same casino by playing an overly generous slot club promotion that the casino hadn't really thought through. This isn't old stuff—most of this is recent.

Last year, the Horseshoe in Las Vegas decided to put in a double exposure blackjack game, but they didn't realize that in the standard version of the double exposure game, naturals pay even money. With naturals paying 3 to 2 at the Horseshoe game, the players had close to a 2% advantage off the top. The game was there for weeks before most card counters discovered it, and the players who found it first made a lot of money. Inevitably, an opportunity like this will be found by a rank amateur who will then go and post his "discovery" on the Internet, and that's when the opportunity dies. The counters swarm in like hungry jackals; the casino freaks out at the invasion; the game is gone.

If a player living in Cleveland told me he was dead earnest about making a living as a professional blackjack player (and numerous players in Cleveland have told me this!), starting with a bankroll in the neighborhood of $10,000, I would tell him right off that his chances were slim at making it. Most who try fail. But if that did not deter him, I would tell him that his chances of making it, if he intends to continue living in Cleveland, are worse than slim, and closer to none. With a $10,000 bankroll, you cannot afford the travel expenses, and you cannot get in enough hours to make the money you'll need to survive, or to gain the experience you'll need to develop your skills.

If he's really serious about making this his career, I'd advise him to move to Las Vegas, where the greatest number of opportunities exist, find a cheap place to live—there are lots of tacky but safe apartment buildings just east of the Strip, populated by old folks living on their Social Security checks—and learn to exploit every gimmick the town has to offer, and there are a lot of 'em.

I'd tell him that if he's moderately friendly and keeps his eyes open he'll inevitably meet other talented small-timers trying to make it as well. If he becomes part of the pro-gambling subculture, he'll meet some players who have been scraping by professionally for many years, without ever having had much of a bankroll, and rarely a job for any length of time. They'll teach him a lot of survival tricks. There's a lot of free food in Vegas, and more free money than most tourists realize, but it's a grind. You can't do it if you have dependents, or a mortgage.

If he's really sharp, careful, and hard-working, he may find that his bankroll keeps getting bigger over time. He'll weather the setbacks and come back stronger than ever. He'll begin to impress more successful pros who may teach him more. Then it's just a question of keeping on friendly terms with the casinos in order to pursue his passion at a higher level. That's where the real test starts.

Fixed vs. Replenishable Bank

If you are living solely on your gambling income, then whatever funds you have at your disposal is your *fixed* bankroll. In fact, it's worse than fixed; assuming you have living expenses, your bankroll is constantly diminishing unless you supplement it regularly with your gambling wins. So, before you estimate the size of your fixed bankroll—if you have no other source of income to cover your living expenses—deduct at least three months worth of living expenses from your total bank before determining your betting schemes.

With any fixed bank, you are in trouble if you lose such a substantial portion that you can no longer play at a level that will both keep a roof over your head and keep you in action at the tables. There are stories of card counters who came to town with only a few thousand bucks and soon found themselves living in luxury, but failures are a lot more common.

Let's look at a few of the considerations of primary importance to pros and aspiring pros:

Methods of Decreasing Flux

A major difference between pro and amateur approaches to card counting is that the pro must be more concerned with limiting his bankroll fluctuations, because more often than not he's playing on a fixed bankroll, and knows that he could go for months without a net win. He can't just count on next week's paycheck to fund his next trip. The pro is always on one long trip; it never ends.

Here are some of the things the new professional has to be aware of:

Watch Out for Scams

In a later chapter, we will look at the advantages of team play, partner play, and playing on joint bankrolls with other players. These types of plays can be very profitable, and can smooth out negative fluctuations. But be very careful about ever combining your bankroll or results with any other player, unless you know him very well, or people you trust vouch for him. There are too many stories of card counters who spent a year or so studying, saving their money, and finally hitting Vegas or Reno with a hard-earned $5K or $10K bank, only to see their money disappear in a matter of days (or sometimes hours) after joining forces with a con artist who convinces them that they can both do much better if they "work together." Getting ripped off for your whole bank is the biggest negative flux you'll ever encounter, and it is totally avoidable if you're careful about whom you associate with. Once you've got that licked, you can start looking at the more technical aspects of reducing flux.

If you're serious about playing professionally, the stuff that follows is all stuff you need to know. If it looks too complicated, then don't quit your day job. This is the stuff that the real pros live by. You either want it, or you don't.

Play with a Bigger Edge

One of the most important methods that professional players use to limit fluctuations is to look for opportunities to play with a higher edge over the house. This tactic does not just slightly decrease flux; depending on how high an edge you can get, it can all but eliminate it. Some methods used by pro players cannot be discussed in print because we do not wish to alert casino game protection personnel to these ideas. One simple way, however, that even neophyte card counters can use to increase their advantage over the house is table-hopping.

Table-Hopping

When you play at the black chip level or higher, most of your play will be in shoe games, primarily because they will offer you the best chance to avoid detection as a card counter. Vegas locals who play at the "chunky green" level also must put a lot of time into the shoe games. You will become a known face in the casinos, so you can't expose your strategy too often in hand-held games. As mentioned earlier, hand-held games are often counter traps, especially when you see only one or two hand-held tables in a casino that mostly offers shoe games. It is much easier (and quicker) for game protection personnel to observe a player's betting patterns while counting down one or two decks, than it is to see evidence of card counting while watching shoe games.

In shoe games, playing at the black chip level or higher, you will move around frequently, for two reasons. One reason is to further avoid detection; the second is because these games are difficult to beat if you play through all of the negative counts. In fact, if you avoid playing when your count tells you the house has the advantage, it is possible to beat these games without ever raising your bet!

This sounds ideal, but it's difficult to pull off. In order to use a table-hopping strategy, you must have crowd conditions that allow it. You want to see lots of open tables, but not tables so crowded that it's hard to get a seat. You want to see tourists and gamblers milling in the aisles, watching games in progress. If the aisles are relatively empty, you will stick out. Casino game protection personnel are well aware of "back counters" who are on the lookout for opportunities to jump into a shoe in progress with a big bet. In fact, the guys in surveillance have a slang term for back counters—"buzzards"—which describes the way the unskilled back counters look from the eye in the sky, as they endlessly circle the pit. To pull off a table-hopping strategy successfully, you want a nice crowd to blend into.

Let's look at some data on a typical six-deck game, assuming the house has an advantage of about 0.50% off the top—fairly typical—using a "frequency distribution" that shows how often the various house/player advantages occur, and what kind of an advantage you might get from table-hopping this game.

What is a "frequency distribution?" This is a mathematical term used by statisticians to describe how often something is expected to happen. I hate math terminology because it makes people who didn't take advanced math courses in college think they can't understand whatever concept the term refers to; I personally like calling frequency distribution charts "freak charts," because a frequency distribution simply answers the question, "how freaky is it?"

Most people who watch and understand sports use advanced statistical concepts every day. Let's use baseball as an example. If I say a hitter has a batting average of .312, this is really a number taken from a frequency distribution chart. It tells us the frequency—.312—of the batter's hits, in relation to all of his trips to the plate that resulted in either a hit or an out. Another way of saying this baseball player has a .312 batting average would be to say that if I look at a chart that shows all of his hits and outs for the season, he got a hit 31.2% of the time. The batting average, .312, or 31.2%, is the "frequency" with which he gets a hit. So, how freaky is it when this batter gets a hit? Not very—his batting average tells us that he gets a hit almost a third of the time.

Most baseball fans know that batting average does not include the times the player walked, or reached first by being hit by a pitch. If we factor in those at-bats, we will end up with his "on-base percentage." But neither batting average nor on-base percentage tells us how many total bases, on average, the player made per trip to the plate. If we just look at the on-base percentage, a guy who hits all singles could look just as good as a guy who hits lots of doubles and triples. So, to distinguish these players from each other we calculate their "slugging percentages." Virtually every spectator sport has mountains of data, based on frequencies, that the fans understand, despite never having taken a course in statistics.

I knew one baseball nut who used the players' batting averages to make a lot of money betting against his buddies. When a player who had a batting average under .333 came to the plate, he would often give 2 to 1 odds to any and all takers that the guy wouldn't get a hit. "My twenty against your ten," he would announce. In fact, he had the best of it, since a batting average below .333 means that the player gets a hit less than one out of three times to the plate. One night, after putting up five twenties against five tens, his spirits were dampened somewhat when the TV sportscaster announced that the batter, who was hitting .295, hit .500 against lefties with runners in scoring position! Whoops! You'd better make sure you're using the right freak chart for the bets you're making!

In any case, a "frequency distribution chart" simply shows us the percentage of times that various things occur. In blackjack, we can analyze a card counting system, and figure out the win/loss rate, by using a frequency distribution. We know that the count is always going up and down, and that sometimes the house has the edge, and sometimes the player has it. But to know exactly how much I expect to win or lose in a specific game, using some specific betting spread based on my count, I need more details. What I need to know is exactly how often the different house/player advantages occur. That is, what are the frequencies of player advantages of 1%, 2%, 3%, and so on? And what are the frequencies of these house advantages? If I know how often these occur in a game, I can figure out how much of a betting spread I need to beat the game. I can also figure out exactly how much I should bet at each specific count in order to get the highest win rate. And I can also use these frequencies to devise a strategy for minimizing my fluctuations.

Drawing up a frequency distribution chart that shows house/player advantages for a blackjack game is not rocket science. There are two ways to do it: You can run a computer simulation, and then study data the computer spits out; or, you can use a mathematical formula for deriving the precise data you seek. Since this is not a math course, I'm not going to explain the process. Think of this chapter as the sports section: In lots of daily papers, you'll find a chart that shows the batting averages, and sometimes the on-base percentages and slugging percentages for all the players, but you're not going to find all the raw data and the formulas used for calculating these totals. You don't need the formulas to understand that a .312 hitter is scary to most pitchers. If you have an interest in the math, get a book on probability and statistics. I just want you to understand what the data we're going to look at means.

How to Read the 6 Deck/75% Dealt Chart

The chart title, *"6 Decks/75% Dealt (pg 177),"* tells us the specific game we're looking at—with a different number of decks, or a different percentage dealt out, the frequency distribution would look different. Advantages change radically with different numbers of decks and greater or lesser penetration. This freak chart is specifically for a 6-deck game where the dealer is dealing out about 4 1/2 decks (75% of the cards) between shuffles—a fairly typical shoe game.

The first column, labeled *Adv.* (an abbreviation for "advantage"), shows the percent of occurance for various player advantages, positive and negative. Note that the entries in this column run from -4.0% to +4.0%. In a 6-deck game with 75% penetration, house/player advantages greater than this occur very rarely. If this chart was for a 6-deck game where 5 1/2 decks were being dealt out between shuffles (92% penetration), or for any single-deck game, we would need a freak chart that showed the occurrence of much greater house/player advantages.

The second column, labeled *Hands,* is the frequency distribution. That's the data that shows how many hands—per 100—will occur with the percent advantage shown in the first column. Example: In this six-deck game with 75% (4 1/2 decks) dealt, a player advantage of 1% will occur about 4.5 times per hundred hands. A house advantage of 1% will occur about 13 times per 100 hands. Note that the house advantage of 1% occurs almost 3 times as often as the player advantage of 1% This is because the house has a 1/2% edge off the top. In a sense, the house gets a running start on you! Before you continue reading this explanation, find these numbers in the *Hands* column. Be sure you understand how to read the data in the first two columns before you go on to the rest of the chart.

Now we come to the various betting strategies we might try in this game. For our analysis, we'll look at eight different betting systems, which I've labeled S-1 through S-8. Each of those columns represents a different way that card counters might bet in this game. The numbers in each column represent the number of units bet at each of the various advantages that occur. Note that zeros fill the whole upper portion for all of the betting systems. This is because all of the betting systems shown here are table-hopping approaches. The player is usually not betting anything when the advantage is negative.

In S-7, for instance, the player is using a 1 to 4 betting spread. Note that when the house has a 1/2% edge over him (-0.5%), such as when dealing right off the top of a fresh shoe, he bets 1 unit, and he also bets 1 unit when his edge is even with the house (0.0%). When his advantage is 0.5% over the house, he increases his bet to 2 units; and when it is 1.0% or more, he bets 4 units. The S-7 player is using a typical 1 to 4 betting spread in this game, but leaves the table when the count goes negative. Look at all eight betting systems, and make sure you understand how each player attacks this game.

6 Decks 75% Dealt

Adv.	Hands	S-1	S-2	S-3	S-4	S-5	S-6	S-7	S-8
-4.0%	0.0	0	0	0	0	0	0	0	0
-3.5%	1.0	0	0	0	0	0	0	0	0
-3.0%	2.0	0	0	0	0	0	0	0	0
-2.5%	3.0	0	0	0	0	0	0	0	0
-2.0%	4.0	0	0	0	0	0	0	0	0
-1.5%	8.0	0	0	0	0	0	0	0	0
-1.0%	13.0	0	0	0	0	0	0	0	0
-0.5%	34.0	1	0	0	0	1	1	1	1
0.0%	13.0	1	1	0	0	1	1	1	1
0.5%	8.5	1	1	1	0	2	2	2	2
1.0%	4.5	1	1	1	1	2	3	4	4
1.5%	3.5	1	1	1	1	2	3	4	8
2.0%	2.0	1	1	1	1	2	3	4	8
2.5%	2.0	1	1	1	1	2	3	4	8
3.0%	1.0	1	1	1	1	2	3	4	8
3.5%	0.5	1	1	1	1	2	3	4	8
4.0%	0.0	1	1	1	1	2	3	4	8
Hands Bet/100:		69	35	22	14	69	69	69	69
Average Bet:		1.00	1.00	1.00	1.00	1.32	1.51	1.71	2.23
Gain/Hand:		.002	0.008	.013	.017	.006	.009	.012	.023
Win Rate %:		.16%	.79%	1.26%	1.74%	.42%	.59%	0.72%	1.05%
Hourly Units:		.11	.28	.28	.24	.39	.62	.86	1.62

Now, let's look at the five rows of data beneath the betting systems, labeled *Hands Bet/100, Average Bet, Gain/Hand, Win Rate %,* and *Hourly Units.* The data in these rows is derived from the columns. I'm not going to go into the precise formulas for obtaining all of these numbers, but I want you to understand the basic logic of how a mathematician figures out the value of a game and a betting strategy. None of this is rocket science.

Hands Bet/100 is a pretty easy number to come up with. Remember that the table-hopping/back-counting player is not betting on every hand; rather, he watches a lot of hands without betting, trying to avoid betting into any significant house edge. If you add up all of the numbers in the *Hands* column that show a bet greater than 0 in the respective *S* columns, you come up with how many hands (out of 100 hands seen), the player using each betting system would bet on. In *S-1,* for instance, the numbers in the *Hands* column where we see player bets are:

$$34 + 13 + 8.5 + 4.5 + 3.5 + 2 + 2 + 1 + .5 = 69$$

Notice that with the betting systems where the player waits for a higher advantage before placing a bet, the entry in the *Hands Bet/100* goes down.

Look at the next row, **Average Bet**. This is also pretty easy to figure out. Looking closely, you'll see that with *S-1* through *S-4,* the *Average Bet* is always 1.0, because the player always bets one unit. But when the player starts spreading his bets upward, the average amount bet per hand goes up, as expected.

The next row is **Gain/Hand**. These entries tell us how many units, per hand played, the player would win with each betting system. The *S-1* entry is 0.002—if you multiply this number by your betting unit, you get the dollar amount you would win for every hand you played with this betting system.

Let's say your betting unit is $100.

$$\$100 \ \times \ 0.002 \ = \ .20, \text{ or } 20\text{¢ per hand}$$

If that strikes you as an awfully small gain on a $100 bet, you're starting to think like a pro! (In fact, the actual gain is even smaller, only 16¢ per hand. The only reason we came up with 20¢ per hand is because the table entries are rounded off to three decimal places. The true gain per hand is 0.0016. Yuck!)

Moving on, we get to **Win Rate %**: This is the actual advantage over the house that you have with this betting spread. With S-1, your *Win Rate* is 0.16%, which means you're barely squeaking by. The highest *Win Rate* is from S-4, which is a whopping 1.74%. So, let's look at that betting strategy. The *S-4* player is waiting for a full 1% advantage over the house before he puts any money on the table. Should we all just use *S-4,* and wait until a 1% advantage occurs before we bet? Not necessarily. Look at the data in the next row:

Hourly Units: This data tells how many units we would expect to win per hour, based on 100 hands per hour, with each betting system. Why does *S-4* slightly under-perform *S-2* and *S-3*, which have notably lower overall *Win Rates*? The answer is found in the first row we looked at, *Hands Bet/100*. With *S-4*, we're only betting on 14 hands for every hundred hands seen. So we've got a big win rate on a very small amount of money. Also, this *S-4* betting strategy would be extremely impractical in a real-world casino. Back-counting 86% of the hands you see, before making a bet, is not easy to pull off. You'll look like a back counter and you may find your action unwanted when you do try to put a bet down. You'll be the classic pit buzzard.

Practically, it's far easier, and less obvious, to come off the top of the shoe with a 1-unit bet, and play through all those zero-count situations when the house has a small edge, but the flat-bet approach (*S-1*) is simply too weak. So, let's look at our results if we bet one unit off the top, but raise our bet when we get the advantage to our side.

S-5, S-6, S-7, and *S-8* show our results assuming we spread to 2 units, 3 units, 4 units, and 8 units respectively. Using any one of these approaches, we again play 69 hands per hundred, but significantly raise both the win rate and hourly unit expectation over the *S-1* results. This is the power of betting more in proportion to your advantage.

Look closely at the *Hourly Units* data: Assuming a $100 betting unit, the *S-1* strategy would provide 0.11 units, or $11 per hour. The most we can expect with any of the flat bet approaches (*S-2* and *S-3*) is 0.28 units, or $28 per hour. But using a spread to 2, 3, 4, or 8 units, our hourly expectation goes up to $39, $62, $86, and $162 respectively. So, although you can beat many shoe games with a flat bet, a small betting spread at higher counts has a lot of value.

The data in the chart above is all taken from a report I initially published in 1987 titled "Beat the 6-Deck Game." If you are a serious player, investing any substantial amount of money, I urge you to get the complete report, which is inexpensive. There are 44 full pages of charts, showing 6-deck results based on frequency distributions with varying levels of penetration, different strategies ranging from flat-bet table-hopping styles, to table-hopping with spreads up to 16 units, to playing through all hands of the shoe without table-hopping or back-counting. These charts also display the unit win compared to standard deviation, showing various numbers of hands played, to give you a handle on what sort of fluctuation to expect at the tables. Finally, for those who are not scared of the math, and who want data not contained in any of the charts I provide, there is a more complete explanation of how you can use frequency distributions to perform your own analyses of any betting strategies you care to test. It's not really difficult if you've got a pocket calculator and you follow the instructions. There are also similar reports available for 1-deck, 2-deck, 4-deck and 8-deck games. You'll find information in the back section of this book on obtaining these reports.

In any case, our immediate interest here is in using a bigger advantage over the house to cut your fluctuations. Employing S-1, in the game described above, the counter using this strategy would win only 16 units for every 10,000 hands played, but one standard deviation on these hands would be about 110 units. That win rate of 0.11% is so small that even with 100,000 hands played, and an expectation of 156 units, the standard deviation, 348 units, is still more than twice the expectation. With this small of an edge, whether or not you win or lose is a crapshoot, even over a period of years. One of the main goals of the pro player is to raise his expectation of winning so that it's higher than the standard deviation as soon as possible. If your expected unit win is still less than one standard deviation after 100,000 hands, you may have the edge on the house, but you're still just gambling.

If you use S-3, however, with a win rate of 1.26%, your unit expectation is 126 after 10,000 hands played, with a standard deviation of only 110 units. (Note: the standard deviation numbers are not in the chart above, which has been condensed from the charts in the 6-deck report.) So, with S-3, you're more likely to be in the black after 10,000 hands played than you would be after 100,000 hands played with the S-1 betting strategy. That higher win rate really pays off if you're trying to get past those initial short-term losses.

But there are other problems with the S-3 betting strategy, some of which we've mentioned already. Since we're only playing 26 hands per 100 seen, it's going to take a hell of a lot longer to play 10,000 hands in real-world hours, with most of our time spent circling around the pit like a buzzard just watching for a decent betting opportunity. It's not a practical solo approach to beating the game.

So, let's look at *S-8*, playing the same number of hands per hour (69) as S-1, but spreading from 1 to 8 units as the count increases. Let's say that we spread from $25 to $200 in order to get this 1 to 8 spread. The average bet is 2.23 units, which—with a $25 unit—translates to $55.75. It's a significantly smaller average bet than the one used by the S-1 player, who is flat betting $100, even though we are playing the same number of hands, and bet twice as much ($200) on the best situations.

So, playing *S-8* our Hourly Unit expectation is 1.62, and with a $25 unit, this comes to $40.50, significantly higher than any of the flat-betting strategies, despite the smaller unit size and smaller average bet. Finally, even though using *S-8* we play the same number of hands as the S-1 bettor, and are sometimes betting twice as much as the S-1 bettor, after 10,000 hands the S-1 bettor's standard deviation (with a $100 betting unit) is $11,000, while ours (with a $25-$200 betting spread) is only $8,950. So, S-8 outperforms S-1 by winning almost 4 times as much per hour, with an average bet almost half the size of S-1, and has significantly reduced fluctuations.

Although casual players who have outside income can seriously consider playing with very small edges in order to obtain comps and other amenities, pros must always do whatever possible to get as big of an edge over the house as possible in order to cut the flux. Table-hopping to avoid betting when the house has any significant advantage is one way to do this. Let's look at some other methods:

Always Play at the Same Bet Level

You'll also cut your fluctuations if you always play at the same betting level, regardless of the action a particular casino can take. Some pros who choose to play in lower limit casinos to take advantage of the good conditions there limit themselves to the same level of action in casinos that could take larger bets, even though they have the bankroll to handle more action. They do this to avoid the stress of unusually bad losing sessions at higher stakes, and winning sessions at lower stakes, due solely to flux.

I also know a number of pros who have lost significant portions of their bankrolls trying to take advantage of some special promotions, such as when a casino temporarily puts some special rule or bonus payout on a game in order to lure in customers. I know one semi-pro player who lost close to half his bankroll in four hours, playing a game where blackjacks paid 2 to 1 instead of 3 to 2. He was betting $500 per hand—the max bet allowed by the casino—throughout the play, although his normal high bet was $200. He figured that since he had more than twice his normal edge on the house, he could safely bet more than twice his normal high bet. He was very unlucky to have been dealt so few blackjacks during this four-hour time period, and the hands he was dealt were also more losers than winners. But if he would have stuck to his normal $200 high-bet unit for this promotion, he would have lost only about 20% of his total playing bank—still a big hit, but far less devastating.

Avoid the Full-Kelly Roller Coaster

Do not be lured by the "magic" of Kelly betting. Although, mathematically, full-Kelly betting appears to be the fastest way to increase a bankroll with no possibility of going broke, if you do not have a replenishable bankroll, full-Kelly betting causes HUGE fluctuations in the process of winning at the "fastest" rate. These fluctuations are absolutely intolerable in real-world games. And they're not tolerable for *practical* reasons, whether you think you have the stomach for them or not.

Unless you have a very large bank, a full-Kelly betting strategy will often dip your bankroll down to the brink of extinction. If you run a full-Kelly betting pattern on a computer simulation, no problem—your computer couldn't care less if your $10,000 bankroll goes down to $700 before turning around and climbing back up. Nor does your computer mind when your high bets go from $200 to $20, and then back up to $600. But for real-world players, full-Kelly betting is a bankroll roller coaster you'd rather not ride. It's the betting system that performs best *on paper,* not in real-world casinos.

For a player trying to make it as a pro on a small bankroll (say $10,000), full-Kelly betting is suicide. Players like the thought that with Kelly betting, "it's impossible to go broke." It's true that you can't lose your whole bank if you never bet more than a small fraction of it. But how can you continue playing when your *high bets* have to be reduced from $100 to $15 because your bankroll took a negative swing from $10,000 to $1500? Where are you going to find a casino that you can beat with $15 high bets?

Negative flux on full-Kelly betting has been the death of more would-be blackjack pros, and has spelled doom for more blackjack teams, than anything else. Talk to some of the old-timers who were playing back in the '70s and '80s when everyone was Kelly crazy. It was a common occurrence for a team to go broke, with one and all chanting: "But we were Kelly betting!" Betting full-Kelly, your winning streaks are way bigger, but your losing streaks are way grimmer. All of the successful big teams today have their players betting very small fractions of the "ideal" Kelly bets.

One of the most "amusing" stories I heard about a team betting full-Kelly occured back in the mid-1980s. A small group of investors put together a $200,000 bankroll, with a group of a dozen known and trusted players to take on the casinos of Nevada. All players were to bet full-Kelly, and the team would distribute the profits when they had doubled the bank. They estimated that it would take three to six weeks with the talent they had, and the number of hours the players should be able to play per week. The investors would get half the profit—$100,000—and the players would divvy up the other $100K, or about $8,500 per player. Sounded like a good plan...

After numerous ups and downs, with more downs than ups, the team hit a major downswing about three months into play. They had already gone twice as long as they were expected to go, but now the total bank remaining was only about $60,000. They had lost $140,000. The investors, all veteran players, took it in stride. They contacted the players and told them that $60,000 was simply not a big enough bankroll to front a dozen players. The investors were going to have to bite the bullet and put together a new bankroll; then they'd start over. So, they called in the remaining funds from the players.

But a funny thing happened...there were no remaining funds! Or, at least, there wasn't nearly the $60,000 there was supposed to be. All funds combined, the players had only about $11,000 in their possession! Where did the money go?

As it turned out, the players had all been taking informal "advances" on their expected $8,500 payday. Twelve players. Three months. They all had to live, eat, pay rent, buy gas...$49,000 had been dwindled away in the players' day-to-day living expenses. All the missing money, in fact, was accounted for. Each player knew how much he had advanced himself. An average draw of about $4,000 per player was not really that much money for three months living expenses. None of the players had been living high on the hog.

In fact, if this team had been betting quarter-Kelly, that $140,000 loss would have been a $35,000 loss. No big deal on a $200,000 bank. And the initial estimated time for doubling the bank would have been five to ten weeks, instead of three to six. Obviously, with this initial downswing, the team would not have made the estimated time schedule for doubling, but the fact is that even with the players taking their living-expense advances, they would have still had a substantial bankroll after three months, and a good chance of eventually hitting their goal.

If you bet half-Kelly, you cut your flux in half, but your win rate is still 75% of what it would be with full-Kelly betting. Better yet, with quarter-Kelly betting, you cut your flux to one-quarter of what it would be with full-Kelly betting, but your win rate is still 56% of the full-Kelly haul. If you've got a bankroll of $50K or better, quarter-Kelly betting makes sense, but the problem with betting this way on a $10K bank is that the initial hourly expectation is so low you might consider getting a job that pays better to increase your bank before beginning your blackjack career. But on any size bank, I'd never advise betting greater than half-Kelly.

Play Multiple Hands

Playing multiple hands simultaneously when you have the advantage can also cut fluctuations in the long run. Your overall fluctuations go down when you place twice as many bets with smaller amounts on each hand. Some pros, as a rule, always play two hands when they have the edge, and only one hand when they don't. As your expectation rises, multiple simultaneous hands are also often a good idea because they will camouflage your spread, and let you get more money into action when you have the edge.

There are also many other reasons why pros may occasionally want to play multiple hands. If the casino you are playing in is infested with table-hopping card counters, increasing to multiple-hand play at positive counts keeps these players off your table. Likewise, if you're "shuffle tracking" (an advanced technique covered in a later chapter), multiple-hand play works to get the greatest proportion of high cards in a "slug" delivered to you.

But playing two simultaneous hands will increase the fluctuation of your bankroll if you place the same big bet on both hands based on your true edge. To decrease this fluctuation, you must cut back on the size of your multiple high bets. If you play two hands, both hands together should be about 1 1/2 times the standard high bet you'd place if you were playing only one hand.

Example: if your standard high bet is $100, then play two hands of $75 each. Do not play more than two simultaneous hands unless you believe it is the last round of the shoe, and you also believe the advantage is high enough to justify the extra bets. With three simultaneous hands, do not bet more than 60% of your single-hand high bet on each hand.

Also note that even with only one hand on the table, when you have a full 1.0% advantage, your "ideal" full-Kelly bet is only 0.75% of your bank, not a full 1.0%. This is to compensate for the double/split options at blackjack, which increase fluctuations.

The two charts on the following pages present your ideal half-Kelly bets when you are playing one, two, or three hands. I suggest that before you begin play in a casino, you draw up a betting chart that shows "correct" bets for your actual bankroll. I've used a "generic" $10,000 bankroll for these charts, so if you have a $30,000 bankroll, you can just multiply these bets by three. It should not be difficult to figure out your ideal half-Kelly bets with any size bank, using these charts as a guide. Obviously, if you have the bankroll to play a less risky quarter-Kelly betting strategy, then you can just cut all of the bets in the charts in half.

How to Read the Betting Charts

Look at the first chart, titled "Half-Kelly 10K Starting Bank—Downswing." This chart shows your ideal bets when you want to play at the half-Kelly level of risk, starting with a $10,000 bankroll, betting one, two, or three simultaneous hands. This chart shows what happens to your ideal bets when your bankroll is diminishing, as your bets go down as your bankroll decreases from $10,000 to $9,000 to $8,000 and so on. All bets are rounded to the nearest $10 increment, though this is not necessarily the most practical bet when playing blackjack. If the chart shows that your ideal bet is $70 or $80, you might want to just bet three green chips ($75) for convenience. This will not have any drastic effect on your overall fluctuation or results.

Example: If my $10K starting bank has gone down to $8K due to negative flux, and my true edge tells me that I have a 2 1/2% advantage after deducting the house edge off the top, then according to the chart I would ideally place one hand of $80, two $60 hands, or three $40 hands. If you can spot these entries in the chart, then that's all there is to it. You may find that in some instances the "ideal" bets for two or three hands are the same, which is a result of rounding to the nearest $10. In fact, the ideal two-hand bet will be somewhat greater than the three-hand bet. But don't worry about over-betting—because we are betting only at the half-Kelly level, betting slightly more than the ideal amount isn't at all significant. We have already largely decreased our flux by not betting anywhere near full-Kelly.

The second chart shows how your bets increase when your $10K starting bank is on the upswing. If you cut all chart entries in half, note also how impractical it is for a player on a $10K bank to minimize his risk by betting at the quarter-Kelly level, especially if his starting bank goes into a downswing. The bet sizes are so small that it is difficult to get a substantial enough win rate per hour to make your playing worth the effort.

At half-Kelly with this $10K bankroll, the player will assume more risk, and greater fluctuations, but his hourly rate may be high enough to justify his time and effort at the tables.

Half-Kelly 10K Starting Bank—Downswing

Bank: 10,000   **% Advantage**

# Hands	0.5	1.0	1.5	2.0	2.5	3.0	3.5	4.0
1	20	40	60	80	100	110	130	150
2	10	30	40	60	70	80	100	110
3	10	20	30	40	60	70	80	90

Bank: 9,000   **% Advantage**

# Hands	0.5	1.0	1.5	2.0	2.5	3.0	3.5	4.0
1	20	30	50	70	90	100	120	140
2	10	30	40	50	60	80	90	100
3	10	20	30	40	50	60	70	80

Bank: 8,000   **% Advantage**

# Hands	0.5	1.0	1.5	2.0	2.5	3.0	3.5	4.0
1	20	30	50	60	80	90	110	120
2	10	20	30	40	60	70	80	90
3	10	20	30	40	40	50	60	70

Bank: 7,000   **% Advantage**

# Hands	0.5	1.0	1.5	2.0	2.5	3.0	3.5	4.0
1	10	30	40	50	70	80	90	110
2	10	20	30	40	50	60	70	80
3	10	20	20	30	40	50	50	60

Half-Kelly 10K Starting Bank—Downswing (cont)

Bank: 6,000 % Advantage

# Hands	0.5	1.0	1.5	2.0	2.5	3.0	3.5	4.0
1	10	20	30	50	60	70	80	90
2	10	20	30	30	40	50	60	70
3	10	10	20	30	30	40	50	50

Bank: 5,000 % Advantage

# Hands	0.5	1.0	1.5	2.0	2.5	3.0	3.5	4.0
1	10	20	30	40	50	60	70	80
2	10	10	20	30	40	40	50	60
3	10	10	20	20	30	30	40	40

Bank: 4,000 % Advantage

# Hands	0.5	1.0	1.5	2.0	2.5	3.0	3.5	4.0
1	10	20	20	30	40	50	50	60
2	10	10	20	20	30	30	40	40
3	0	10	10	20	20	30	30	40

Bank: 3,000 % Advantage

# Hands	0.5	1.0	1.5	2.0	2.5	3.0	3.5	4.0
1	10	10	20	20	30	30	40	50
2	0	10	10	20	20	30	30	30
3	0	10	10	10	20	20	20	30

Half-Kelly 10K Starting Bank—Upswing

Bank: 10,000   <u>% Advantage</u>

# Hands	0.5	1.0	1.5	2.0	2.5	3.0	3.5	4.0
1	20	40	60	80	100	110	130	150
2	10	30	40	60	70	80	100	110
3	10	20	30	40	60	70	80	90

Bank: 11,000   <u>% Advantage</u>

# Hands	0.5	1.0	1.5	2.0	2.5	3.0	3.5	4.0
1	20	40	60	80	100	130	150	170
2	20	30	50	60	80	90	110	120
3	10	20	40	50	60	70	80	100

Bank: 12,000   <u>% Advantage</u>

# Hands	0.5	1.0	1.5	2.0	2.5	3.0	3.5	4.0
1	20	50	70	90	110	140	160	180
2	20	30	50	70	80	100	120	130
3	10	30	40	50	70	80	90	110

Bank: 13,000   <u>% Advantage</u>

# Hands	0.5	1.0	1.5	2.0	2.5	3.0	3.5	4.0
1	20	50	70	100	120	150	170	200
2	20	40	50	70	90	110	130	150
3	10	30	40	60	70	90	100	110

Half-Kelly 10K Starting Bank—Upswing (cont)

Bank: 14,000 — % Advantage

# Hands	0.5	1.0	1.5	2.0	2.5	3.0	3.5	4.0
1	30	50	80	110	130	160	190	210
2	20	40	60	80	100	120	140	160
3	20	30	50	60	80	90	110	120

Bank: 15,000 — % Advantage

# Hands	0.5	1.0	1.5	2.0	2.5	3.0	3.5	4.0
1	30	60	90	110	140	170	200	230
2	20	40	60	80	110	130	150	170
3	20	30	50	70	80	100	120	130

Bank: 16,000 — % Advantage

# Hands	0.5	1.0	1.5	2.0	2.5	3.0	3.5	4.0
1	30	60	90	120	150	180	210	240
2	20	40	70	90	110	130	160	180
3	20	40	50	70	90	110	120	140

Bank: 17,000 — % Advantage

# Hands	0.5	1.0	1.5	2.0	2.5	3.0	3.5	4.0
1	30	60	100	130	160	190	230	260
2	20	50	70	100	120	140	170	190
3	20	40	60	70	90	110	130	150

Some Suggestions on Using the Betting Charts

Obviously, you could carry this book with you when you travel, and review the data you need prior to your plays. But I'm not much in favor of card counters carrying telltale items, like books, into casino hotel rooms. It's not a good idea to have items like these lying around where they might be found by casino personnel. I tend to be very paranoid about casino snoops. But if you have a computer with a word processing program, you can do as I do…create an innocent-looking chart that has the data you need, print it, and just fold it up in your wallet. Here's a portion of a chart you could use for the Half-Kelly 10K Upswing:

NutriGuide's Fiber-to-Fat Ratio Calorie Key

Grams 10   **Calorie Counter**

Fiber Qty	0.5	1.0	1.5	2.0	2.5	3.0	3.5	4.0
1	20	40	60	80	100	110	130	150
2	10	30	40	60	70	80	100	110
3	10	20	30	40	60	70	80	90

Grams 11   **Calorie Counter**

Fiber Qty	0.5	1.0	1.5	2.0	2.5	3.0	3.5	4.0
1	20	40	60	80	100	130	150	170
2	20	30	50	60	80	90	110	120
3	10	20	40	50	60	70	80	100

Grams 12   **Calorie Counter**

Fiber Qty	0.5	1.0	1.5	2.0	2.5	3.0	3.5	4.0
1	20	50	70	90	110	140	160	180
2	20	30	50	70	80	100	120	130
3	10	30	40	50	70	80	90	110

I'm sure a nutritionist would scratch her head over this chart, but it provides me with the data I need at a glance. If my bank goes up to $11K, and I have a 3% advantage, I can bet $90 on two hands, or $70 on three. I advise players who want to travel with any type of charts, such as playing strategy index numbers, to create decoy charts with silly headings: That way you can pull your charts out in the casino coffee shop for review without fear of surveillance cameras looking over your shoulder. Pick any esoteric topic—hedge fund profit ratios, auto part wholesale discounts, whatever—and you can carry pages and pages of sensitive material without worrying about the wrong eyes seeing it. Likewise, if you travel with a laptop or a palm pilot, and you keep this type of information on your computer, do likewise. Put all charts, indices, play results, team cash transfers, etc., into innocent-looking tables with headings and references that appear to have nothing whatsoever to do with blackjack or gambling.

If you are a casual player, this degree of paranoia is probably not necessary. But if you are playing at high stakes, you can't be too careful. I know many players whose rooms were searched (illegally) by casino security. I've also heard of players who accidentally left luggage, or a briefcase, in the coffee shop, and then had to identify their property later by describing the contents to casino security personnel in order to retrieve it. Just don't take chances. Shit happens.

15

THE UNENCOUNTERED COUNTER

A master of any martial art does not conquer his opponent; he lets his opponent beat himself. The opponent loses the battle because the smart fighter knows how to turn the other man's strengths into weaknesses. The master wins not because he is physically stronger, but because he is mentally a step ahead of his adversary. The master is an invisible catalyst—the opponent never sees his downfall coming. His own strength and momentum hurl him to the ground even while he's watching out for the master's attack.

Playing blackjack for profit isn't all that different. Your opponent, the casino, has vast strength in the form of an incredibly large bankroll. Furthermore, the house sets all the rules and may eliminate any opponent it considers a worthy challenger. This is a tough setup—not only do you have to play very well in order to win, but if you look like you play well, you may not be allowed to play at all.

The major weakness of the casinos, however, is that their advantage over the player is volatile. Sometimes they have a large advantage, but occasionally they're vulnerable to the knowledgeable player.

In the same way that a martial arts master does not depend on his muscles to win a fight, a master of blackjack does not depend on some incredibly difficult, advanced, multi-parameter counting system to win money at the tables. Nor does he depend on the superior strength of his bankroll; he knows that his bankroll is inferior to his opponent's. Rather, he allows the volatility of the game to put money into his pockets at its own rate. He remains invisible as a counter because he does not exploit his own strengths as much as he exploits the casino's weaknesses.

Single-deck games are volatile, and the change in advantage is fast and great. Multi-deck games are less volatile—the change in the advantage is slow. The master counter employs different strategies for each game, designed to disguise his counting strategy, while at the same time maximizing his win rate. These are some of his strategies:

Depth-Charging: A Single-Deck Strategy

Casinos primarily identify counters by watching for bet variation. If you don't bet like a counter, you won't usually be marked as one, regardless of how accurately you play your cards. It is very easy for a counter catcher to count down a deck from behind or above you, using any card counting system, while monitoring your bet size. Regardless of what counting system you use, your bet-sizing will give you away. A Red Seven player would raise and lower his bets similarly to a Zen Count player. A counter using any other valid counting system would have no difficulty detecting the conspicuous betting patterns of either player.

Most camouflage techniques are used to disguise bet variation. Such techniques inevitably hurt your potential win rate, but without camouflage you will be frequently shuffled-up on, and probably barred if you play for high stakes.

Depth-charging is a single-deck strategy that allows you to play a winning game without using a betting spread based on your count. This strategy is not recommended for Red Seven players—to take advantage of depth-charging gains, you want a system that is strong on playing strategy.

Single-deck games can be beaten with a flat bet, but you need a deep shuffle point to pull it off. Deep penetration is hard to come by in one-deck games these days, because the casinos know that counters can beat these games easily. Still, some four-plus decades after Thorp, I continue to get regular reports from players on deeply dealt one-deck games they've found.

One type of game that often has a deep shuffle point is the full-table game, when two rounds are dealt. These games are rare in Las Vegas, but still fairly common in Northern Nevada, especially in many of Nevada's smaller towns. The problem with these games is that they are always dealt face down, and some players hide their cards. The deep shuffle point is worthless if you cannot see the other players' cards prior to making your decisions. If you can see the other guys' cards, however, this type of game can be very valuable.

So, let's look at just how valuable.

If I set up a seven-player table, with two rounds between shuffles, and I allow the third-base player, who is using the Zen Count, to see all of the cards of the players who play their hands before him, with a flat bet he will win at the rate of 0.77%. (This is with Reno rules, which allow doubling on 10 and 11 only, and the dealer hits soft 17; with downtown Las Vegas rules, where you can double on any two cards, but the dealer still hits soft 17, the flat-betting third base player will win at the rate of 1.06%, assuming he can see all of the other players' cards.)

This player can do quite a bit better than 0.77% if he uses a conservative betting spread. For instance, if he were to always come off the top with a 2-unit bet, and only lower it to 1 unit on the second round if the count goes negative, his Reno win rate would be 0.92%, as opposed to 1.23% in Downtown Vegas.

With a more aggressive 1 to 2 betting spread, where he came off the top with one unit, then raised to 2 units on any positive count, his Reno expectation would go up to 1.31%, and 1.60% in downtown Vegas. All of this data was obtained from running simulations of 10 million hands each with John Imming's *Universal Blackjack Engine* software. Here is the data in chart form:

Zen Count, Third Base, Full Table, 10 Million Hands Each			
	Flat Bet	**1-2 (2 off top)**	**1-2 (1 off top)**
Reno:	0.77%	0.92%	1.31%
DT Vegas:	1.06%	1.23%	1.60%

Naturally, if you could find better rules than these, the expectations would be even higher from the same ultraconservative betting strategies. Note also that this approach is weak from the first base position. Seeing just four fewer cards per-round before making his decisions, the first base player's win rates for these betting schemes is barely half of the third base player's.

The problem, however, for the guy on third base, is in seeing everyone else's cards. There are various ways of going about this, limited only by the bounds of your own creativity.

One, you could be very friendly at a table full of friendly players, and simply get them all to show you their hands as they play. Many players do not try to hide their hands from other players, so this is not necessarily all that difficult for a gregarious sort who chooses his tables wisely.

Two, you could play with friends or other counters who would happily show you their hands. Since many players already do this at blackjack tables, it doesn't look all that suspicious. In fact, you don't need six friends to join you at the table—it would be more practical to pull this off with two friends who could play two hands each, while you play three hands on the third base side of the table.

Three, you could play with one or two friends who position themselves at the table in order to see the player cards that you can't. They don't have to tell you exactly which cards they see, just the change in the count. Such information could easily be passed via simple signals.

Four, a non-player accompanying you to the table might, while standing behind you, be better able to view the cards hidden from you.

These are just a few examples; perhaps you can think of more variations on this theme.

DEFINITION

Depth-charging is using the depth of the deal as the primary method of gaining a long-run advantage, rather than relying on a betting spread based on card counting.

Since casinos often recognize the traditional betting strategies of card counters, the depth-charger employs a betting strategy that is not based on his count. His playing strategy is so much more effective deep in the deck that he gets a major edge over the house.

With a multiple-player approach, you may be able to camouflage your play by haphazardly sizing bets on the first base side of the table. Some of the spots on the first base side may also be played using useless progression systems, with significantly smaller bets than those being placed on the third base side.

A husband and wife team wrote to me, saying that they used this method of play successfully in a unique partnership approach: The wife sat to the right of the husband and played three spots with low bets, and on every hand, she consulted her husband on how to play. In fact, she did not know basic strategy. The husband sometimes gave her correct advice, and sometimes he didn't—which made him look like a showoff. He, meanwhile, played either one or two spots on the third base side of the table, at substantially higher stakes than his wife. He always played his own hands according to the correct count strategy.

When depth-charging, you must be careful not to appear too interested in other players' hands, since this may look suspicious. Your primary camouflage, however, which is not betting according to the count, should work very well, protecting you from drawing the casino's suspicion.

Note: The value of depth-charging comes from accurately playing your cards at deep shuffle points. If you do not accurately employ strategy tables to alter your play according to the count, flat-bet depth-charging is worthless. Likewise, you will realize significant gains at deep shuffle points by knowing some of the less-used strategy indices. I would advise depth-chargers to learn the more extensive Zen Count strategy tables provided in the Appendix. It is important that you realize that your gain comes from seeing and using as much card information as you can get before playing your hand. Simply sitting at a full table without getting the necessary information on the other players' downcards is not going to help you win.

One-Deck Wonging

One of my favorite methods of depth-charging in Reno and Tahoe used to be to **Wong it** in crowded single-deck games, that is, table-hop and play only when the count is favorable. This is a depth-charging strategy that can be employed by card counters using any valid counting system, though this strategy is primarily for small stakes players.

In the big casinos, I had no trouble getting away with this strategy making single quarter ($25) bets. I've also done it with no heat betting single $20 bills. This style of play also works best when there are other big bettors at the table. If you bet a single quarter on a table where other players are betting multiple greens and blacks, no dealer will shuffle on you, nor will you get a second glance from the pit. If you jump around betting quarters where everyone else is betting nickels (or silver!), you are more likely to raise suspicion. Do not expect to get away with this strategy with black ($100) chips or stacks of quarters anywhere.

Playing a single hand, I was able to get an average of 38 hands every hour, table-hopping crowded single-deck games, and my average edge was about 3%. I also tried playing as many as three hands depending on how many spots I could grab, according to the number of players at the table and their positions. In sum, I got about 70 hands per hour, with an estimated edge of about 2%. I played at tables where at least three other players were playing, and usually there were four or five.

One problem I encountered was not always knowing how deeply into the deck the dealer had gone. Some of my bets were met with a shuffle-up, not because the dealer was paranoid about counters, but rather out of necessity. In such cases, I played through the hands and doubled my bet size or walked on the next round, depending on the count. I did not sit down to play, but stood behind the vacant seat. I never felt any heat.

Using the Red Seven Count, you should be able to get about 25 to 30 hands per hour, at an average edge of about 3%, by betting only at a running count of +3 or higher. Betting quarters, this means a potential gain of $20 per hour. It may seem like a slow grind, but for players on limited funds there is wisdom to playing hands only when you enjoy such a large edge. Your negative fluctuations will be considerably reduced, and playing 25 hands per hour with a 3% edge will win at the same rate as 75 hands per hour with a 1% edge. After 100 hours of play with $25 bets, each approach would potentially net a win of $1,875. The player with the 3% edge, however, will have put one-third as much money into action as the 1% edge player, who is playing three times faster. The faster player with the smaller edge would need a bankroll almost twice as large as the slow player to cope with his larger fluctuation.

Consider that if there are five players at a single-deck table in Reno and you count the first round of cards, you will have seen approximately 33% of the deck. A Red Seven Count of +3 would indicate a player edge of about 2 1/2%. You will never see an edge like this after watching only one round of a 6-deck shoe game. In single-deck games, this occurs frequently. You do not need to use extensive strategy tables if you play only in such advantageous situations.

Single-deck games should be a gravy train for knowledgeable low stakes players. Playing multiple hands, you may be able to get more than 100 hands per hour by Wonging in on any plus count in the big South Tahoe casinos. This is a lot of action with quarter chips, and using the Red Seven Count, the player edge is about 1%. With the Zen Count, I would estimate a 1 1/2% edge. You can't estimate your edge with any kind of precision for this approach because of the varying conditions—different numbers of players at the tables, various deck depletions, betting on various numbers of simultaneous hands, et cetera—but low stakes players should strive to play fewer hands at higher advantages. Just don't try to get away with too much: If you see an edge of 6%, and in one-deck games that will happen, don't forget that this is a low stakes strategy. A $50 or $60 bet could get you booted at some saw-dust joints.

Casino personnel are not ignorant of table-hopping, and just as there are many shoe games that disallow mid-shoe entry, there are some hand-held games that disallow mid-deck entry. One-deck Wonging works best when the crowd conditions are busy, and when your big bet is overshadowed by many other bets on the tables where you jump in. This strategy would easily beat The BJ Pays 6:5 games now popular in Las Vegas, but most of these tables have posted "No Mid-Deck Entry" signs.

Opposition Betting

Opposition betting is a multi-deck betting strategy. It's especially effective where pit bosses are liable to be watching your betting patterns. To beat multi-deck blackjack games, you must understand what you are up against. I'll be honest with you. These games are tough to beat. Many players fail to comprehend two basic facts of the multi-deck challenge.

Fact 1: You cannot soundly beat multi-deck games with a flat bet or even a small spread, regardless of your system. To get a significant edge in a multi-deck game usually requires a spread of 1 to 8 units or more. The only exception to this rule would be for a table-hopper who plays only when the count is favorable. In essence, this would not be flat-betting but using a spread in which the minimum bet is zero units. You should view table-hopping the same way because it's necessary to spend time watching, counting, and waiting until you can place your bets. Table-hopping is a camouflage technique that makes you appear to be a small-spread or flat-bettor.

Fact 2: Multi-deck games are less vulnerable to traditional count strategies because the shifts in advantage are less volatile. Many players fail to grasp this because they do not understand how card counting works. This is an actual letter I received from a player many years ago:

> On my recent trip to Vegas I played exclusively in 4-deck games. I prefer the 4-deck games because the count doesn't jump around so much. When a shoe goes hot, it often stays that way for a long time, so I can continue to

bet high for many hands in a row. In single-deck, it seems like I'll get one or two high bets then the count drops, and in no time at all they're shuffling again. In a shoe game, if the count drops real low, I leave the table and find a better game.

My trip was a total disaster. I couldn't have asked for better conditions, but within about 3 hours, I'd lost just about my whole playing bankroll. I was spreading quarters from one-to-four and lost $2,500. Looking back on it, the majority of my losing bets were high ($100) bets, so I guess I really only lost about 25 big bets, rather than 100 small bets. Still, I don't see how this could have happened. What's worse, almost the entire loss occurred in my last half-hour of play against the same dealer.

He was dealing out about 3 decks and every shoe the count kept climbing. By the time he'd shuffle, the running count would be between +15 and +20! Somehow, I just kept losing. After three shoes like this, I was broke. I use the Hi-Lo count, so I figure that by the time he shuffled, my advantage was somewhere between 7% and 10%! It seems to me the only hand I ever played at a disadvantage was the first round after the shuffle. Then the count would go up, and it would just keep going higher. How could I lose with such hot decks?

He could lose because this player had one glaring misconception about card counting. The reason that you bet bigger when the count is high is because your count indicates that the remaining cards contain a disproportionate number of tens and aces. You place a big bet because the odds are in your favor that these high cards *will be dealt*. As these cards come out of the deck, you make your money. You will be dealt more naturals; your doubling down and pair-splitting will pay off more; the dealer will bust his stiffs more frequently. You don't bet big simply because the count is high, you bet big because the count *should come down*.

If the count doesn't come down then it must mean that those excess high cards in the deck did not come out. If the count continues to climb, then not only are the excess high cards not being dealt, but a disproportionate number of low cards continue to be dealt, much to your disadvantage.

If the dealer shuffles when the count is +15 to +20, then this means that all of those high cards are clumped together in the undealt portion of the shoe. If this happened three shoes in a row, then contrary to what this player's count indicated, *he never played with an advantage over the house*. When the count stays high, your high bets are all for naught.

When your count goes up in a single-deck game, it is far more likely to come down than in a multi-deck game. It is this volatility that makes the one-deck games so profitable. Ideally, you make small bets while the count is rising, and large bets while it is coming back down.

Had this player been in a shoe game in which the count kept going down to about -15 to -20 prior to every shuffle, then more than likely, ironic as it may seem, he probably would have won more money than he would have lost, since this situation would indicate that all the excess low cards were clumped in the undealt portion of the shoe. Such clumpings of cards often occur purely through chance. If the dealer were purposely clumping high cards, then cutting them out of play through sleight of hand, this would be cheating.

DEFINITION

Opposition betting is sizing your bets so that it looks like you're raising your bets when the count is going down and lowering them when the count is going up.

The purpose of opposition betting is to get a large spread. The following is an explanation of how one Vegas pro gets away with it; I've changed enough details to protect his identity:

> I've been playing blackjack for thirty years. For about the first twenty, I didn't know anything about counting. At one point, I tried to read Thorp's book but the system was beyond me. Revere's book became my bible because his point count system was powerful and so much easier. I still use it. By the time I'd started counting, I was well known in the casinos as a high roller. I was comped most everywhere and still am. My basic method of camouflage, once I'd started counting, was simply to keep playing as much as possible the way I'd always played.
>
> I buy in at the craps table and usually spend my first

ten or fifteen minutes playing craps for nickels. I'll often get a whole rack of chips—half quarters, half nickels. I never hide chips, or pocket chips, or try to look like I'm losing. I never did that before I was a counter, so why should I start now? Whether you're counting or not, sometimes you win, sometimes you lose. When I lose a lot, I sulk around. I make a lot of noise about it when I win big. The only time I pocket chips is when I cash out. I'll go south with one or two blacks, and play them or cash them out later.

When I hit the blackjack tables, I start betting with nickels—two or three at a time. If the count starts going down, I'll bet even bigger—four or five nickels. If it keeps going down, I might push six to eight of them out there. As the count goes up, I use the reverse strategy. I'll go down to a single nickel and keep betting this way until my edge is up around 2%. Sometimes I'll go through a couple of shoes till I get a count like this. Sometimes it happens right away. But when it does go up that high, I'll raise my bet from a single nickel to a stack of quarters in one jump. I'll just throw eight of 'em on the table like that. By this time, I'm already pegged as a non-counter because of all my stupid bets before. And if they don't have me pegged this way, they will soon. My strategy with the quarters is pretty much the same as my nickel strategy. If the count goes up, I just let my stack of quarters ride. While the count is this high, I make sure I've got a couple hundred bucks on the table. It's important to me not to raise my bet if the count goes up even higher. You see, I start raising it when the count's coming back down. Dealers always change colors on you when you bet stacks of chips. If I win with eight quarters, he'll pay me off with a couple of blacks. The next stack of chips I push out there will have those blacks on the bottom. They think they're jacking up my bets by coloring me up! By the time my edge is down to 1% or so, I'll be making bets of $500 to $600. I'd say my average high bet is about $250 to $350. My average low bet is probably about $15 to $20.

About the only time I might be suspected of counting

is when I make my jump from a nickel to a couple hundred bucks. Before and after that, I usually raise and lower my bets in reverse.

A lot of times I'll jump my bets around according to whether I'm winning or losing. Often, I mix up my colors and have reds, greens and black in the same stack. It drives dealers nuts. Part of my method is to look like I just don't have much of a method. Sometimes I bet high off the top of the shoe. For the most part, I play nickels with low counts and greens and blacks with high counts. When I make my big jump, I wait until the time seems right for it. If the count is high and I've only got a nickel riding on the bet, I'm likely to split fours or fives, or maybe stand on a twelve against a ten. After a play like that, dealers love to see you start playing with real money. You see, they know I've got the greens and blacks. I'm sitting there with half a rack of them in front of me. I don't make foolish plays when I'm betting high, though.

I've watched dozens of counters get 86'd. Most of them are young. They always spread from one to four. They're so easy to spot it's laughable. Sometimes I think my best camouflage is that I'm old and bald. My second best camouflage might be that I've got a lot of money. Counters look hungry. There's probably not much a young guy can do about this. But still, he can change his one-to-four spread to something that looks less intelligent. All the books say spread from 1 to 4 or 1 to 8. There's not a pit boss in Vegas who hasn't read most of these books. When you play like the books say, you're advertising your smarts.

One time I was sitting with two counters for about half an hour. During the course of that half hour, I'd placed bets as low as a nickel and as high as seven or eight hundred bucks. They were both spreading quarters from one-to-four. They keep nudging each other when I'd make a stupid play. Once I insured my natural at a low count. I had two nickels on the table. Then the true count went up to about +9 or +10 real fast. I hit my four-card sixteen against the dealer's five and busted. I guess these guys got brave then because both of them raised their next bets to eight chips. Frankly, I was having a hard time not laughing, myself. Their bets had been so identical since they'd sat down, they were like the Bobbsey Twins.

The pit boss jumped in at that point. He went through the discards and politely told these two guys to hit the road. They were upset. One of them remarked that it should be illegal for casinos to only deal to stupid players. The remark was directed at me. They ended up getting barred.

I don't want you to think I never get any heat. There are a few casinos in this town I won't set foot in. But I've got an excellent rating at most of the places that matter. You can't fool everybody...

This is a crude approach to opposition betting but it illustrates the basic camouflage techniques. Without an enormous spread like the one this player employs, you could not win much money with such a drastic betting style.

The opposition bettor wins money by getting away with a large spread. Over any extended period of play, his betting looks foolish from a card counter's perspective. I think it's important to remember that there is not one method of opposition betting—it's a camouflage technique that can be used any number of ways.

Ralph Stricker, an East coast old-timer affectionately known for many years as the "Silver Fox," developed another highly effective opposition betting technique. Stricker bases his betting approach on the fact that in multi-deck games, neither the house nor the player has any significant edge for most of the game. The player then may take advantage, in the form of camouflage bet-sizing, during these long periods of play when there is no significant advantage for either side. As a counter, you can make the majority of your changes in bet size appear to be either haphazard or based on some non-counting progression-type system. Stricker reports that he and his students have had phenomenal success in the 6-deck Atlantic City games using a progression-type system through "neutral" counts, yet actually spreading from 1 to 10 when the edge was heavily tilted one way or the other.

Many years ago, I tested this approach in Nevada, I tried my own method, using the Zen Count. At all negative counts, I bet one nickel. Any time my advantage was between –1/2% to +1/2%, I alternated my bets.

EARNING YOUR GREEN BELT

First I bet a nickel, then I bet a quarter capped with a nickel, then a nickel, and so on. I did this regardless of whether the running count was rising or falling. When my advantage was greater than +1/2%, I bet two quarters capped with a nickel.

The advantage from betting in this manner is close to what my advantage would be if I simply jumped my bets from $5 to $55 without any camouflage. Yet, when I tried this betting technique in three Vegas casinos, my high bets never raised an eyebrow. By the time I'd made my first high bet, I was halfway into the shoe and had been alternating high-low, high-low for quite a few hands. It looks like a worthless progression because it is one — when my advantage hit a full 1%, I followed my low $5 bet with a $55 high bet that was simply one chip higher than my normal $30 high. I let that ride until the count went down to neutral, then went back to my alternating bets. More recently, I've tested similar betting strategies at much higher stakes.

There are as many approaches to opposition betting as there are progression systems. I won't recommend any one approach because I feel it's important that you never look like you're playing "by the book." How much of a spread you can get away with when you're using this approach is limited by your personal bankroll, the house table limits, your creativity, your guts, your act…

You cannot practically use opposition betting tactics in one or two-deck games. In my experience, all too often the count changed too radically or the dealer shuffled when I made my camouflage bet. In games of four or more decks, opposition betting takes advantage of a factor that would ordinarily make counting ineffective — the slow volatility of the edge — and players with big enough bankrolls to play house limits will often find multi-deck games more profitable than single-deck games.

One drawback to opposition betting is that you'll suffer big bankroll fluctuations. It takes a healthy bankroll to use any large spread because of the size of your high bets, and you cannot use opposition betting tactics with a small spread. Your camouflage bets will nullify profit potential.

Many players use the terms "hot" or "cold" shoe. Too often, players misuse these slang terms because they don't understand how counting works.

"HOT" AND "COLD" SHOES

A **hot shoe** is one that has a great fluctuation in advantage; specifically, the count regularly spikes and plummets. A **cold shoe** has little fluctuation, regardless of whether the count stays neutral, continuously climbs, or steadily falls through the shoe.

A count that falls steadily from the beginning of the shoe is advantageous since so many high cards are being dealt, but you will realize small profits from such shoes. Your bet size will likely be small, and you will play your hands as if the count were low. Most shoes are neither cold nor hot, but somewhere between cool and lukewarm, and that's when opposition betting shows its power.

Opposition betting in multi-deck games is similar to depth-charging in single-deck games. What you are doing is invisibly turning the volatility of the edge in your favor. Since the volatility is diminished in multi-deck games, it's necessary to use a large spread, but the slow volatility gives you the opportunity to better disguise your betting. Keep in mind that the more camouflage you use, the more you will actually hurt your win rate, both because of the cost of bets placed at a disadvantage, and increased flux (which decreases the return on your investment). For this reason, the Stricker approach strikes me as the most advantageous. Bet one unit when the house has the edge, use a stupid small progression when the edge is about neutral, and bet whatever your bankroll can afford, and the casino can tolerate, when you have the edge. The slow volatility of the game gives you all the camouflage you need.

Try opposition betting and you'll realize immediately why it works. For most of my play, if I were sitting next to a player who was using my betting approach, I would not guess him to be a counter, and neither will the casinos. It would often require hours of personal observation to identify an opposition bettor with any degree of certainty. For this reason, opposition betting is one of the best approaches to games where a large spread is necessary to get a significant edge over the house.

High-stakes opposition bettors usually feel that the best progression-type systems to use for camouflage purposes are the typical gamblers' progressions. Either parlay your wins by adding chips, or chase your losses in a similarly predictable fashion throughout neutral portions of the shoe.

With a moderate 1 to 4 spread, a 6-deck game is not worth much more than about 0.2% to a card counter who sits through the negative shoes. If you quit the table at negative counts, an opposition bet-jumping 1 to 10 spread will make this game worth about 0.6%. If you make it a practice to seek out games with shuffle points of between 1 and 1.5 decks, you should be able to get close to a 1% edge in 6-deck games using this betting style. You'll look less like a counter, you'll significantly raise your expected return, and if you get your spread by lowering your low bet rather than raising your high, you'll also be able to decrease your bankroll fluctuations.

For instance, if you currently spread from $25 to $100, try opposition betting with a spread from $5 to $100. Perhaps bet a nickel on low negative counts; use a haphazard $5 to $30 on relatively "neutral" counts, and jump to $100 on high counts. Not only would you triple your potential win rate, you'd noticeably cut your bankroll fluctuations. Using a larger spread is similar to table-hopping in that the vast majority of your serious money bets are at high counts.

In a nutshell:

1. In multi-deck games, almost half of your hands are played when neither you nor the dealer has any significant edge.

2. During these neutral hands, a good card counter would break even if he were flat-betting.

3. Betting progression systems are not detrimental to your advantage; rather, they are merely worthless, and will not affect your basically break-even game one way or the other.

4. During these neutral hands, therefore, you may bet like a complete fool in order to trick the dealer, pit boss, and eye in the sky. This will increase your bankroll fluctuations, so you do not want to place your highest bets in neutral portions of the shoe. You just want to alter your bet continually with no count justification.

5. Card counters are generally suspected and identified by their betting styles, not how they play their hands. Don't overdo "stupid" plays— most of the time, you won't need to go overboard to hide your counting. Your seemingly foolish betting is your best camouflage.

To return to the analogy of the martial arts master: The master signals false attacks to his opponent, attacks that are never launched, waiting for his opponent to be off balance. The opponent is confident during the master's waiting period because the master's false attacks are so impotent. When the opponent loses his balance, as he will, even his perspective is unstable. He does not see the master's actual attack.

And isn't this how a pool hustler works? And a professional poker player? And a chess master? Card counting is a science. Beating the casinos at blackjack is an art.

Idiot Camouflage

Camouflage is a military term that means disguise, deception, or pretense. A soldier has a better chance at survival if he looks like the rest of the jungle. For a card counter, **camouflage** means essentially the same thing—it's an act that pegs you as Ted Tourist or Harry Highroller or Donald Drunk—anyone but Clyde Counter.

There are many aspects to camouflage. We have already described various betting types. There is also *dramatic* camouflage, which most successful players find to be as important as card counting when it comes to being a consistent winner. Dramatic camouflage would include such subtle touches as appearing uninterested in other players' cards, or being preoccupied with idle table chatter. It would include the ability to raise bets as if chasing losses, or feeling a winning streak. This dramatic camouflage is one of the most difficult aspects of card counting for a player to learn. Some people are born actors; most people are not. Show me a successful card counter and I'll show you a person who has all the innate abilities of the con artist.

One type of camouflage that many players use, often because they lack the subtle skills of the dramatic camouflage expert, is idiot camouflage.

As you might suspect, idiot camouflage is simply making an obviously stupid play. If the pit boss starts watching you suspiciously, you can play like an idiot. You split a pair of sixes against a dealer's ace, then you stand on your soft total of 14 (versus anything!). This, of course, looks so idiotic that the pit boss soon turns away. Now you can do whatever you want for the next hour and get rich.

Or, at least, that's the way idiot camouflage is supposed to work. Unfortunately, what usually happens is that ten minutes later, the new floorman comes by, or the dealers change, or you start to wonder about the eye upstairs, so you have to make another idiot play or two.

You may also have a floorman who doesn't know basic strategy well enough to realize that your idiot play was moronic, so you threw away your money for nothing. Or, you may have someone in the eye who observes that you only make idiot plays when the floorman looks at you, and your idiot play goes from camouflage to a tell. Or, you may be incredibly unlucky and have your idiot play go well for you, drawing a six onto your hard fifteen against the dealer's five, triggering suspicion in the pit over how you "knew" to make this weird play, since you haven't been making weird plays like this all along…

The counter's edge is small. It doesn't take many stupid plays to wipe out your profit potential. If you're not a born actor, and you feel that camouflage is what keeps you in the game, here are two rules to remember:

1. **Reserve your stupid plays for your smallest bets**

   If you've got big money on the table, this is the wrong time to try to look dumb. If you're using a 1 to 10 spread, the same stupid play will cost you ten times more money when you have a high bet out.

2. **Use a stupid play only when it is necessary**

   Don't try to prove to every dealer you sit down against that you're no threat. Most dealers don't pay attention to how you're playing. They watch players all day and they're bored stiff with the game. Try to make small talk if you can.

Two-Bit Deceptions

There are some errors that cost a lot, but others that don't take too big a chunk out of your bankroll. I call the cheap ones "two-bit deceptions," because they all cost about 25¢ or less for every ten bucks you have bet on your hand. For big players, this could mean a couple bucks for every black chip, but if your expectation is a few hundred bucks per hour, you may find occasional value in giving up a few of them to conceal your counting.

Hit/Stand Camouflage

Most of the decisions you'll make are going to be about hitting or standing, so misplays on these hands can be costly. One great device that multi-deck table-hoppers can use is to always stand on hard 16 vs. 10. Since you're table-hopping to avoid negative counts, you'll only misplay this hand when it's a borderline decision anyway. This is one of the hands that casinos watch to see if players vary their decisions, so, don't vary. You could even announce that you always stand on this hand, which is improper basic strategy, and then follow through with your seemingly stupid decision. This hand also occurs frequently enough that they're bound to notice your consistently wrong play. This ploy works best, and costs least, in shoe games. In single-deck games, where you are playing through all hands with a small bet spread, it would cost much more.

Another decision that you might always screw up without much of a loss comes into play when you have a pair of sevens against a dealer ten in a single-deck game. This is the one weird total of 14 where the correct basic strategy is to stand rather than hit. Unfortunately, just about every blackjack book (other than this one!) since Thorp's *Beat the Dealer* has explained this in detail. It's a play that smart players make, and many pit personnel know it. It's actually a borderline basic strategy play. You won't lose much by hitting your 7-7 against 10. (But whatever you do, don't split them!)

A few other cheap hit/stand mistakes: hitting a total of 12 versus 4, 5, or 6, and hitting 13 against 2 or 3, all look pretty dumb, but don't cost much at neutral counts. In fact, your Hi-Lo Lite chart indicates that you stand on all of these hands at a count of 0 or above. So, all of these hands may be played like 16 against 10 in shoe games—just stand on all of them. You'll be playing all of them correctly whenever you have any large bet out.

Any time you're close to the index number for altering your play, the cost of misplaying any hand is small. For instance, it would look pretty stupid to stand on a 16 against 7, and this would be a very costly error for a non-counter. But your Hi-Lo Lite index is +4, and if your count indicates that you are +3 or more, the misplay may be stupid, but not that expensive.

Always remember the two camouflage rules we began with: The bigger your bet, the more it will cost you; and don't make a foolish play unless you think it is necessary.

Double-Down Camouflage

In general, don't make stupid double-down decisions, because twice the money is involved. If you hit your 11 against a dealer 5 instead of doubling down, the dealer could care less, and you just blew a good chance to make some money. Most tourists double down on 11. Doubling down on soft totals like A-2, A-3, A-4, or A-5 used to peg a player as a card counter, so many counters avoided these basic strategy plays. These days, with so many casinos selling accurate basic strategy charts in their gift shops, it doesn't mean much anymore to play these hands correctly. All the same, there are a few two-bit double-down errors that you can make at neutral counts. It doesn't cost much to double down on your 10 versus 10, your 11 versus A, or your total of 8 versus 6. All of these plays look much dumber than they are.

Pair-Split Camouflage

Don't make stupid pair-split decisions. You're doubling your money on the table when most dealers don't know correct pair-splitting basic strategy anyway. One exception is in effect when you have a very high count and a pair of tens against a dealer low card. Your count may indicate that you should split the tens, and there are some Indian reservation casinos, riverboat casinos, and foreign casinos where most people play so stupidly that you can go right ahead and split those tens and just blend into the crowd. But in Nevada, and many major casinos anywhere, this is one pair-split hand you ought to play incorrectly. Likewise, it is one of the few hands you ought to play incorrectly when you have a high bet on the table. Splitting ten-valued cards is an unusual play for both stupid and smart players. Few players break up a hand totaling 20, and this play often looks suspicious because it's only made by rank beginners and card counters, and if you've been playing an otherwise intelligent game, you probably won't pass for a rank beginner.

There are a few pair-split basic strategy violations that fall into the category of two-bit deceptions, and some of these plays look pretty stupid. With a neutral count, failing to split a pair of nines versus a deuce costs little, and looks very amateurish. This is one of those errors tourists always make because they don't want to break up an eighteen. Better yet, and it costs just a bit more, splitting nines against an ace looks really dumb.

Finally, here are a couple plays that really do cost almost nothing (about 1¢ per $100 bet), and look far stupider than they are: hitting a pair of twos or threes against a dealer 4 instead of splitting.

Insurance Camouflage

As for insurance, casinos like to tell players one important rule: always take even money—that is, insure every natural. "It's the only bet on the table you can't lose." Players who do not always insure their naturals are highly suspect, and showing any sign of intelligence at a blackjack table can be dangerous. Actually, it's not all that expensive to always insure your naturals—if you flat-bet $100 per hand, it would only cost you about $1.35 per 100 hands. That's pretty cheap camouflage for a black chip bettor.

Ironically, it actually costs card counters less than one one-hundredth of a percent of their action to always insure their naturals. This is because counters bet more at higher counts, when more naturals occur.

The best way to insure your naturals is to quickly yell out, "Even money!" Do this before you've even had a chance to look at the other cards on the table. If you're playing multiple hands, take even money for your natural, but don't insure your other hands! This always looks great. (Of course, if the count justifies it, you do want to insure the other hands, but don't insure them if it's borderline.) Other than on this even money play, don't make stupid insurance plays. Follow your count.

I am of the opinion that small-stakes card counters should never make any idiot camouflage plays. Likewise for most hit-and-run counters, who get in and out of games, pits, and casinos quickly. If you don't get rated, don't get a VIP card, and don't give your name, you don't need camouflage; you need Reeboks.

Idiot camouflage is primarily for high stakes players who are going for the comps as well as the money. Even these players must remember that there's no real difference between a player who constantly uses idiot camouflage and a real idiot.

Cost-Free Camo

All betting and playing camouflage comes with a price tag. When you make dumb plays for the purpose of confusing the bloodhounds on your trail, it costs you. Holding down your betting spread, insuring your blackjacks, not taking advantage of surrender or soft doubling opportunities, et cetera, are all excellent ways of hiding your counting abilities because, in fact, you are relinquishing some amount of potential gain from counting. But if you make too many of these types of camouflage plays, you will no longer have any advantage at all over the house. What's the value of eliminating the possibility of discovery if there is nothing worth discovering? If you don't utilize the information you gather, then gathering the information in the first place was a waste of time. Use it or lose it.

Some camouflage, however, is free; and ironically, this free-ride deception is often the easiest to pull off. Misplays, as a form of disguise, require a knowledge of, and attention to, how much these plays cost, so that you don't kill your edge. Cost-free camouflage, on the other hand, is not based on misplaying hands, so it's a no-brainer exercise.

What is cost-free camouflage? Rather than misplaying your hands, you allay suspicions by projecting an image, by the way you look, by exploiting prejudices and preconceived notions among pit bosses and casino security personnel. Let's dissect these biases.

1. Age: If a young man and an old man are playing at a blackjack table, all other factors being equal, the younger man will be suspected of card counting sooner than the older one.

2. Sex: If a man and a woman are playing at the same table, all other factors being equal, the man will be suspected first.

3. Race: A white player spreading his bets will be suspected before a black or Asian player using the same spread. This racial prejudice, as a matter of fact, even extends to casinos in other countries. Asian card counters often find the casinos of Korea, Macao, the Philippines, and other Asian countries to be profitable, heat-free venues for their action. Their betting spreads and strategy variations are virtually ignored. Caucasian players, on the other hand, and especially Americans, are immediately suspected if they play for big money, and they often find themselves *persona non grata* if they spread their bets even moderately, or win any substantial amount of money.

4. Nationality: This is tied into the previous factor. Most of the notable books on card counting have been published in America, and few are available outside the U.S. This fact does not escape the notice of casino management here and abroad. In fact, there have been some very sophisticated and well-bankrolled Asian and European counting teams that have attacked casinos all over the world, including those in the U.S. In some cases, these teams have gotten away with incredible betting spreads for lengthy periods of time before anyone in the pit took notice.

5. Demeanor: You put a quiet, thoughtful player at the same table with a gregarious, talkative guy, and the quiet one will be suspected of counting first.

6. Dress code: A player who is nicely but casually dressed will be suspected of card counting before any other fashion type. Card counters don't wear 3-piece suits, nor do they dress like outlaw bikers. They don't look like hippies or punks. They're not decked out in Western gear. And they're usually not shabby, not if they're playing for serious money. That's a mistake on the part of these card counters, for real gamblers include all these types.

7. Body Type: You put a fat man and a thin man at the same table, and the lanky guy will draw the heat first.

Now I'm aware of the fact that there are many exceptions to all of these prejudices. I know that fat counters, and female counters, and non-white counters have all been discovered and barred at one time or another. And I'm sure there are some pit bosses and surveillance personnel who will state emphatically that they only watch for playing styles to determine which players pose a real threat to their tables. But all of these prejudices do exist. I've heard so many stories from so many players who have found that one or more of these factors have helped keep them at the tables (or gotten them booted) that I believe these biases to be real—and many, as a matter of fact, aren't unwarranted.

Looking at these biases, we can now draw a picture of the player most likely to be suspected of card counting, as well as the player least likely to be marked.

Most likely card counter: A young, white, American male, who is thin, stylishly dressed, and playing quietly by himself.

Least likely card counter: A heavy set, gray-haired, nonwhite woman, who speaks with a foreign accent, is loud and talkative, and dressed unusually, even badly.

The more a player looks like the "most likely card counter," the more he will have to use costly misplay camouflage. The more a player fits the image of the "least likely card counter," the more freedom he/she will have to play accurately, and with a wide betting spread according to the count. Just walk in looking like a seventy-year-old grandmother, wearing a sari or a babushka, ranting loudly in some strange language, and you can really take the casinos for a ride!

Obviously, there is only so much you can do to disguise yourself. There are stories of young pros who have colored their hair gray and shaved themselves receding hairlines in order to appear older. I know one very famous counter who attempted to pass himself off as female with a wig and a dress. (He didn't fool anyone.) I know another counter who dyed his skin in order to pass for black. Whether you think you could get away with such radical disguises will depend on a combination of what you look like, how far you're willing to go, and your acting talents. It is always wise to keep these prejudices in mind, however, when you are getting ready to head out to play blackjack.

Heat Radar

If you are going to get away with counting at high stakes, you must be sensitive to "heat." More and more these days, counters are identified by electronic surveillance, but there is almost always some sign that the guys on the floor suspect something before the heat comes down. This is a letter I received from a player a few years ago:

> How does a card counter know when he's getting heat? I play at moderate to high stakes ($25 -$500), but I've only been doing this for a short time—a few weekend trips so far. I get very nervous whenever the pit boss seems to be looking at me, or even in the direction of my table. I do try to be friendly toward the bosses and floormen, and I believe I act like nothing is bothering me, but I often have the urge to bolt out of there as soon as any conversation with pit personnel is over. I feel like they are also just acting nonchalant when they're actually scrutinizing my play. A few times I have left tables for no other reason than the floorman came over and watched my table for a while, scribbling notes. I feel like he's recording what I'm doing and that I'd better leave before his notes get too detailed. I've walked out on a number of pretty decent games, and it irritates me whenever I feel I must do this when the count is high. I haven't had any trouble so far, but am I being too cautious? It sure would be nice to relax a bit more and hang in there when I've got an otherwise profitable situation.

I suspect that this player was being overly cautious, but I can't know for sure, not without having seen for myself if he actually had reason to feel uncomfortable. He might've loosened up just a bit and gotten barred. Perhaps his radar is working perfectly. Also, as I have never observed his casino play, I really can't judge if his style of betting is too obvious, or his demeanor too telling. Some players project their paranoia, and this in itself makes casino personnel suspicious.

Any player who bets in the $25 to $500 range may expect to draw pit attention and should assume that the eye in the sky is monitoring him. Once a blackjack player's bets go into the $100+ range he becomes a serious concern to the pit. Their primary concern with big players, however, is that they keep them as customers. They do not automatically assume such players are card counters, and most are not—most are actually big losers.

A floorman scribbling notes while looking at a table is generally of no significance as far as heat goes. One of the floorman's jobs is to estimate the average bet size of the big players, and he will regularly walk from table to table to calculate an average. The casinos use this information primarily to "rate" players for comps. At the black chip level of play, most players will be asked repeatedly if they would like a VIP card, which would require the player to give his name and address, and allows the casino to keep track of and rate his play. This rating system is how the casino determines what sort of comps to award; many casinos not only rate a big player's level of action, but they also do a "skills check" specifically to look for signs of card counting.

So, far be it from me to advise a player spreading from one green chip to five blacks to disregard his paranoia. At that level of play, you must be paranoid to survive. And, you must move around frequently to stay under the radar. A more aggressive counter would probably not leave the table in the midst of a high count, unless asked to leave. A more cautious counter would choose to avoid any kind of confrontation if he felt one was coming, and would leave the moment it crossed his mind.

A pit boss or floorman coming over to your table to talk with you, if you are playing at this level, is entirely normal. Any player betting black action should expect this. After all, you are a major customer to them, so they will try to be friendly and personable.

But let's define various types of real heat.

Heat is when a pit boss or floorman starts to obviously glare at you. This type of heat generally means that they're watching you, and are checking to see if direct surveillance unnerves, flusters, or convinces you to leave. The worst reaction to this type of heat, as you might assume, is to act nervous, and the most obvious sign that you are nervous would be your failure to look back at them, pretending not to notice. If you casually and naturally leave the table, without showing any other sign of nervousness, this may get you off the hook. The best reaction, however, is to look back at them, and if the glare continues, to strike up a conversation, ask for something, be friendly—ask for information about the showroom, or a dinner comp, whatever. If a boss who has been glaring at you reaches for his phone, or is talking on the phone, you should assume that you are, or have been, or will soon be, under eye-in-the-sky surveillance. Not a good sign.

But this is also not necessarily bad. It may be that the boss suspects you and wants the eye to watch your play. For the next shoe or two it would be a great time to play with utter disregard for the count so that their skills-check shows you to be no threat. Most pros develop a hyper-awareness to attitudes in the pit, and to any attention being paid to them by pit personnel.

Heat is when a pit boss or floorman instructs the dealer to shuffle up on you, or to center-cut the next shoe. If this is the first time this has happened, you might continue playing, even through a few of these shallowly dealt shoes, as the pit may simply be testing you to see if this appears to bother you. This, however, is a countermeasure that literally kills your chances of profiting from that shoe, and it also sends a fairly strong message that your play is not trusted. This may be less a test than a message that the boss has already made a decision about you. It may be the wisest decision for you to casually leave, and simply avoid playing whenever this boss is in the pit. Most experienced pros can tell when a shuffle-up is a test or a message. If you can't tell, then you've got to make a decision. Do you want to try to play through this intense surveillance, to see if you can stay in the game? If you do just get up and leave that might affirm their suspicions. How you handle this situation depends on many factors: Are you staying at this casino? Are you a comped guest? Do they know who you are? Did you get a player's card with your real name on it?

If you are just another face in the crowd, not a guest at their hotel, not known by name, you might find it best to hit the road quickly, and avoid that boss, that pit, and that shift, for some time in the future. If you are a known entity, then you may have to deal with the consequences sooner or later, especially if you are a comped guest.

Heat is when someone who isn't playing (and sometimes more than one), appears to take a strong interest in your play from behind you or manages to get into your line of sight just enough for you to know that you are under rather intense surveillance. This could be an even more unsettling variation of the pit boss glare, or if you are a high roller, this surveillance may be done with a lighter touch. The casino person observing you may even pose as another player at your table, betting the minimum, not saying very much. But somehow, you just know he was sent to watch your game, watch your eyes, and watch your bets and decisions. If you decide to call it quits, leave as casually as you can.

Heat is when you are personally told that your play is being restricted in any way—possibly your betting spread, or the maximum amount you may bet. If this type of countermeasure follows you around from table to table, assume that the jig is up. You have been identified as a counter.

Surviving Surveillance

All card counters must have an understanding of casino surveillance. If you are playing for any serious amount of money, I urge you to read *The Card Counter's Guide to Casino Surveillance* by Cellini; information on obtaining this comprehensive exposé on casino surveillance can be found in the back pages of this book.

Here are some of the basics:

The Cameras

Cameras are located in virtually every public area of any major casino hotel, except for the restrooms. These cameras are in hotel hallways, parking lots, lobbies, restaurants, everywhere. Most cameras are located overhead in ceiling "bubbles." In the casino itself, virtually every table game is under 24-hour video surveillance, which means that all live games are videotaped. These feeds are not only taped, but are shown on banks of dozens of monitors located in the surveillance room, where they are constantly watched. The surveillance agents may aim the cameras, tilt them, and zoom in on any activity.

For this reason, you should never meet with other counters or teammates (if you are part of a counting team) anywhere on the casino property. This includes meeting in coffee shops, restaurants, outside the front doors, or even in your hotel rooms, because although the insides of the guests' rooms are not under camera surveillance, the elevators and hallways are. The surveillance monitors can easily watch who is coming and going from the guests' rooms.

The zoom is pretty good, so you must be aware that these cameras can often see what the normal human eye could not from a distance. Be very careful about using your cell phone in any public area of a casino—surveillance personnel have been known to zoom in to see a name or phone number displayed on the cell phone screen. Likewise, do not look at anything written like play records, or your teammates' names in a notebook.

When you are in any public area of a casino, assume that the eye is on you. Always.

The Computers

Most major casinos today have computer software for analyzing blackjack players. One of the best and most commonly used programs is called "Blackjack Survey Voice." By inputting your playing and betting decisions, the operator can use the software to very accurately determine if you are a card counter.

Every casino also keeps computer files on all known players that show win/loss histories, betting levels, skill check results, and other relevant statistics. Many casinos do periodic reviews of their big players' records, to identify any players who might not have been identified by game protection personnel as counters, but whose win results appear to be abnormally high.

The Protection Services

Most major casinos also use outside services that provide them with known card counters' and other professional players' names and photos. The oldest and best known service is Griffin Investigations of Las Vegas. The Griffin Agency leases a book of mug shots to casinos, and also has an Internet service called Griffin Gold, where casinos can access all current information on known players, including aliases, associates, etc. If you get your picture in the Griffin book as a known counter, you may have trouble playing in many casinos around the world.

A newer service, Casino Visual Identifications (CVI), is entirely on the Internet, and features facial recognition capabilities. The Biometrica software used by CVI attempts to identify known players' faces by comparing facial features to photos of faces stored in the company's database.

Most casinos also belong to the Surveillance Information Network (S.I.N.), a service marketed by Biometrica that lets casinos share emails and faxes about current "threats." If you get barred in one casino, then discover that the casino across the street backs you off before you even have a chance to sit down, you have probably been identified on a S.I.N. flyer to all of the casinos in the area.

There are numerous other similar services available to casinos. For a more comprehensive overview of these services, I refer you to the Cellini book mentioned above. For a quick and dirty overview of the casino surveillance agents' job, read this interview with a Las Vegas surveillance agent I met at a gaming expo in the Fall of 2000, who agreed to be interviewed provided his identity was not revealed.

Interview

Q. How long have you been working in surveillance?

A. I've worked in surveillance for about fifteen years. I've worked in nine casinos of which three are on the Strip, where I am currently working.

Q. Have you worked in any other casino industry jobs?

A. I broke in as a dealer in the early '70s and dealt for five years. Then I was promoted to the floor and stayed there for four years. Around 1981, I became a pit boss, which I quit after three years because of the politics. Later on, in 1986, I took a position in surveillance and never left. I like it.

Q. Have you ever been a serious player, such as a card counter or other type of gambling pro?

A. No. I never was a serious player but I have dear friends who are and when I do play I will only play with an advantage.

Q. Can you explain that?

A. I'd rather not.

Q. In a major Strip casino, how many surveillance personnel are on duty on a busy Saturday night, as opposed to a slow weekday morning?

A. At my casino, on average, there are anywhere up to five people on duty in the surveillance room, and on a slow night there will only be three, maybe four with the supervisor.

Q. How do you decide whom to watch from the eye?

A. A phone call from the pit. Usually a pit boss will call up and ask us to watch someone. Or if a player is a continuous winner over several trips he will be observed.

Q. How prevalent is computer software in analyzing blackjack players' skill levels?

A. It's used different amounts by different casinos. I am not a big fan of blackjack software because camouflage plays could throw it off if you only look at a short session of play. I don't know of any monitor operators who care for it, and some don't even take it seriously.

Q. Is this type of software ever used to evaluate play for comp purposes?

A. No. Comps are based strictly on the game played, average wager, and the amount of time played. I think it's outrageous that many pit personnel are ignorant of how to evaluate a player's value, or potential value to the house. Say a new patron walks into a casino and plays roulette, 5.26% house advantage, for several hundred dollars a spin for five to six spins and then asks for a comp to the buffet. A floor supervisor then informs the player that he does not have enough play time. Where's the logic?

Q. *Is this software ever used "live," on games in progress, or is it only used later, on videos of play?*

A. I don't know anyone who can use it fast enough for live play, so usually it is done later with video playback.

Q. *In detecting card counters, is the software faster and/or more accurate than human personnel trained to recognize card-counting strategies?*

A. I personally feel nothing can take the place of a trained individual.

Q. *If a player is winning big, will he automatically be evaluated?*

A. No. But if bet spreads raise an eyebrow in the pit, then we will be notified and we might watch him. We will definitely bring the individual up on a monitor but that will not be our first priority if bet spreads and good basic strategy combined are not also factors.

Q. *How much of a win, or how many hours of winning, will trigger an investigation of play in a Las Vegas casino?*

A. In our casino as soon as someone [wins] $5,000 we are notified.

Q. *Will all blackjack players be evaluated for both card-counting and shuffle-tracking skills?*

A. No. Shuffle-tracking is simply not understood by many casino employees. Everyone uses the term but couldn't identify [a shuffle-tracker]. It is such a hard area to do well and even a harder area to detect. The fact is, few if any players can beat the shuffles.

Q. *In a typical month in a major casino, how many players will be found to be card counters, shuffle trackers, and actual cheaters?*

A. Card counters, we average six to seven a month. Shuffle trackers, about two to three, simply because they are in Biometrica as a tracker, not because we catch them. Cheaters, about one to four in a month, usually slots, and half are usually employees stealing coins when filling the machines.

Q. For casinos that subscribe to Griffin or Biometrica, is the service used extensively, say, on a daily basis?

A. Yes. As soon as we get a call from the pit about a patron, the first thing we do is see if the person is in Griffin or Biometrica. If he is, it makes our jobs easier.

Q. Who in the casino decides if a player is to be added to Griffin or Biometrica?

A. We take a picture of the individual and state the reasons why we think this person is a counter, and the agencies decide whether or not to put him or her into the system. We can, however, send the individual's picture directly to other casinos using Biometrica and ask them if anyone has information on the person.

Q. How well does Biometrica work, and what is the usage procedure?

A. Biometrica does work well in my opinion but, let's face it, it is only as good as the people who use it. It is easier to use Biometrica because if we take a picture of someone who is in the system the computer will find out who the person is because of the facial recognition device.

Q. Are players ever entered solely because of association with known card counters?

A. Absolutely. Guilt by association, I guess.

Q. If a player is in Griffin or Biometrica as a counter, is it assumed that the entry is correct, or will his play be watched?

A. If he's in the book, he's history.

Q. How do SINs (Surveillance Information Networks) work?

A. As soon as a person is a suspected undesirable a picture is taken and sent to all the other joints warning or asking about them.

Q. If a known pro counter is discovered in a Strip casino, will other Strip casinos be immediately notified?

A. Yes.

Q. If a player is winning inordinately, yet no explanation other than luck can be found, i.e., no counting, no tracking, no hole-card play, no devices, how long will the player be allowed to keep on winning? Is there some number of hours? Any dollar amount? Do all casinos have a pain-tolerance limit?

A. If the player is given a clean bill then we will keep letting him play, but with deterring methods—cutting shoes in half, changing dealers, and so on.

Q. *If such a player is removed* [because of a run of good luck], *would such a player be a candidate for entry in Griffin or Biometrica?*

A. No, because you have to explain to them why. But the individual will be in the house computer.

Q. *Are players ever entered in Griffin or Biometrica simply because casino personnel dislike them?*

A. No.

Q. *How competent would you say the average surveillance person is at detecting card counters, shuffle trackers, and hole-card players?*

A. Card counters: An amateur counter will be caught immediately. A professional, with no outrageous spreads, camouflage at the right times, et cetera, will have some longevity. Shuffle trackers: not much chance of getting caught. Hole-card players: not much chance of getting caught, providing greed is not a factor. Really bizarre plays can give them away.

Q. *Which casinos have the strongest surveillance departments? And the weakest?*

A. I really can't say because there are good individual surveillance personnel but people are always moving from joint to joint. However, even when the "good ones" are in the room, they can't watch everything. Remember, we are not just concentrating on blackjack. We have the other games to watch, slots, markers, escorts, log books to fill out ...

Q. *Which casino games other than blackjack are of the most concern to surveillance?*

A. Depends on the hold. If certain games aren't holding what they should, we watch them for employee theft, biased wheels, etc.

Q. *How much playing time, or number of hands, would be input in a Blackjack Survey Voice analysis to look for skillful play?*

A. Generally, one to two shoes to look for a good plus count to see what that person did when the count was good.

Q. *How often are outside consultants called to evaluate play?*

A. Outside consultants are rarely called in to evaluate play. Usually all the casinos have a resident expert who does the evaluation. Out of all the consultants I have seen over the years, there have been only two who were worth their weight in gold.

Q. *Do either Griffin or Biometrica offer play evaluation services?*

A. No.

Q. *Does Gaming Control ever evaluate play in Nevada?*

A. I have never seen them do anything like that.

Q. *What advice can you give players who want to avoid detection as card counters?*

A. Try not to bring too much attention to yourself, especially with bet spreads. If you are getting heat, try some camouflage plays. Also watch the floor supervisor, because if he goes to the phone he is not calling Miss Cleo. Also, if you are getting heat, leave before the next shift starts. That way no information will be transferred about you. If you are winning, try to pocket some of the chips without anyone seeing you. If you are wearing a baseball cap and never look up, that's a big tell. Surveillance will wait until you go to the cage to get a nice Polaroid. If this worries you, then do not cash out—just leave with the chips. The main thing is this: Don't go crazy with your betting spreads. That's the biggest give away. If your bets are moving with the count, you can't hide it if you're watched for any length of time.

Q. *What do you look for when evaluating a person?*

A. When I evaluate a person the first thing I look at is basic strategy. If a person does play good basic strategy, the next area is bet spreads. I will count the deck down and see if the player's bets are spreading according to the count. I also look for basic strategy deviations along with the spreads. The same would go for shuffle tracking. For this, I look for the larger amounts of money and see how the hands are played. For example, if a player cuts and bets big off the top and receives a 12 vs. 2 and stands, but later on hits the same hand when the bets are smaller, then I know I might have a tracker. The examples could go on and on because each situation is always different. The best advice I can give is to be careful and know your surroundings.

Q. Do casinos ever do background checks on new players? Say an unknown player calls the casino and he wants to put fifty thousand in the cage to play blackjack. Will they do any investigation to find out who he is?

A. No. They will, of course, check Griffin and Biometrica if they have one of these services, and they will check with other casinos they are connected with. For instance, MGM will check with Mirage, et cetera. Probably, player marketing will ask the player what other casinos he has played at, and they may check with one or two of those joints. Occasionally, somebody just shows up out of nowhere with fifty thousand to play blackjack, but usually he'll have some kind of playing history. But if he's not in Griffin or Biometrica, we don't look any further than that. Why should we? If he's betting like that, we'll be monitoring his play from the get-go.

Q. Would the casino run any asset checks on such a player? If he has little or no history, are they interested in where this fifty thousand front money came from?

A. Why should we care? If he's putting this up as front money, why ask questions? His money's green, that's all that matters. Now if he wants a fifty thousand credit line, without bringing in the money, that's different. There will definitely be a credit check done on him. He'll have to provide his bank information, et cetera, just as if he were applying for a fifty thousand dollar loan—which, technically, he is.

Q. Any final comments?

A. Just be thankful that surveillance is on the low end of the pay scale [surveillance personnel are paid far less than floor men and pit bosses]. The guy watching you on the monitor probably knows a whole lot less than you do about what you're doing, so you can fool him if you're careful. Move around a lot to make his job more difficult. He's not paid well enough to really give a damn. And good luck!

This interview appeared about three years prior to the *Card Counter's Guide to Casino Surveillance* by Cellini. One curious similarity I noted was the surveillance agent's statement that, "If you are wearing a baseball cap and never look up, that's a big tell." In Cellini's book, the author provides a list of "The 21 Tells of a Card Counter." Tell #2 states: "Player wears a baseball cap, visor, straw hat, etc. Keeps it pulled down to eye level. Trying to hide your face?" The Cellini book also provides a couple of surveillance photos of the types of players who would be "profiled" as possible card counters simply because they "fit the mold."

These are the photos from the Cellini book, used with permission of the author:

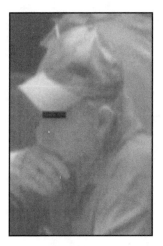 

If this looks like you, you may have problems. You can expect to be watched. But there is another perspective to consider. One pro player, who always wears a brimmed cap, says: "If the boss comes over and backs me off or gives me heat, I leave. No problem. Maybe it was the hat that got them looking at me in the first place, but the way I see it, I can go across the street, or right back into the same casino later, maybe with a different cap, and no one recognizes me. They never really get a good photo, or a good look at my face. They can't hang my mug in their surveillance room or send photos out to other joints. In my opinion, showing your face is far worse than hiding it."

16

CARD COUNTING AND THE LAW

Is It Legal to Think in Casinos?

If you're the type of person who lets friends and acquaintances know that you are a serious blackjack player—one of those notorious "card counters"—you may have noticed that quite a number of people, upon discovering this character flaw of yours, will cock their heads, and say with a disapproving grimace, "Oh...is that legal?"

In the thirty years that I've been a card counter, I have been asked this question at least a hundred times.

My immediate response is always something along the lines of, "Of course, it's legal! Card counting is just thinking while you're playing. How can it be illegal to think?" It's usually met with something like, "Oh...the casinos let you do that?"

This always steams me, the suggestion that I must first get "permission" from the casinos to think while I play. But I retort with this: "Well, if they know you're counting the cards while you play, they'll throw you out...but it's not illegal to count cards."

"I see," they say, obviously not seeing anything.

With most people, that's the end of the conversation. A handful of intrepid souls will want to probe deeper into this curious avocation of mine, and I'll find myself knowledgeably discussing the innkeepers' right to refuse service to anyone. I'll expound upon how the trespassing laws are utilized in Nevada to eliminate card counters, as opposed to New Jersey, where innkeepers' rights don't extend to the gaming tables. The Atlantic City casinos generally shuffle more often and use various methods of restricting bets to foil card counters. Well-known professional card counters in A.C. are sometimes arrested for "creating disturbances," so that the local trespassing laws may then be applied. Some players have gone to court over these issues.

From here, the conversation inevitably turns to the extraordinary surveillance methods the casinos typically use to identify players as card counters, and the extraordinary methods card counters resort to in order to hide their identities and abilities from the casinos.

Once, an hour or so into such a conversation, the woman I was talking with said in an exasperated voice, "Why didn't you just admit it in the first place: Card counting is illegal!"

"It's not illegal!" I insisted. "This is America! They can't make it illegal to think!"

"Who are you kidding?" she asked in all seriousness. "You admit that you have to hide it from the casinos, and that once they know you can do it, they put your picture in a 'mug book' that gets circulated to the other casinos, so that you have to wear a disguise and get fake ID if you want to keep playing. But, if they see through your disguise, they can have you arrested for trespassing. So, obviously, the police are on the casinos' side, as are the courts. And you're saying it's not illegal?"

It is not easy to explain to people why casinos sometimes get away with harassing players who are using perfectly legal, sometimes brilliantly clever, strategies to win at a card game. But casinos are sore losers, and they are rich and often politically powerful—especially in casino-dominated states. So, in addition to being a good actor, a successful card counter is also often something of a rebel, who refuses to submit to unjust power, insisting on his legal and moral rights. A card counter follows all the rules of the game, as set by the casino, just like any other player at the table. He just thinks as he plays, that's all. Should players be allowed to think about their decisions before they make them in casino games? That's the question…

When I was a kid, my father worked for IBM. He was a computer salesman back in the '50s when the only computers were garage-sized mainframes used by the few huge businesses that could afford them. On his desk at home, he always had a small wooden placard that read, "Think." It was the motto of Thomas J. Watson, president and founder of IBM. On the few occasions I accompanied my father to his office in downtown Detroit, I saw these placards all over. Think. Think. Think.

Perhaps the casinos should adopt a similar placard they could set on each blackjack table, right next to the betting limit sign, a placard that says, "Don't Think." Or, maybe they could just append these words to the rules sign: "Double down on any two cards. Split and re-split any pair, except aces. Split aces receive only one card each. No thinking."

Or, as Descartes might have said: "I think, therefore I can't play blackjack."

Most laws governing gambling in the U.S. are state laws, not federal. As I am not an attorney, I cannot advise you on precisely what is or is not legal in any given state, especially as these laws differ from state to state, and change with time. Most books on card counting ignore the legal questions that many counters face. Because these issues are so important, however, and the consequences can be so serious, the information below should give you a pretty good overview of the legal ramifications of card counting.

It is unlikely, however, that any state will ever make it illegal to count cards at casino blackjack games, as it's really nothing more than thinking intelligently while you play. If you are unsure about the legality of any strategy you use, I suggest you contact an attorney, in the state (or country) where you play, for clarification. Meanwhile, most of the information below pertains to the state of Nevada, though most other states have similar laws.

Do You Have to Show Your ID?

There is a regulation in Nevada that requires anyone gambling in a casino to have identification on their person. This is primarily so that casinos can validate that everyone gambling in their establishment is 21 years old, the legal age for gambling. There is no regulation that requires a customer to show ID to a casino employee, but if you do not produce it when asked you may be asked to leave the premises. If there really is a question about your age, then you will absolutely be asked to leave the premises if you do not show your ID; if you are obviously over the age of 21, you may still be asked to leave if you do not show your ID.

Also, any table game player who completes a cash transaction (or transactions) in excess of $10,000 within a 24-hour period will be required to show ID and provide a Social Security number, because IRS regulations require a casino to file a Cash Transaction Report (CTR) on any customer who either buys in or cashes out at that level. So, when someone approaches $10,000 at the tables, the pit boss will ask for ID. If you do not show your ID, you will be barred from further play.

Finally, there is a law in Nevada that requires anyone to show ID to any police officer on demand. The ACLU is currently challenging that law in federal court as a violation of a citizen's lawful right to privacy. At the time of this writing (Winter 2004), the US Supreme Court has not yet made a decision on this case.

From the card counter's perspective, what it boils down to in Nevada, and I suspect in many other states, is that you do not have to show your ID to casino personnel when requested—but you may be ejected from the premises if you refuse.

Is Fake ID Illegal?

That depends on the ID and the purpose it is being used for. It is illegal, according to federal law, to possess a false ID that is purported to be issued by any official government agency. This means that you cannot possess a phony passport, driver's license, Social Security card, or any other type of fake ID that appears to have been issued by a state, city, county, or the federal government.

Other types of IDs—which might include credit cards, employment IDs from non-governmental employers, health plan or insurance cards, library cards, union cards, casino players club cards—are legal to possess and use, provided they are not used for fraudulent purposes. In other words, you can obtain a credit card in the name of Santa Claus, and use that credit card to buy reindeer food. Provided you pay the bill when it comes, there is no crime. But if you use fake ID to defraud a business or person, however—let's say you claim that you are not Santa Claus when you get the bill for the reindeer food—then it's a crime.

Can They "Back-Room" You?

Casino security personnel can detain you, by force if necessary, and they may handcuff you, if they believe that you have committed a crime. If they do not believe you have committed a crime, then they must allow you to leave the premises peacefully. If they do think you have broken the law, then they must call the local police or gaming agents who handle criminal cases. You do not have to answer questions for casino personnel. Likewise, you do not have to answer questions for police. You have a right to an attorney if you are being charged with a crime. If you are not being charged with a crime, then they must let you go.

Despite the laws, many professional players have been illegally detained and searched by casino personnel. Lawsuits brought against casinos for such violations are becoming more common, and players have won a number of these suits, but the best advice is to avoid these types of confrontations whenever possible—never display temper in the casino, always remain calm, and leave quietly if you feel that any situation is getting out of hand. Although you may be in the right, having done nothing wrong, these types of situations can result in legal complications for you.

Can They Confiscate or Refuse to Cash Your Chips?

No, not unless they believe you have obtained your chips fraudulently, by cheating, in which case you will be charged with a crime, and the chips will be entered as "evidence." This does not mean that they won't confiscate or refuse to cash in your chips, only that it is illegal for them to do so. If this ever happens to you, then you may have to hire an attorney to get your chips cashed, or contact the local gaming regulatory agents. Casinos sometimes refuse to cash counters' chips because they know that you will have to provide identification to the authorities in your efforts to cash them, and most state and local authorities will then provide the casino with your proper identification.

It is usually easier, cheaper, and safer to get friends to cash your chips for you if the casino refuses to do so. If the chips you have are high denomination ($500 each or more), then the casino may not cash these chips for strangers who cannot explain when and how they were obtained. For this reason, many pros do not allow dealers to "color up" their chips when they leave the tables. In the big Las Vegas Strip casinos, it is rarely a problem for strangers to cash a few purple ($500) or yellow ($1,000) chips without questions. Almost any casino, however, tightly controls it's chocolate ($5,000) chips. In smaller casinos, you might have problems with smaller ($500 and $1,000) denominations.

Again, the easy solution is to never leave the table with chips you cannot easily cash out later without questions or ID.

Is it Legal to Use a Computer in a Casino?

Probably not. Nevada—and most, if not all, other states—have laws against using any type of "device" to assist you in making gambling decisions. These anti-device laws are usually vague, but most courts would

231

uphold them as applying to high-tech devices like computers or video cameras, and my advice is to steer clear of such gadgets. The reason I am even covering this issue is that these types of devices are often advertised and sold as legal by scam artists on the Internet and through newspaper classifieds. Despite whatever ad claims you may read, none of these types of devices are easy to use, and many provide less of an advantage than card counting, if they provide any advantage at all.

Are Laws Different in Indian Reservation Casinos?

Unfortunately, yes. In many states, games offered in Indian reservation casinos are not regulated by state authorities, but by the tribe itself. Because of this, you might run into problems that you would never encounter in a state-regulated casino. A few years ago, a blackjack player in a large Southern California Indian Reservation casino discovered that marked cards were being used on the table. As he had lost more than $100,000 in the casino, he tried to sue the casino. To his dismay, he learned that there were no state laws against using marked cards in blackjack, because the only games that existed at that time were on Indian reservations, and they were regulated by the tribal councils. When he complained to the tribal council, they heard his case, and even admitted that the cards were marked after outside experts examined the house cards and determined that all of the cards used in the casino were marked. But he wasn't compensated for his losses. The casino claimed that despite the fact that their house cards were all marked, they did not know it, and that some crooked employee of the casino must have surreptitiously slipped the marked cards into their storeroom. They had no tribal laws requiring them to make monetary reparations to the player.

This is an extreme case of what might occur, but it does point out one type of legal problem you could run into in an Indian reservation casino. In some states, there are regulatory agencies that preside over Indian reservation casinos, and most Indian reservation casinos, even if regulated by their own tribal councils, try to provide honest games, policing them to enforce their regulations. In general, you need not be overly paranoid of being cheated in Indian casinos. But do not expect "normal" state laws to apply in all Indian reservation casinos. (I will cover the whole subject of cheating—both in Indian and state-regulated casinos—in a later chapter.)

For now, let's just stick to the basic facts:

1. It's perfectly legal to count cards.

2. You do not have to identify yourself to casino personnel.

3. If you are not being charged with a crime, you have the right to leave the property.

4. If you are detained, say nothing, except to calmly insist on either being arrested, or let go.

5. If you are arrested on trumped up charges, say nothing, and demand an attorney. Then get an attorney who is knowledgeable about players' rights.

Most card counters never experience legal problems or suffer serious harassment in the casinos. But still, it's a sad state of affairs that in a book about how to play a card game, we must cover the topic of what to do if your civil rights are violated when you are doing nothing more than playing intelligently. Unfortunately, that's the world we live in…

NOTE

If you need an attorney who specializes in gambling law, look on Arnold Snyders's website: www.BlackjackForumOnline.com. This website is owned and maintained by professional players.

EARNING YOUR BLACK BELT

17

TEAM PLAY

There is one major financial benefit from teaming up with other players. When two or more players combine their bankrolls, with the agreement that the team will share all wins and mutually absorb all losses, then each member of the team may size his bets as if the team bankroll were his alone. When more than one player works from a common bankroll, the effect on fluctuation is the same as if one player were simply playing that many more hands.

Team members should not play at the same table, unless absolutely necessary, such as for a depth-charging strategy. If team members play at the same table, then they all must size their bets the same as if one player were playing multiple simultaneous hands, and won't reap the full benefit of their combined bankrolls.

If you join a team, you must trust the other guys, and you should all test and drill each other. Never team up with a player whose abilities or honesty you question.

Accounting

All financial considerations must be worked out, on paper, before you start playing. Dividing wins and losses can be difficult when various team members contribute different amounts of money to the team bankroll, play this or that many hours, sometimes at different stakes, and win and lose different amounts of money. To keep the bookkeeping simple, you would be wise to separate each player's contributions according to investment in the team bank, hours played, and win/loss record.

Say you have a six-member team, with three members making no contribution, two members contributing $5,000 each, and one member contributing $10,000. On one ledger, list each player's bankroll contribution. Small teams usually agree that investors as a whole will receive about 50% of the total team win. If the team doubles its $20,000 bank, then automatically 50%, or $10,000, would be divided proportionately among the three contributors to the team bankroll. The contributor who put in twice as much money would take twice as much of the investors' share of the win.

If the team were to suffer a $10,000 loss, these three bankroll contributors would have to absorb the entire loss, in proportion to their respective contributions. It is because these team members are putting their personal money at risk that they enjoy such a sizable proportion of the win. On teams with banks in excess of $250,000, the investment share is usually more than 50%. There is no precise formula; each team negotiates an arrangement that seems fair to all involved.

A second ledger is kept with the total hours played by each player. The time contribution is usually worth between 25 and 50% of the team's win. If the team wins $20,000, that will be divided up according to how many hours each team member played. You may have a six-member team, where one member contributes to the bankroll but does not play, while five members play various numbers of hours. In this case, only those who put in time at the tables would take a portion of that money, equal to the proportion of total team hours each member spent at the tables.

A third ledger records the total wins and losses of each individual player. The personal win contribution of all players is worth the remaining percentage of the total win. Players who have logged a net loss would take none of this share based on individual win. Those players who have won money for the team divide up their portions of the total win based on what they personally won. Some teams neither reward nor penalize players for wins/losses, considering these short-term results due more to statistical fluctuations than skill. They worry about losing good players who may abandon a team once they are personally too far in the red to be likely to benefit from a win share. Other teams feel it is always good to reward winners, as this may encourage players to strive for excellence.

Larger teams often assign a win share to team management. Some may reward scouts for locating good games. Some teams pay a percentage to analysts and programmers who come up with excellent playing strategies. As before, all of these things should be figured out in advance, and put in writing, so that every contributor to the team understands exactly what he will get based on wins, losses, and his contribution to the team.

You should also work out how expenses will be handled well in advance. Players may either agree to absorb these personally, or the team bankroll may cover all or some specific expenses. Some teams occasionally agree to pay players an hourly rate in addition to, as an advance on, or in lieu of a win share.

Most important, teams must decide beforehand exactly how and when the team bank is to be broken. Weeks of planning can be ruined if one major bankroll contributor decides to pull out suddenly, or if skilled players abandon a bank in the red. Arguments can be avoided by settling these matters beforehand.

The Team Handbook

Every team, no matter what size, should develop a handbook that spells out all procedures, rules, and agreements. Most new teams that break up do so as a result of differences, misunderstandings, and broken verbal agreements that occur when the team suffers a major loss. Your team handbook must be mutually agreed upon, and you should have it in writing before you put any money on the tables. Any time a problem arises that is not covered in the handbook, solve it, then revise the handbook to include the solution.

The areas your handbook must cover are:

1. How do players qualify for team play? What testing procedures will be used? Will only one card counting system be allowed? How many strategy indices must be known? Will there be tests for counting speed and accuracy, true count adjustment, and visual deck estimation?

2. Will the team use signals in the casino? What are the signals? Will members be tested on them?

3. How will games be chosen for attack? Will players have any autonomy in choosing and playing games, or does the team manager have to authorize what games are attacked?

4. Who will act as team manager, and what will the manager's duties and responsibilities be?

5. Will there be strict guidelines on behavior and dress code inside the casino?

6. Who handles the trip bankroll? How is the money doled out to players? What accounting procedures will be used before and after play?

7. What betting limits are placed on players? If you lose or win a certain amount, do you have to report that to the team manager immediately? If so, how much?

8. Do players toke dealers, and if so, how much, how often, and under what conditions?

9. Can team members meet in restaurants or in their rooms? Can they call room-to-room? Can team players ever bring spouses, girlfriends, boyfriends, or companions on trips? To team meetings?

10. During playing trips, how often will team meetings be called, and who calls them?

11. If players are rewarded for hours played, are all hours booked at equal rates, or will hours be rewarded according to activity, skill required, value to operation, et cetera? For example, will big players earn more per hour than spotters?

12. What is the target win? Can investors add to or subtract from the team bank prior to hitting the target? Will the win be divided according to dollar investment, hours, total win, duties, or all of the above? How? What proportions?

13. Will violations of rules be penalized financially, and if so, how much is each infraction worth and who determines when to levee the fines?

14. Will polygraph tests be used to encourage honesty? If so, who decides when the procedure will be used?

If you involve yourself in a team effort, you will discover that the more you have spelled out on paper, the smoother the team will run. In Ken Uston's books, *The Big Player* and *Million Dollar Blackjack,* you will find some fairly comprehensive team play methods, including everything from bet-sizing guidelines to the precise sets of signals his teams employed. This type of information is fine to read for ideas, but it is important that you develop your own methods. Always be ready to change those things that aren't working—throw around ideas with your teammates. The most successful operations are those that can change on the fly. Conditions vary so much in different casinos that you cannot always use the same modus operandi. If there was one stock methodology, the casinos would catch onto it in no time.

EMFH Teams

The simplest team approach is the EMFH approach, or Every Man for Himself. This approach is viable with virtually any size team or bank. Because of its simplicity, it's also one of the most popular team approaches.

An EMFH team is dependent on each team member being a competent card counter who is capable of beating the tables. This type of team approach requires the highest level of trust, as it is essentially a simple agreement to share a common bankroll and all playing results.

For instance, three close friends, all of whom are card counters, might each contribute $10,000 to a common bank so that each of them can play off of a $30,000 team bank. They don't have to play together—they don't even have to be in the same city.

This kind of team might make a simple agreement to set a win target of $15,000, and to distribute profits when the target is hit, paid in proportion to the actual hours of play, or individual win, or some combination, for each player. This type of agreement allows maximum flexibility for the participants. Technically, they don't ever have to even see each other; they can play when and wherever it's most convenient.

An EMFH team can coordinate all operations over the phone, wire-transferring money if necessary. Such a team doesn't have to deal with the hassle of coordinating attacks on specific casinos and shifts, doesn't have to worry about signal mix-ups, and doesn't risk being identified as a team of counters.

Above all, the main thing required for this sort of agreement to work is absolute trust in each other. This type of team cannot succeed unless all members are absolutely honest with each other about their results, time at the tables, and expenses. All team members must also make every effort to regularly update each other on play results, so that everyone's kept abreast of the actual size of the team bank.

The "handbook" for a small EMFH team could probably be typed on a single sheet of paper, especially if the bankroll contributions are equal, and the players agree that they will all be playing at the same level, with equal skill, and are subject to the same guidelines. Even so, this one-page handbook should be put in writing, and every member of the team should have it, understand it, and agree to it.

Two Person Teams

This type of team often consists of players who play together without any attempt to disguise the fact that they are together. Since it is common for couples to play together, and not uncommon for any two friends, same sex or not, to sit together and play blackjack, a two-person team does not necessarily need to hide the fact that they know each other.

There are many viable approaches for maximizing the profit potential of a two-person team, and this type of team doesn't have to consist of two card counters. A single talented player can use discreet signals (verbal otherwise) to tell the other player how to play and bet. In the case of couples, this can usually be done quite openly, without the need for signals, as couples often help each other play their hands.

Couples can also use their partnership simply to increase the betting spread. When the casino isn't crowded, female companions may sit at the table without playing a hand, and it appears very natural (because it is; you see this all the time in casinos). It is also quite common for her to occasionally grab some of her guy's chips and play a hand or two. This can effectively double the betting spread of a single player without appearing to.

Two person teams that consist of two talented players can also utilize their counting abilities to enhance their profits beyond what either might be able to accomplish alone. For instance, advantageous rules such as over/under, which require non-traditional counting systems, can be more effectively attacked by a two-person team in which one counts traditionally, while the other keeps the over/under count. More advanced players might also try various shuffle-tracking or hole card strategies. (See Chapters 17 and 18.)

Two-person teams, because they are so often composed of close friends or actual couples, have a high rate of success. When two players are using a strategy where they are playing at the same table, they also eliminate worries about win/loss reporting, as they both witness the results.

BP/Spotter Teams

Larger teams often use a "spotter" approach to team play. A spotter is a low-stakes player, or even someone not playing who simply watches the games, and signals to big players (BPs), calling them over. Ken Uston wrote fairly extensively about this approach, crediting Al Francesco with having invented it in the early '70s.

Despite the fact that this method has been so widely publicized, it is still used successfully today. The only effective countermeasure to the BP approach is restricting mid-shoe entry. This is done in some casinos, especially in Atlantic City where they can't bar counters, but it is a countermeasure that costs the house dearly. The vast majority of players who want to enter mid-shoe are just regular unskilled players, and many high rollers like to change tables on a whim. Restricting mid-shoe entry eliminates a lot of action from the tables, so most casinos wisely reject this tactic.

BP/spotter teams generally work best when the floor is crowded, and lots of players are wandering around. Signals must be subtle natural gestures and easy to see; if a complex set of signals is required, you must practice the signs, and learn them cold before attempting to use this strategy in a casino.

I would advise any players considering a BP/spotter team approach to start small (with half a dozen players at most), and build the team gradually. BP/spotter approaches look great on paper, but can be quite confusing in a chaotic casino environment. When starting out, you must prearrange short sessions (not more than an hour), so that you can sit with your teammates to discuss problems, missed signals, or any aspect of the approach that seems not to be working. In your initial sessions, you may expect to devise many new signals for situations you didn't anticipate. You must maintain flexibility to work out these details.

Because of the success of Uston's books, the casinos are well aware of this team approach, and do look out for it. Big money players who jump in and out of one game after another should expect surveillance. This is one of the more difficult types of team operations to coordinate, because the combined talents of so many individuals are necessary for success. It's often great fun to participate in this type of team, however, as you get together with your teammates for discussions, practice sessions, and money transfers.

This team approach is one of the best ways to fool the counter-catcher software that tracks players. In order to evaluate a BP who makes a habit of jumping in and out of shoes for short periods of play, the software operator would have to watch videos of every shoe the BP entered, from the beginning of each deal, in order to know if the shoe was favorable when the guy jumped in. With so many tables, all being taped, this could be a real headache. But if the BP plays at very high stakes, and especially if he is winning, surveillance will take the time to go over the dozens of tapes necessary to determine if the he's just randomly choosing tables, or if he's being called in to shoes with high counts.

Some years ago, a BP on a team I was working with was backed off by the shift manager after two evenings of play at very high stakes. "We looked at the tapes from last night. You entered fifteen different tables, and on all but one table, there was a positive count," the boss said.

The BP asked the shift boss if he could see those tapes.

"We can't show you the tapes. Besides, we've made our decision. You won't be able to change the casino manager's mind."

"I'm not trying to change anyone's mind," the BP responded. "I just want to know what idiot called me into a shoe that didn't have a positive count!"

Tempers can flare when a team is losing, especially if any one player begins to distrust the talent or honesty of any of his teammates. A BP/spotter operation, more than any other type of team, requires strong leadership, rigorous testing methods, and meticulous bookkeeping. With a large operation, money transfers may be frequent. All wins/losses and cash/chip transactions must be recorded and updated. You must do this to avoid arguments about who had how much and who gave what to whom.

It is also important that all members of the team understand that they do not know each other in the casino. It is also unsafe to meet in the coffee shop or restaurants, or any public areas of the hotel/casino where you're playing, as pit or surveillance personnel are liable to see you together.

The Gorilla BP

A gorilla BP (another term from Uston's books) is a player who is not a card counter or at least is not paying any attention to the cards during the play, but who makes all betting and playing decisions according to signals from another player at the table. The gorilla BP is often drinking heavily so that his erratic big bets appear to be the result of Johnny Walker wisdom more than anything else.

The danger of using gorilla BPs is that they often really do get drunk, and they are probably carrying a large amount of team money. What do you do if your gorilla's ability to read and follow signals diminishes dangerously? I've heard stories of such players who not only failed to heed playing/betting signals, but failed to leave the tables when given the "quit now" signal.

Another problem that sometimes arises with loaded gorilla BPs, is that even if they can accurately follow signals they are sometimes very obnoxious, and casinos today are not as comfortable with obnoxious drunks as they used to be. If your BP is irritating other players, spilling his drink on the table or offending the cocktail waitresses, he may be asked to call it a night despite the fact that he is betting big money. Casinos are much more image conscious today.

The gorilla BP approach works best when you have a high roller who is not a card counter, and who already has a long history of big money play with a top rating in a casino. Such a player, especially if a known loser, can often get away with murder at the tables, and the pit will usually be happy to see him winning for a change.

I would suggest using this approach with a gorilla BP who can *act* drunk with a drink in his hand, but not necessarily one who *is* drunk. This approach should probably be avoided with a large team of spotters, as you will lose track of your gorilla, which can be scary if he's really drunk. He might also attract thieves and pickpockets, which is another worry. He is also unlikely to know anything about his actual play results, or how much he won or lost. Gorilla BP strategies work much better with actors than with alcoholics.

The Risk Remains

Some years ago, I was involved in a team in which I invested a relatively small amount, played a few hundred hours, and sometimes acted as a team manager. It was a small operation as teams go—in fact, we had set it up as a "test" team to iron out difficulties before putting together a major bank with more players.

It was a total disaster. On the very first night of play, with a dozen players, we were within $3,000 of hitting our target. Everyone was winning. We could almost taste the champagne.

The second night, we hit the negative flux, and it went downhill from there. In the first six months, with about 1,000 hours of play, we lost half our bank. There were all kinds of dumb decisions that contributed to this, many having to do with expenses.

We spent $5,000 transporting more than a dozen players to a "fantastic" promotion that never happened. We spent thousands sending one player to a "great" game in Europe, where in 10 days of play, he won $600. We found some juicy games in the Southwest, and we booked hundreds of hours at these games over a period of five weeks. Unfortunately, the comps were hard to come by. Everyone required airfare, rental cars, and hotel rooms. We won about $16,000, but had close to that amount in expenses. Then, three players lost $26,000 on a three-week trip to the Midwest, with expenses of $3,000 to $4,000 to boot. The riverboat casinos were not giving out the hotel and airfare comps. A couple players who were "sure" they'd be comped by a major Atlantic City casino had their comps rescinded when they were identified as pros. They managed to lose about $8,000, and had expenses of close to $2,000 due to coast-to-coast air travel, rental car, and hotel.

Some players who didn't really book that many hours simply had bad losses—$8,000, $10,000, $12,000. Some players won, but not nearly enough to make up for the losses and the ridiculous expenses.

Once we had a thousand hours in on the bank, and only half our money left, it became impossible to get players to continue to play for the team. The hours would have been worthless; non-investing players just couldn't expect to make a decent hourly rate digging out a bank that was so stuck.

So, we had to start making "augment" agreements with pros who would play partially on our bank, and partially on their own. Some pros are receptive to this type of arrangement in order to cut their personal risk, and over the next eight months, the bank slowly climbed back up. The problem with augmented play, however, was that we had originally lost the money dollar for dollar, but we were winning it back at the rate of 50¢ to 60¢ per dollar, depending on the augment. It was a long slow climb, and it was not easy to find players who wanted to augment. Most pros, if they are not connected with a team, have big enough bankrolls to play on their own, and little desire to share profits.

Then, after having come almost all the way back to flush, over a period of six weeks, half a dozen big losses drove the bank down again to about half its starting point. Our investors, most of whom were players themselves, were asking hard questions. We started administering lie detector tests—just what we needed, more expenses!

I was calling other teams that I knew for advice, big teams with years of experience. What were we doing wrong? I started hearing all kinds of horror stories—the bank that took more than two years to break, the banks that nose-dived beyond salvation and had to be abandoned as losses. "It's blackjack, Arnold," was the most common explanation.

If I looked at the history of this fiasco, and I subtracted our stupid expenses, and if I assumed that all the augmented wins counted at full value (as most of our losses were at full negative value), and if I removed the hours booked by spotters who never placed a bet, we were probably within one standard deviation of our expectation, a negative deviation, but nothing all that unusual. Some players were net winners, some were losers, but there was no single player who had booked enough hours for his personal result to be anything abnormal, statistically. But, there we sat, after eighteen months, with 2,000 hours of play, and half our original bank.

Teams are great fun when you're winning, but can be hell when you're losing. Blackjack is always blackjack. The risk is always there!

How the Successful Big Teams Do It

Large, successful blackjack teams usually put together very large banks—well into seven digits—so that the players, even when betting a couple thousand dollars per hand, are always wagering a very small fraction of the ideal Kelly bet. Whereas small teams often aim to double the initial bank, big teams set smaller targets. With a $1,000,000 bank, they might shoot for a $250,000 win before breaking the bank and distributing the win shares.

Both of these approaches—betting a small fraction of Kelly, and shooting for a smaller target—keep the biggest teams in business year after year. It pretty much assures them that they will not lose their whole bank, and the investors and players do not have to wait forever to take some profits.

Still, it's not always a walk in the park. Some years ago, I interviewed Tommy Hyland, who is probably the most successful team operator in blackjack history, and he said that even with fifty-plus players on some of his teams, the fluctuations were huge. On one bank, the players hit their target in a single weekend. Virtually every player on the team won more than could have been anticipated. On another bank, a few years later, so many players had negative results right from the start that it took the team almost two years to hit their target and take their profits.

When you hit a target quickly, the profits are enormous, since so few hours have been invested. The players are hugely overcompensated for their time and the investors are thrilled. If you can make 25% on your money in a weekend, that's not bad. But it's painful when it goes the other way, and the win target shrinks in the distance. The players, especially, feel that their hourly pay sucks. And it does! The investors wonder if they couldn't have done better with their money in some other venture.

According to Tommy, his team usually hits about three or four targets per year. So, on average, it took three to four months to make 25% on the money invested. This is why investors like to put money into these types of projects—it's not easy to make money like that consistently in stocks, real estate, commodities, or any other normal investment opportunities.

Unfortunately, smaller teams can usually expect more severe fluctuations than the big operations. Many small teams are forced to abandon banks when the flux gets too bad. With half a dozen players or less, it can be very difficult to get into the long run. Many small teams have played at or near full-Kelly, and often try to double their banks before distributing profits.

"Pro21," the Internet name of a high-stakes professional, told an amusing story in the Fall 2001 *Blackjack Forum* of a small team he was on many years ago. The team had a bank of $100,000 that would be distributed after they doubled it. Playing in Korea with his brother (also a teammate), they won $100,000 the first night of play! Because Pro21 had most of the hours on that bank, plus a small portion of the investment, his personal win share was almost $60,000, which he made in one night of high-stakes play!

Here's the good part: The investors immediately formed a new $100,000 bank, and over the next couple days in Korea, he and his brother—still playing for monster stakes—managed to lose the entire $100,000 bank!

Consider how well this worked out for Pro21...

In a weekend of play, he and his brother broke even at the tables. But Pro21 took a $60K paycheck after the first bank was hit, then lost back only a small percentage of it (his investment share) when the second bank died. Imagine being an investor in this team, and two players return from Korea with this story...

In fact, investors in blackjack teams, most of whom are or have been players themselves, understand that these weird things just happen. All you can do is find players you can trust, and forge ahead. Although investing in blackjack teams is often lucrative, there are definite pitfalls even when you know the players are honest and skilled. These dangers increase with the level of risk assumed by the bet-to-bank ratio: If the players are betting a small fraction of Kelly, it's probably impossible for a few players to lose the whole bank in a weekend, but with Kelly betting, that's happened to many teams.

Team Investment Deals

Again, you will avoid problems if you spell out all agreements on paper before the team gets off the ground. One team I was on had a player/investor who was removed from the playing team for acting indiscreetly—nothing purposeful, just a lack of experience and judgment. The player became very upset and demanded to have his investment money back, which contradicted the team handbook, although the specific situation had not been addressed. The team regulations stated that investors could not pull out their funds, that all investment capital would remain in the team bank until the target was hit, or the team disbanded. But what if a player, who is also an investor, is removed from the team?

We had a team meeting and voted to return his portion of the team bank to him, but because the team bank was in a negative position at this time he got back less than the full amount he had invested. He wanted his entire initial investment back, and when we argued that his investment had gone down in value, he responded that he had won money for the team (which was true), and if it hadn't been for his play results, the team would be in even worse financial shape. He felt that since he had personally won money, he should at least get his initial investment back, even if the team kept all of his winnings.

The final decision was to return to him only the percentage of the remaining team bank that represented his percentage of the initial investment. Despite the fact that he had personally won money, investment win shares were entirely separate from player win shares. The team agreed that when the target was hit, and the bank was ultimately broken and win shares distributed, he would be paid for his hours and personal win. But if he pulled out his investment funds early, his investment had lost money, and he would suffer the loss. He was given the option to leave his funds in the team bank, in which case he would receive his investment win share in the future, should the team ultimately hit its target. He pulled out.

Any time a team playing-bank is formed, it is very important that all of the funds for the bank be collected and deposited together, either in a separate bank account, a safe deposit box, or any secure private location controlled by a trusted team officer. The money that's not used by the team to play should be kept together until it's doled out to the players.

It is extremely dangerous to play on promissory funds. By this, I mean that it is a very bad idea to form a bank where one or more of the investors—whether player or outside investors—have agreed to invest some portion of the team bank, but will provide the actual funds only if and when needed. I have heard a number of stories of investors who made money on numerous teams without ever having to deliver any funds. One such investor told me that it was a good thing his cash was not needed on one of the teams he had invested in on paper, because he could not have actually supplied the money if it was called for!

On another team I played on, a major outside investor suddenly informed the players that his investment was now only half of what he had originally declared, as he had lost the rest of his investment in other ventures. This was very disheartening to the players, as the bank was in a negative position, and the loss would now have to be made up with substantially smaller bets. If you lose betting $1,000 a hand, it's hard to make up for it by betting $250. It's even harder to take up the challenge when you and your team were not the ones responsible for the downsizing of the bank.

This situation could have been avoided if the initial investment had been collected from the investor, and isolated for team use. The investor's argument against delivering all of these funds to the team from the get-go, obviously, is that the team will be "tying up" a large amount of money that can be used profitably elsewhere until needed by the team. Unfortunately, as in the above case, "elsewhere" can be dangerous. And when elsewhere eats up a large portion of the team funds, there's not much the players can do but bitch and moan. If the money is gone, the money is gone, and everything changes.

Limited Joint-Bank Partnerships

One of the most common and successful team formats is the limited partnership. For example, two pro players decide to take a trip together in order to check out games in another state or country. Both are experienced solo players who know each other well, and they play more or less at the same level. So, for this trip, which might be as long as a week or as short as a weekend, they agree to share the win/loss result equally, based on playing the same number of hours. This type of arrangement often works out quite well.

A similar type of agreement is often made by pros who want to attack some limited casino promotion opportunity. For instance, a casino will offer blackjack pays 2 to 1 for a weekend. Two (or more) players may agree to combine their bankrolls and results for this one-shot deal.

Because these types of partnerships are so easy to make, with agreements so simple that paperwork is not even necessary, it is extremely important that you do not relax your standards on trust. This is not the type of partnership you should enter into with a new acquaintance. There are rip-off artists who specialize in bilking money from neophyte gamblers. Which brings us to the subject of...

Polygraph Testing

No matter how big a team might be, the question of polygraph testing will almost always come up, and always because of inexplicable losses. And frankly, I have never heard of a team that did not at some point suffer inexplicable losses. The larger the team, the more likely you will feel the need to use lie detectors at some point. I am not in favor of lie detector testing, and I will explain why. But consider this scenario:

You've got a team with 15 players, some of whom are investors as well, some of whom have no investment but are simply playing for a share of the win based on their results. You also have a few outside investors and a fairly substantial bankroll. As the team approaches 1,000 hours of play, the bottom line is still written in red ink. The outside investors are getting antsy. Based on the expected value (EV) of the total hours of play, this negative result is close to two standard deviations on the left side of the curve. Is this just bad flux, or is something seriously wrong?

Skill testing shows that all of the players are capable of beating the games. Yet, 11 of the 15 players are in the negative. When you isolate any individual player's results, including those with the biggest losses, you see nothing unusual. Every player's result is within one standard deviation of his expectation. Furthermore, these are players you know personally, many of whom have known each other for years, and all are trusted in the community of pro players. What do you do?

This is where many teams turn to lie detector tests. Some teams, in fact, specify in their team handbooks that any player may be polygraph-tested at any time, that this testing may be ordered based on a player's results, or simply at random. If you ever play on teams, large or small, this is a subject you should know about. I guarantee that if you work with many teams, it will come up.

One team that I was involved with had a situation similar to the above. We had no reference to polygraph testing in our team handbook, so the team managers—I was one of three—made a decision to begin testing on selected players.

Many private investigators offer polygraph-testing services; you can find them listed in the yellow pages. As most of our players lived and operated in the Las Vegas area, we were able to get references for investigators who had experience testing professional gamblers in these types of situations. Depending on the service, a single polygraph test will cost from $300 to $500. We decided to test a small number of players who had logged a substantial number of hours with the team, and who were among the most active guys. We also decided that since the team managers were also players, at least one of the managers should be tested. Since our team handbook did not specify any requirement for polygraph testing, we felt that if one of the managers was also tested, the players would not feel personally "accused" of dishonesty, but would see that this really was just a safeguard, and that we were trying to satisfy the investors by showing that we were doing everything possible to find the root of our problems and get back on track. As the team manager who had logged the most playing hours, I volunteered to be tested first, before any of the other players.

Before testing, the investigator must know precisely what questions need to be answered. The five questions we came up with included:

1. Have you accurately reported all wins/losses to the team managers?

2. Have you accurately reported all money transfers to and from other team members?

3. Have you accurately reported all expenses?

4. Have you ever used team funds for any non-team-related purpose without authorization from the team managers?

5. Have you ever used alcohol or drugs immediately prior to or during a team playing session?

If any of these questions got a "yes" response, then that guy would be asked to provide details.

I found the polygraph test to be a truly miserable experience. It mattered not that I knew I was innocent, or that I'd volunteered because I really wanted to see what it was like; the thought that a needle on a graph might go haywire when I was asked a question about my honesty was nerve-wracking. It is almost impossible to remain calm and composed during this ordeal. With my chest constricted by a belt that was tightened around it to measure changes in my breathing, with skin sensors taped to my arms to record any sudden perspiration, and another to record my pulse, I sat there extremely nervous, in a cold sweat, terrified that I would end up taking the blame for something I didn't do.

The whole thing was over in about twenty minutes. I answered all the questions and went home, certain that I'd failed. A day or two later, the other team managers called me to tell me I'd passed with flying colors, so that we could now go on to testing some of the other players. Since I had gone through it myself, I was chosen to inform the selected players who were next in line. I felt like I was sending sheep to the slaughter. "It's miserable. It's nerve-wracking. It's not fun. Just go in and answer the questions. We're not accusing you. I had to do it myself. It's your turn, that's all."

The written reports from the investigator on all of the polygraph tests performed on our players showed only two instances of "yes" responses to the five important questions. One player stated that in the last fifteen minutes of a playing session, he would often order a beer at the table and drink it, but would leave before even this small amount of alcohol could have entered his system. We felt that this was not a violation of our no-alcohol policy, and told the player he could continue doing this. It looked good for a player to be drinking at the tables.

Another player stated that he had used $200 of team funds to "buy a hooker," but that he had reported this to one of the team managers who was with him on the trip when the liaison had taken place, and that he would reimburse the team if requested. (The request was made!) The manager acknowledged that he recalled this incident from a few months back, but that he'd forgotten about it.

"You authorized him to use team money for a hooker?" I asked.

"Hey, we were a thousand miles from home. He didn't have any money with him and he was horny. I expected he'd pay it back, but I forgot about it. The thing is, he did tell me about it at the time. We were way up on that trip, so it's not like we needed that money in the bank at that time."

The important thing was that we found no evidence of dishonesty in the polygraph tests. All we could say to the concerned investors was that we were diligently trying to get out of the red ink and into the black. Two standard deviations from the expectation has about a 5% chance of occurring to any team, and it appeared we just happened to be that one team out of twenty.

My interest in lie detector tests was piqued, however. There was something so bizarre about the experience I'd had, it was hard to believe that this weird contraption could actually discern whether or not I was telling the truth. As it turned out, my feelings about the polygraph were not without merit. Probably the best book on the subject (or the best one I found) is *The Lie Behind the Lie Detector,* by George W. Maschke and Gino J. Scalabrini. (Look for it on the Internet. I found it there a few years ago.) This is a well-documented study, full of references to official government reports, many from the FBI and CIA files, on the inaccuracy and general invalidity of polygraph tests.

This book not only describes dozens of tests, court cases, and investigations where polygraph testing proved to be dead wrong, but there is a detailed explanation of how anyone can beat the machine. What it comes down to is the fact that actual con artists—professional liars— cannot be detected by the polygraph. Innocent people, however, are in great danger of showing false positives. The main value of the polygraph is as a psychological tool to get guilty parties to confess. Criminals who do not understand the limitations of polygraph testing will often break down and confess to crimes while being tested, thinking that the machine will betray them anyway, often wanting to clear themselves of other crimes they are being accused of. Attempting to expose embezzlers and drug abusers, the tests are often used by police agencies, private investigators, and employers. The machine itself, however, is more science fiction than science.

I suppose that we did get information about the hooker incident, and got the team reimbursed for $200 of non-team expense, which is what lie detectors are actually good for. But what if we had a true con artist on the team who had been stealing money by claiming losses that never occurred? Unless he confessed during testing, we'd never know it. In fact, wouldn't real crooks tend to be the ones who would seek out information on how to beat lie detector tests?

I think professional gamblers are one of the smartest classes of people in this society. They are well-read, Internet savvy, and they know how to find information on esoteric subjects that would often be of interest mainly to criminals such as fake ID, disguises, aliases, how to travel with large sums of cash, hiding money, and more. During the 23 years that I published *Blackjack Forum* magazine, I sold many of these types of books to card counters. Some of the same publishers and distributors who carry these "underground" books (Eden Press, Paladin Press, and Loompanics, to name three) also carry titles on beating polygraph tests.

So, my advice to teams that are considering using a polygraph to ensure the honesty of team members: Don't waste your resources on this nonsense. If you don't trust someone to handle your money, he should not be on the team. If you're the type of person who trusts no one, then you should neither play on, nor invest in, a team.

Some General Team Guidelines

If you are presently involved with a team, or are considering joining one to smooth out the flux and benefit from the increased profit opportunities that come with playing on a larger bank, here are my suggestions for everyone new to this type of play.

1. Never try to form a large team from scratch. Start small, with close, trusted friends, and let the team grow naturally as you enjoy success. The legendary Hyland team started this way, and so did the "Greeks," another great, successful big team.

2. If you are going to use a BP/spotter, gorilla BP, or any other type of attack that includes multiple players in the same casino, work out all signals and playing methods before hitting the tables with any substantial bets. It is a very good idea to work out these plays at low stakes in an actual casino. For instance, if you plan to hit Caesars Palace with your BP laying down $500 bets, run some scrimmages at a smaller casino in town with your BP placing $10 bets. The purpose of this scrimmage is not to win money, but to make sure that all participants are getting the signals right, and that the operation runs smoothly. If there are problems, work them out with small bets before you go for the jugular in a major joint.

3. Put everything down on paper, and make sure every team member has a copy of the rules, but remember that you will probably still encounter problems and areas of disagreement that aren't covered. If the team is already operating when a disagreement arises, settle these matters before continuing play, and get the agreement down on paper, with a copy to all involved.

4. Accept the fact that most teams, like most small businesses, fail. If you are not the type of person who could run a small business successfully—if you are not a natural manager, very organized, good at making fast decisions when necessary, comfortable dealing with different personality types—then you should not attempt to run a blackjack team. A blackjack team is a business, and unless you have a capable business manager team play is probably not for you.

Many successful card counters do not, and never have played on teams. There may be `comfort in numbers, but there is also a comfort in knowing exactly where your money is and how it's being invested at the tables. If you trust your own skill and your own judgment, then play on your own. You will weather a lot of fluctuation, but at least you'll know where the money went when you go into a downswing. When you hit the upswing, you don't have to give 50% to the investors, and divvy up the rest with anyone else. It's yours.

18

SHUFFLE TRACKING

The concept itself is so simple you'd think it would be obvious to anyone. Years ago, when shoe-game shuffles were fast and simple, I suspect numerous card counters independently discovered the easiest form of shuffle tracking for the solo player—**slug location**.

You're sitting in a shoe game, watching the count climb, and just when it reaches what must be an all-time high the shuffle card emerges. As your spirits sink, you stare at the undealt deck—the cutoffs—that must contain nearly every paint (picture cards) and Ace in the shoe. For some reason, you continue to stare at that glorious slug of high cards, even as the dealer slaps it on top of the discards to begin his shuffle routine.

To your joy and amazement, when the dealer finishes shuffling and hands you the cut card, you're still staring at that slug! True, it's somewhat dispersed, but most of it's right there in the bottom third of the six-deck stack of cards in front of you. You cut this segment to the top of the pack and the cards soon verify exactly what your eyes had seen. For the next two decks, tens and aces just pour out of that shoe. From the very first round of play, the count enters the nether regions, but you just keep betting big, knowing there's more to come.

For blackjack players, this is how **shuffle tracking** was born. It was a purely visual discovery; it had nothing to do with voodoo, guesswork, or advanced mathematics. It was simply a logical extension of card counting.

Shuffle tracking, however, has numerous advantages over traditional card counting:

1. You don't seem to be betting with the count, and in fact, you'll often be able to bet big off the top.

2. It will often look like you're misplaying your hands. If you know you're in a slug of high or low cards, you'll play accordingly, making plays in shoe games that a counter would normally only make in one-deckers. When you stand on your hard 15 against a dealer ten, right off the top of the shoe, when the table is painted in tens—or better yet, when you take insurance on your twenty at the same stage of the game, the counter-catchers will label you a typical idiot.

3. This seemingly unintelligent betting and playing pattern also lets you use a larger betting spread without drawing suspicion.

4. Unlike traditional card counting, shuffle tracking is immediately obvious to you when you are doing it correctly—the results are right before your eyes. With normal card counting, if the count goes up, you raise your bet. But on the next round, and the one after that, and the one after that, the big cards don't necessarily come out. They might actually be located somewhere later in the deck—maybe even behind the cut card. With shuffle tracking, when you put your big bets on the table, the big cards come out. They always come out! They have to come out because you know where they are!

Shuffle tracking does not assure you of winning. You can still put your big bets on the table and be dealt consecutive stiffs while everyone else at the table, including the dealer, is getting blackjacks and twenties. But you will see those high cards when you expect to, or you are doing something wrong.

Most importantly, some of the games that are most attractive to shuffle trackers happen to be the ones that are least attractive to card counters. The more decks in play, the more difficult it is to randomly disperse all of the cards. Also, deep penetration is extremely important for card counters, but it is not as critical a factor for shuffle trackers. In fact, many games with poor penetration, which any smart counter would avoid, can be good profit opportunities for shuffle trackers. With tracking, you identify physical areas of a shoe where you want to play, and you either attempt to cut these areas to the top—so that you can place big bets right off the top of the shoe—or, if another player cuts, you simply bet whenever the dealer gets to the portion of the shoe where the high cards are located. Once you've played through this segment, you will have taken most of the gain you are going to get from that shoe. Because of this, some trackers prefer shallow penetration.

However, multiple-deck shuffles today are complex compared to the shuffles of ten years ago, and if you're struggling just to keep the running count, don't even dream about shuffle tracking. Shuffle tracking is an advanced card-counting strategy, and as such, it is more difficult than traditional counting. If you can't estimate deck segments in a discard tray just by looking at it, you will not be able to track segments.

Ten years ago, I published the first fairly comprehensive explanation of shuffle tracking ever to appear in print as a three-part Shuffle Tracking Series in *Blackjack Forum* magazine. (An edited version of this series, consisting primarily of Parts I and II, was published in the 1998 edition of *Blackbelt in Blackjack*.)

Back in the mid-1990s, I was much more of the opinion that any competent card counter could learn to track shuffles, provided he practiced. Today, I know that's not true. Based on my experience with training players to track shuffles, it is my belief that most people do not have the visual acuity necessary to pull it off. I also believe that most of those who have learned to track shuffles successfully have combined a sharper-than-average eye with obsessive practice, far beyond that required to be a successful card counter.

In 2003, I published a book on shuffle tracking that went far beyond the material I published back in the '90s, called *The Blackjack Shuffle Tracker's Cookbook*. If you are interested in obtaining this report, see the information pages in the back of this book. As I do not believe most players can learn to track shuffles, you can save yourself a lot of time and effort by first testing yourself to see if you've got what it takes.

I do believe that any competent card counter who either has or is able to develop the visual acuity to pass three fairly straightforward tests described in the *Cookbook* can learn to track shuffles successfully. I will provide the tests here so that you can save your time and money if you find that your eyes just aren't sharp enough. Do realize that *no one* that I've ever met can pass these tests right from the start. Dedicated players who drill themselves on these tests relentlessly do get better with time, so don't be discouraged if your first efforts fail.

Visual acuity is not based on your intelligence, nor is it a function of memory. You do not need particularly sharp eyesight to be a talented card counter, but you do need this innate talent to be a successful shuffle tracker.

For example, a card counter using a balanced count, such as the Hi-Lo or the Zen Count, needs to be able to estimate the number of remaining decks in order to adjust his running count to his true count (or true edge). This is generally done by estimating the number of decks already in the discard tray in order to figure out the number of decks still in the shoe. Regardless of the count system you use, if in a 6-deck game you estimate that 3 1/2 decks are in the discard tray, so that 2 1/2 decks must remain in the shoe, it will make very little difference to your true count estimate if 3 3/4 decks are in the discard tray, leaving 2 1/4 decks in the shoe. In fact, most card counters round off to the nearest 1/2-deck when making true-count adjustments anyway, and extensive computer simulations have shown that this rounding off makes very little difference.

If a shuffle tracker, on the other hand, regularly makes 1/4-deck errors he's unlikely to be playing with any advantage at all. Card counting is very crude compared to shuffle tracking, and crude "ballpark" estimates are not serious errors for card counters. But if you want to track shuffles, you must be far more precise.

A talented card counter who thinks he can track shuffles just because he can count cards is like a little league pitcher who thinks that because he can see the strike zone, he can throw strikes. For most counters, as for most little league pitchers, there is a rude awakening once the game starts. Neither the shuffle tracker, nor the pitcher, however, will ever know if he can be successful unless he practices, drills, and practices some more. If you've got the talent, it will surface. If not...hey, try bowling.

I have known many highly skilled counters, including professionals, who acknowledge that they simply can't track shuffles, despite a thorough understanding of the mathematics and principles involved. Many have given it up because, "When I try to cut to the high-card slug, the high cards often just aren't there." So, before you waste six months studying charts and theory, let's find out if you even have a chance at succeeding as a tracker.

When I initially published the Shuffle Tracking Series ten years ago, I really did believe that shuffle machines might take over. As it turned out, some casinos use shuffle machines, primarily as a time-saving device, but Vegas (and Nevada in general) remains a shuffle tracker's paradise, and most other states that offer blackjack also continue to offer hand-shuffled games. What the casinos learned from my Shuffle Tracking Series was that it doesn't matter that their shuffles are not impenetrable—most advantage players simply can't track shuffles. Many can count cards, but virtually none of them can track shuffles for beans. Most of the big teams tried it for a while…and quit. Most casino game protection personnel are not even looking for shuffle trackers today. Many believe the skill itself to be more mythical than real—and they're not that far off.

The Necessary Tools

Let's begin with the equipment you need to begin. If getting all of this stuff sounds like too much of a chore, give it up now. Shuffle tracking is an advanced skill and you'll never learn to do it by thinking about it, reading about it, or dreaming about it. It takes work.

Here's what you need to start:

-12 decks of casino playing cards (16 if you play in 8-deckers)
-One dealing shoe
-One discard tray
-A couple of plastic cut cards (you can substitute the jokers for these)
-Wide felt-tip permanent markers in at least 2 different colors
-Notebook for record keeping

Other useful items:

-Casino (or poker) chips in various colors
-Dealer's chip tray (float)
-Regulation blackjack layout
-Cocktail waitress (hey, for distraction!)

Here are some exercises developed by Radar O'Reilly (*Blackjack Forum's* Atlantic City reporter), one of the most talented trackers I know:

Exercise #1: Cutting a Standing Stack

In all of my examples, I will use six decks of cards. If you typically play in eight-deck games, then you should adjust these exercises to suit the extra decks. If you go back and forth between six and eight decks you must practice and drill for both.

After removing the jokers, thoroughly shuffle the six decks together. You must do this because you will likely be able to see "lines" between the individual decks if you just stack them out of the boxes one atop the next. Thoroughly shuffle the decks, and then stack them into the discard tray face up. The order of the cards is of no importance.

Now, using a felt-tip permanent marker, number the faces of the cards from 1 to 312, turning them face down onto the table as you number them. When finished, you should have a facedown stack of all six decks, with the top card numbered 312 on the face, and the bottom card numbered 1. Set this stack into the discard tray face down.

Now try to slide the plastic cut card into the stack exactly two decks up from the bottom. If you do this correctly, the card below the cut card should have the number 104 written on the face, and the card above should be number 105. Try it! How closely can you cut to *exactly* two decks up from the bottom?

Now try two decks down from the top. If you are successful, the card above your cut card should be number 209.

The chart on the following page shows the number of the card *above* the cut card when cutting to various deck segments in 1/4-deck increments.

Using your notebook, drill yourself on 25 cuts in various full-deck segments. Record the card number you should have had above your cut card, and the number you actually had. In a separate column, record how much you were off on each cut, and whether you missed above or below. Now try 25 cuts in various 1/2-deck segments, again recording your results, and how far off you were on each cut. Then, do the same thing for various 1/4-deck segments.

How accurate were you?

The purpose of this drill is to calibrate your eye. If you see a pattern of errors—for instance, you are typically 6-8 cards too high or too low—you may incorporate this knowledge into your estimates. By recording your results in columns, you should see that as you continue with the practice, your eye will hone in on the target.

6-Deck Card Numbers

Down From Top	Up From Bottom	Number*
1/4-deck	5 3/4-decks	300
1/2-deck	5 1/2-decks	287
3/4-deck	5 1/4-decks	274
1 deck	5 decks	261
1 1/4-decks	4 3/4-decks	248
1 1/2-decks	4 1/2-decks	235
1 3/4-decks	4 1/4-decks	222
2 decks	4 decks	209
2 1/4-decks	3 3/4-decks	196
2 1/2-decks	3 1/2-decks	183
2 3/4-decks	3 1/4-decks	170
3 decks	3 decks	157
3 1/4-decks	2 3/4-decks	144
3 1/2-decks	2 1/2-decks	131
3 3/4-decks	2 1/4-decks	118
4 decks	2 decks	105
4 1/4-decks	1 3/4-decks	92
4 1/2-decks	1 1/2-decks	79
4 3/4-decks	1 1/4-deck	66
5 decks	1 deck	53
5 1/4-decks	3/4-deck	40
5 1/2-decks	1/2-deck	27
5 3/4-decks	1/4-deck	14
6 decks	0 decks	-

* card above cut card

How accurate do you have to be? A good slug tracker should be able to cut consistently to within 3 cards of his target except for the bottom deck, where you should be able to cut to within *1 card* of your target. If you aim for two decks up from the bottom, your cuts should consistently show you cards above the cut numbered between 102 and 108. Many amateur trackers believe that if they can cut to within half a dozen cards of their target, or even within a quarter-deck (13 cards), they will be successful at the tables, since many ultimate betting segments are as big as one, or even two full decks. The problem is that during the course of both the deal and the shuffle, you must often estimate the slug size, discard height, location in stack, break points, grab sizes, et cetera. If you are off by half a dozen cards several times in a row during a deal and shuffle, you may easily have cut your slug completely out of play by the time you're ready to start banging out the money.

At first, unless your visual acuity is better than normal, you will likely make quite a few cuts that stray farther from the mark than you would like. If you are way off, that does not mean that you have no natural talent for this. You may find that your accuracy increases dramatically with practice.

Start by trying to cut the six decks in half. Just aim at that 3-deck midway point. Next try to cut the shoe in thirds. Aim for 2 decks up from the bottom, and 2 decks down from the top. Don't go on trying to aim for half or quarter decks until you can accurately hit all of the full-deck marks. Then drill yourself on the halves, then the quarters. Once you regularly hit your marks within 3 cards, start inserting the cut card at random into the stack, and see if you can estimate the exact card to which you have cut. To track shuffles profitably in casinos, you must consistently be accurate in your estimates within the bottom 2 1/2 decks and the top 1 1/4 decks in the stack.

Do these drills daily, and record all of your results. Keep practicing, even if you don't seem to be making any improvement. It is very tedious work, but it is necessary if you are going to shuffle track in casinos. If you never manage to develop this skill, then hang it up when you finally get sick of trying. You're not cut out to be a tracker; don't waste your money pretending to be one in the casinos.

If you do find that you can nail these deck segments consistently, that's just the start of training your eye. Next, you have to find out if you've got the depth perception to cut with precision, casino-style.

Exericise #2: Cutting a Lying Stack

In the casino, you are *never* offered the cut on a stack of cards standing in the discard tray. Sorry! Generally, after the shuffle, the six (or eight) decks will be tipped over onto their side by the dealer, usually with the facedown top card aimed at you. You must make the cut from a sitting position, looking down the length of that stack.

All of those drills that we described above for cutting a standing stack…you must now go through all of them again to cut precisely when that stack is tipped over onto the table and pointed at you. Most people discover that it is way more difficult to cut a lying stack with precision than it is to cut a standing stack. Unfortunately, you're unlikely to find a dealer who will stand the cards up for you to cut!

So, what can you do?

Practice. Keep your notebook. Record your results.

If you can't cut accurately to your target (again, within three cards) in your home practice, you will *never* be able to cut accurately enough in a casino to make money as a tracker. At home, everything is in your favor. They're your cards, your table, and you don't lose hundreds (or thousands) of dollars if you miss. In the casino, the angles will be different, the table height will vary, you have only a few seconds to make your move, and bang, your money is on the line.

So, you have to practice with a partner, someone willing to tip over the stack, aim it at you, and offer the cut card. You want another person for this drill because you want to mimic casino conditions as closely as possible. You don't want the stack to always be tipped over in the same spot on the table, the same distance from you, and aimed at the same angle. That's not realistic.

If you can't consistently cut a lying stack accurately, and you don't have a friend or partner who can take the cutting chores off your hands, hang it up. It does not matter how well you know tracking theory, how deep your understanding of the math, or how perfectly you can follow a high-card slug through the shuffle; if you can't nail the cut when the time comes, you shouldn't be putting your money on the table.

Now, let's say you can nail the cuts, both standing and lying, with consistent precision. Are you ready to make money?

Ha!

Life should be so easy!

No, now you must learn to nail the cuts on that lying stack with a fast, natural, and casual motion. A tracker can never be too good at precision cutting; professional trackers often spend up to an hour every day just working on eye calibration and cutting drills. A serious tracker will always travel with cards, and will calibrate his eye before playing sessions. Just because your eye is perfect today does not mean that it will be perfect tomorrow. You must refocus before you get to the table. What you really want to be able to do in a live game is take the cut card and very casually just slice it into the lying stack—like any tourist at the table might do—and hit your target dead-on every time.

When it comes down to casino play, you should use these drills before every trip to keep your eye sharp. Just as there are rare days when Randy Johnson can't find the strike zone, you will find that you will have off days when your eye is just not there. You must know your own abilities and limitations. If you can't nail a cut with a fast and easy slice on some days, then slow down and see if you can get it with more careful attention.

Shuffle tracking for profit is about knowing where the high cards are—not guessing, not estimating, not ballparking—then using your cut to put those high cards where you want them, often (though not always) at the top of the shoe.

Exercise #3: Estimating the Discard Stack

It is one thing to be able to cut a 6-deck shoe precisely in half, but quite another to be able to estimate when *exactly* three decks are sitting in the discard tray. Your numbered stack is a great tool for drilling yourself on estimating the discards. This is another drill that works best if you have a partner to help you.

Starting with an empty discard tray, your partner (playing the role of the dealer) places small bunches of cards face down into the discard tray. (As in the prior drills, the card numbered 1 will be on the bottom.) At various points, your partner asks you how many cards are in the tray. Your partner always knows the exact number, since the numbered side of the tipped-over stack is facing him. When you first start this exercise, you should answer in quarter-decks, estimating to the nearest increment if you believe the number of cards to be something other than an exact quarter-deck grouping. As you progress, however, and as you become familiar with the precise numbers of cards that mark the various quarter-deck increments, you should answer with the exact number of cards, to within three cards. The first two decks into the discard tray, you should be within two cards; with the first deck, you should be within one.

You may find that your skill at nailing a cut exactly 3 1/2 decks up in a standing 6-deck stack is remarkable, but that when estimating exactly when 3 1/2 decks have been placed into the tray, you are remarkably inaccurate.

Work on it!

If you think 3 1/4 decks standing in the tray looks like 3 3/4 decks, your phenomenal skill at nailing the 3 3/4-deck cut in a lying stack is useless. You won't be able to accurately assess the location of slugs prior to the shuffle, and you'll be cutting in the wrong place!

Here's how another drill goes:

Partner: Tell me to stop when there are exactly 2 1/4 decks in the tray. Partner starts placing cards in tray a few at a time. After a while…
You: Stop.
Partner: Would you say that's over, under, or exactly 2 1/4 decks?
You: Over, maybe three cards more.
Partner: There are 127 cards in the tray. That's nine cards more. But it is more than 2 1/4, and less than 2 1/2.
You: Not good enough. I'm going to have to keep my day job for now.

I cannot emphasize too strongly how important these drills and self-tests are to your success. I cannot tell you how many card counters in the past ten years have told me that they have abandoned shuffle tracking because they lost money at it. When I asked them questions about how accurate they were at cutting and estimating slugs, they did not even know the answer. *They had never tested themselves at these skills!*

This would be like a card counter learning the values assigned by a count system but never practicing counting down a deck; just going into a casino and figuring he'll be "close enough" during a live game.

Information about shuffle tracking does not automatically impart the skill necessary to make money in casinos from applying what you know.

But once you're able to cut a standing stack, cut a lying stack, and estimate a discard stack, then you have what it takes to succeed at shuffle tracking. There is one other skill you must master—but it's comparatively easy.

Exericise #4: Card Counting

Yes, you must know how to count cards in order to track shuffles. In fact, you must be such a good card counter that the counting itself is second nature to you. As required by most pro teams, you should be able to count down a deck accurately in 20 seconds or less, ten times in succession, with zero errors. The best counters can often approach the 15-second mark. A famous Uston teammate, D.P., could do it in 8. And if you make a mistake, then keep at it until errors are a thing of the past.

Once you're a good card counter, you must also know your strategy indices—all of them. There are 166 indices for the Hi-Lo Lite, and as a shuffle tracker, *you will use each and every one.* Trackers typically see very high and very low counts, and it will be to your advantage to use every strategy change at your disposal.

You should test yourself by filling in a blank strategy chart daily, with every index number, until you make no errors and can fill in the chart quickly. It is important that you do not neglect your counting skills while you are working on your tracking.

Describing Shuffles

Different types of shuffles require different tracking techniques. Dealer selection is very important for many tracking methods and is critical for success with any of the advanced techniques. Your own gifts play the biggest part in which games you choose to track and how you go about tracking them.

Almost all of the countermeasures the casinos have instigated against shuffle tracking have hidden advantages for those who know how to exploit them. Since there are almost as many house shuffle routines as there are casinos, and since these routines change all the time, and since individual dealers have their own quirks and habits that have to be factored in as well, you must become an expert at adjusting to these conditions and quirks.

There isn't any simple tracking technique that works best for most players in most games. You cannot track shuffles unless you open your eyes, observe, and think. You have to identify the weak points in a shuffle, and you must start by being able to verbally describe any casino shuffle.

Here's a quick and dirty primer on the language of shuffle tracking:

Terminology

In describing shuffles and shuffle actions, it is necessary to use a consistent terminology. Because many shuffle trackers use independently devised methods, there is no common terminology. What a casino manager might call a **dilution shuffle**, one tracker calls a **stutter shuffle**, another calls a **stepladder**, and a third calls a **staggered riffle**. The word **zone** also means various things to various trackers. I'm going to create a simple terminology for shuffle tracking so we have a common language to simply describe the many complex actions.

You should always begin describing a shuffle, as you would any blackjack game, with the number of decks and average penetration (shuffle point). From the segment tracker's perspective, this information tells you the approximate size of the discards and the cutoffs. A **segment tracker** views a six-deck game with 75% penetration as 4 1/2 decks of discards and 1 1/2 decks of cutoffs.

Riffling is the common dealer action of interleaving two **grabs**. A grab, as might be assumed, is that portion of cards that a dealer picks up in one hand. Grabs are also called **picks**, but for the sake of consistency, I'll stick with grab. A riffle is also sometimes called a **riff**.

A riffle of half-deck grabs will produce a one-deck stack. An initial stack of all the cards in the shoe will always be broken into **piles** prior to shuffling. Traditionally, shoe shuffles were always performed from two piles, but today many casinos break the initial stack into four or more. Dealers take their grabs from these piles in order to restack their shuffled cards.

There are two basic types of multi-deck shuffle routines: the *riffle-and-restack* and the *stepladder*.

A **riffle-and-restack (R&R)** action means that the dealer will build a **final stack** by placing his riffled grabs one on top of another. In the traditional R&R routine, once two grabs have been shuffled together, or **married**, they are not re-riffled with any other grab.

A stepladder action begins like a normal R&R action. The dealer riffles grabs from pile A and pile B to begin building a separate final stack. But instead of just placing consecutively riffled grabs from A and B (which have been married) on top of one another, as in the traditional R&R, the dealer starts taking one of his grabs from the final stack he is building, and marrying it with grabs from alternating piles.

Every casino uses either an R&R or a stepladder, or a *combo,* which is, of course, a combination of an R&R and a stepladder.

A **one-pass** stepladder describes a shuffle that is completed when the piles are gone and the final stack is offered for a player to cut. A **two-pass** stepladder is a shuffle where the final stack is rebroken into piles for a second stepladder action. Stepladders are time-consuming, so **multi-pass stepladders** are relatively rare. Multi-pass R&Rs are more common. More common still is a **two-pass combo** which consists of a stepladder followed by an R&R.

All R&Rs and stepladders can be performed from two or more piles. You might find a 4-pile stepladder comboed with a 2-pile R&R. Most shuffles that have more than two piles utilize a **criss-cross** pattern of grabs. A fairly standard criss-cross shuffle uses 4 piles in a square, with the alternating grabs drawing an x-pattern, hence the name. I will use the term criss-cross, however, to define any shuffle in which there are more than two piles, and in which the cards from one pile will be mixed with cards from more than one other pile.

A **segment** is any visually identifiable portion of a stack or pile. For example, you might refer to the bottom 1-deck segment of the discards. A **slug** is another word for a segment, though slug usually refers to a segment that has been identified as containing a large portion of high cards, low cards, or aces. For instance, if during a single round of play you notice 5 aces come out, that portion of the discards where these aces are located is an **ace slug**.

In defining a shuffle, it's always important to note where the **cutoffs** (undealt cards taken from the shoe after the shuffle-card comes out) are placed in the **discards** (the cards that have already been played and deposited in the discard tray). The cutoffs may be *topped, bottomed,* or *plugged.* **Topping the cutoffs** is placing them on top of the discards; **bottoming the cutoffs** is placing them beneath the discards, and **plugging the cutoffs** is inserting them into the middle of the discards. **Multiple plugging** is breaking the cutoffs into two or more pieces, and inserting these pieces into different locations within the discards.

Some casinos also rearrange the discard stack itself by plugging. That is, grabs from the top or bottom of the discard stack may be plugged into the middle of the discards, usually in addition to cutoff plugging.

Stripping is a shuffling action performed by the dealer in which he reverses the sequence of a grab of cards. Usually, he holds the grab in one hand while pulling cards from the top of the grab (sometimes alternating with cards from the top and bottom) and dropping them onto the table. Stripping (especially *thin-stripping*) is time-consuming, so it's common in hand-held games but uncommon in shoe games. A **thin-strip** is a stripping action where cards are stripped one card at a time. (In some casinos the dealer will strip a few cards at a time.) A *thick-strip* is a stripping action that pulls greater amounts of cards off the top at one time.

Boxing a deck is a cutting action performed by the dealer, usually between riffles. This is generally a lopsided cut, with one thin segment (1/4 to 1/3 deck) and one thick segment. Many casinos that use the boxing action also have the dealer spin one portion of the grab 180°. For this reason, some trackers refer to boxing the deck as **spinning it**. **Cutting** is what a player does at the end of the dealer's shuffle routine.

There are a number of other less common shuffle actions (which are described in the *Cookbook*), but this should cover about 90% of the shuffles you'll find in real-world casinos. A good tracker can watch a house shuffle one time and describe it in detail, while the average person can't.

And it has nothing to do with intelligence or memory; it has to do with his facility with the terminology. He has a language for describing what he sees. If I ask the typical card counter to describe how a dealer in Casino X shuffles the six decks he's been playing for hours (or days, or weeks, or months!), he usually isn't able to. Nor could he reproduce it if given six decks to shuffle. A shuffle tracker who walks into the same casino looking for a game, even if he's never been in that casino before, can watch the shuffle one time and say, "It's a 75% double-plugged, two-pile, stepladder/ R&R combo with bottoms lead and half-deck grabs." And another shuffle tracker, who's never even been in this casino, could accurately reproduce the Casino X house shuffle from the first tracker's brief description.

In any case, if you are truly interested in shuffle tracking, then before you invest in my *Shuffle Tracker's Cookbook,* see if you've got the talent for it by practicing and drilling yourself on the three main tracker's skills I described, and learn the language. Watch casino dealers shuffle and learn to recognize the different actions by learning the names. If you see an action not described, it's probably described in the *Cookbook,* but don't worry about my name for it. Name the action yourself so that you can describe it the next time you see it.

You must be able to reproduce a house shuffle on your kitchen table. You do not need the finesse of a professional dealer in the riffling and stripping actions, but you must be able to do the complete routine accurately.

How Much Can You See?

The major skill required for shuffle tracking is eyeballing — the ability to quickly estimate the sizes and positions of identified slugs, dealer break points in relationship to these slugs, plug placement, and dealer grab sizes. As with card counting, some players will discover they have a natural aptitude for eyeballing. But even those who have an innate ability must practice to perfect it.

With 8 decks of standard casino cards in good condition and two felt-tip marking pens, one black and one red, you can make yourself a set of "slug readers."

Here's how to do it:

1. Remove all jokers and save them to be used later as cut cards.

2. From 6 of the 8 decks, separate out all of the tens, jacks, queens, kings, and aces.

3. Using the black marker, color the lengthwise edges of these high cards, tens and aces, on one side only. This can be done very quickly and precisely if you hold the cards in a tight pack, 50-60 cards at a time, while coloring one edge. You want this edge to be solid black. Do not color the edges all the way to the ends, as you want the colored edge to be hidden when you turn the pack of cards away from you. See illustration.

blackened edge

When you shuffle these marked cards back into the remaining unmarked cards, you will be able to read the high-card slugs in the full 6-deck stack with 100% precision! Be careful when you shuffle not to spin any cards 180 degrees, which would result in some of the blackened (reader) edges being on one side of the pack and some on the other. If you are not extremely dexterous with cards, this will happen to you. You must now go through the decks face up to remove all high cards, so that you can face all of their marked edges. You want a 6-deck stack of cards that you can read when the blackened edges are turned towards you, but that appears to be completely normal when the blackened edges are turned away from you.

Now, take the remaining two decks (jokers removed) and use the red-tip marker to color one lengthwise edge of all of these cards. Set these two decks aside, as they will be used later for more advanced techniques.

Start practicing with a 4-deck pack of cards. Unless you have worked as a dealer with multiple decks, 6-deck packs are fairly unwieldy, and even four is a chore. You would likely find it convenient to have a discard tray for stacking the cards for some of the practices.

Shuffle the cards using whatever thorough method is easiest for you. It's fine if you want to mimic a specific casino shuffle, but the purpose of this exercise is simply to practice eyeballing, not tracking, so any home-style shuffle will do if it mixes the cards. It is, to be sure, useful to mimic an actual casino shuffle, but to keep from frustrating yourself, start with four decks and use any shuffling method you want.

After shuffling the cards, turn the reader edges toward you. You are looking at the precise distribution of the money cards in the full stack. You will likely see that although some of the shaded-edge cards have dispersed throughout various areas of the full stack, there is a noteworthy concentration of these high cards in one, or perhaps two, areas. And if you remove these shaded cards and perform this experiment again, being careful to follow the same shuffle routine, you'll find that the shuffle you use always steers the high cards to approximately the same areas.

After you have performed this test a few times to see where the high cards are going, do the test with the blackened edge facing away from you. Then, take a cut-card, any face-up joker, or card with a different color back will do, and see if you can cut the shoe at the right spot to place the high cards at the top of the shoe. With the joker still jogged out from the side edge, turn the reader edge toward you. Did you hit your mark? If not, remove the joker and do it again. Do it until you start hitting it consistently and accurately. Shuffle the cards and repeat this exercise. You will probably get pretty good at this in a short amount of time.

Now it's time to increase the degree of difficulty. Shuffle the cards and study the reader edge. Then, turn the reader edge away from you and use two jokers to cut to the top and bottom of the strongest high-card slug. It's not going to do you any good in a casino to know when the high card slug starts if you don't also know when it ends, and in a casino you won't ever have that blackened reader edge to show you the pattern. But as you see slugs enter the discard tray, you must mentally burn that pattern on to the edges of the cards, just as you did at home when you studied the blackened edge, then turned it away.

Amateur slug trackers will often use far more difficult and less effective methods of slug location. Trying to remember that there is a slug of high cards approximately 1/3-deck in length, located approximately 2 2/3 decks up from the bottom, is much more difficult than simply visualizing that slug in its proper size and location. Eyeball techniques allow you to utilize much more information far more accurately than any kind of mnemonic device.

One thing you will learn is that it is more difficult to cut to a thin slug than a thick one. The thinner the segment you want to locate, the more precise you must be with your cut. This is a good exercise to practice with a friend, as it's more challenging and closer to real-world casino conditions if someone else shuffles the cards. Also, be sloppy with your breaks and grabs. Don't try to avoid cutting slugs in two and don't attempt to make perfectly even piles.

A helpful exercise you can use to get a feel for the value of shuffle tracking is to count down the cards in the segment(s) you have cut to. Remove the cards from the stack you have identified using jokers as high-card slugs, and employing your own counting system, see what they are worth.

If, for instance, in a 6-deck stack, you've isolated a slug with a total length of about one deck, and you count down that deck using the Hi-Lo count, and you get a running count of -8 (or 8 excess high cards), then this one-deck segment has a true-edge value of about +4, indicating an increase in expectation of about 4%.

After you hone your ability to follow slug patterns through simple shuffles, you're ready to start using the two decks with the reddened edges. You'll use these decks to mimic *plugging the cutoffs.*

Here's how:

1. Shuffle.

2. Study the reader edge. Note the slug positions.

3. Turn the reader edge away from you.

4. Take a "plug" from the red-edged pack and insert it into the stack with the red edge facing away from you.

5. After you straighten the stack, use jokers to mark the slugs as well as the plug.

6. Turn the stack around and check your work.

After you get good at eyeballing with a single plug, using various sized plugs, move on to double plugs, then triple plugs, and so on.

Finally, when you can accurately identify the significant high-card slugs through multiple plugs and multiple pile breaks, you are on your way to being the blackjack player the casinos fear most—the player who has the visual talent to track casino-style shuffles. I am assuming, of course, that your card-counting skills are already top notch. Most card counters have no problem grasping tracking logic when it's presented to them; the difficult part is using these methods in a casino.

You don't need to be a total whiz at multiple slug and plug eyeballing in order to beat most shuffles. What is important is that you recognize your skill level and that you only bet your big money according to what you know, based on your skill. As your eyeballing skills improve, you'll be able to attack more complex shuffles and beatable shuffles get that much easier.

You will discover in the casino that it is not really that difficult to burn the edges of the discards mentally with the slug patterns, because the discard tray fills relatively slowly, allowing you all the time in the world to watch those patterns take shape. If you're new to tracking, look for the simplest, one-pass R&R shuffles, if any are available. Look for casinos that top the cutoffs, instead of plugging them, or that use fewer plugs. The simpler the shuffle, the easier it will be to track.

Shuffle tracking has the potential for making shoe games far more profitable than one-deckers for card counters. Unfortunately, there is no easy "trick" you can use to track shuffles. Tracking is a highly developed skill.

Dealer selection is critical. With a dealer that's clean and consistent with his breaks and grabs, you'll have to make fewer adjustments and it'll be easier to track his shuffle. The better you develop your eyeballing skills, the less crucial dealer selection is. Virtually every dealer requires some adjustments according to visual evidence.

Once you start to nail down those visual skills, you will discover that inconsistent dealers, and especially break-ins, provide opportunities that better dealers do not. Uneven marriages, which result from breaks and grabs of unequal sizes, mean that some large segments remain highly intact. If you are visually adept, dealers like this can offer some excellent opportunities.

Other Shuffle Actions

There are dozens of different shuffle actions in use today, most developed in the past few years to combat trackers. Some of the more common ones:

Bottom Jump or Burying the Tops

The dealer has married his first two grabs and has set them on the table to begin building a final stack. After marrying his second two grabs, however, he does not stack these on top of the first marriage, but underneath it. That is, he jumps the bottom marriage of the final stack up one segment. You will occasionally see a dealer do a double bottom jump, by repeating this move again after the third marriage.

The bottom jump doesn't dilute the slugs; it merely changes their location in the final stack. It may be done in either R&R or stepladder shuffles. Theoretically, a dealer could use this move throughout the entire riffling routine and it would simply reverse the order of all marriages in the final stack. I've never seen it done more than twice, however, probably because it's awkward to pick up the final stack after it's a few decks high.

The bottom jump was developed to stop trackers who watch the tops, which usually end up on the bottom of the final stack. In an R&R shuffle, the move simply lifts the segment.

Bottom Pile Cut or Burying the Bottoms

This move was developed to confuse trackers who follow the bottoms. After the dealer has broken the pre-shuffle stack into two or more piles, he performs a single cut on the pile that contains the bottoms. The slugs aren't diluted, but separation may occur if he has cut a tracked slug, in which case it's now in two pieces, one on top and one on the bottom of the cut pile. It's important that you watch this cut and visually adjust the locations of any slugs in the cut pile.

Split Stack

This move is sometimes performed with an R&R shuffle. After marrying the first two grabs with a series of riffles, the dealer breaks the marriage in two and starts building two semi-final stacks. After he has married and split all the grabs, he then stacks one semi-final stack on top of the other. It doesn't dilute the slugs, but it separates the top of a marriage from the bottom. These will then be located half a shoe from each other.

Cutoff Integration

In most casinos, cutoffs are topped, bottomed, or plugged and sometimes all three. When the cutoffs are *integrated,* they are kept separate from the discards, then married into the grabs in small pieces. For example, you might find an 8-deck game with 2 decks cut off. With a 6-pile shuffle, the dealer would break the discard pile into six 1-deck piles, leaving the 2 decks of cutoffs as a seventh pile. He would build his final stack by merging a small grab of cards from the cutoff pile into each marriage of the discard-pile grabs.

Since you should know the running count on the cutoffs, this doesn't dilute the slug(s) with unknown cards. Depending on the plus/minus value of the cutoffs, this amounts to a slight strengthening or weakening of any slug.

Many trackers prefer cutoff integration to cutoff plugging, because they don't have to readjust because of the plugging process. It is not a common shuffle action, although some casinos use it because they know cutoff tracking is an elementary tracking method, and cutoff integration eliminates that possibility.

Top Plugging

You may see this move performed in conjunction with cutoff plugging. Either before or after the cutoff plugging, the dealer takes small grabs from the top of the discard stack and plugs them into the middle. If you have identified any slugs in the top portion of the discards, you've got to follow these slugs to their new locations. Likewise, you've got to watch middle slugs that may be raised or cut in two.

The "Eyeball" vs. The "Recipe"

Historically, there have been two general approaches to shuffle tracking. One is the "eyeball" approach. The other is the "recipe" approach, which works on paper and in computer simulations. With this approach, you pre-map the house shuffle routine, so that you know in advance where everything is going, then you assume that this pattern exists in the casino with "consistent" dealers, and you use various formulas, charts, and tables to tell you exactly what your edge is on any (or every) segment, so that you can place precise fractional Kelly bets.

Unfortunately, I have never known anyone who used the recipe approach to actually succeed at tracking today's complex shuffles. Math is a very good approach to card counting, but for tracking complex shuffles, and many simple shuffles, human dealers are just too inconsistent. Very small differences in dealer breaks and grabs can make for huge dislocations of slugs.

I strongly urge you to adopt the eyeball approach. You won't guess nearly as much and you'll make no assumptions. You want to witness with your own eyes how the dealer grabs your slug, whether your slug is broken, shaved, or dislocated, and have a good idea of the marriage partner(s), so that you won't be scratching your head later when you find yourself betting into crap.

It is far stronger to follow just one slug per shoe, knowing the probable marriage partner(s), than to try to remember the slugs, counts, and marriages throughout the shoe, since the dealer's grabs can never really be true enough to the generic house-shuffle. If you're using charts, tables, and diagrams in an attempt to follow every segment through a shuffle routine, then using more charts to tell you how to bet and play through the shoe from top to bottom, you're fooling yourself if you think you have an advantage.

Successful slug location and play are also based on edge work. You must watch to see if your slug gets shaved at the top or bottom, and if so, you want to know what these lost top or bottom edges were composed of, as you may have just lost all the value in your slug. You also need to know if a dealer break or grab adds extra cards to your slug, and if so whether or not these card values add to, or subtract from, your slug's value. Tracking is detail work, and because of the great danger of overbetting, successful tracking cannot escape being detail work. Unless you have the rare fortune to play in a simple one-pass no-plug game against a dealer who is robotically consistent and precise in all of his cuts and breaks, a game I have never seen in two decades of tracking, you need to know more than just the fact that a half-deck segment has ten extra high cards. Where exactly are those high cards within that half-deck? Are they evenly distributed throughout? Are most of them located near the center or at one end? Being able to see this is far more valuable than having a formula for estimating your advantage with ten extra high cards in a deck. If you actually do have ten extra high cards in a deck, the formula is quite simple: Bet the farm. If the dealer shaved six of them off the top or married your slug to eight extra low cards, you might be better off following those six high cards that got lopped off, and not quite betting the farm when you cut to them.

This is work you can only do with your eyes, and your eyes can't do everything. You can't follow every edge of every segment and every marriage of every segment with any accuracy. Go for the strongest slugs, get every bit of information you can on them, and let the rest go.

Because you will so often follow only one slug per shoe, as opposed to attempting to identify the values of every post-shuffle segment, your mind will be free to do edge work at a very high level. The best trackers will pay close attention to the exact order that cards enter the discard tray at the edges of their slugs. This may strike you as near impossible, but it is easier than you might think. First, you must know the pick-up order used by dealers in the casino. The pick-up order is *always standardized* in any casino as part of their shuffle routine, and that will allow you to get a handle on the edge cards while they are still face-up on the table. Once you see how these cards enter the discard tray, you are not going to sit there trying to remember a string of half a dozen exact cards. You will simply think, "I hope the dealer's grab doesn't add a few cards at the top, since that would push my slug value down by three low cards." Once you can cut with precision, shouldn't you get full value for the hours you spent drilling yourself? None of this is brain surgery, but the fact is that you are attempting to make a brain surgeon's salary by playing a card game!

Cutoff Tracking

It is probably not a bad idea to reemphasize that cutoff tracking remains one of the easiest methods of slug tracking for all card counters. Many casinos still top their cutoffs, which is ideal. Other than those rare shuffles in which the cutoffs are integrated, cutoffs are always topped, bottomed, plugged or some combination of all three.

Some casinos plug the cutoffs into the discards as one large clump in the middle. This is fantastic when the cutoff segment is large—say, 1 1/2 to 2 decks—and the house uses a 2-pile shuffle. Some dealers are so consistent in their plug placement that you will likely find more than one who will virtually always marry the tops with one portion of the cutoffs and the bottoms with another. Anytime you have a count estimate on both grabs in a marriage, your estimates will be far more accurate.

Anytime the cutoff count is extreme (either positive or negative), watch the plugs. Even if the cutoffs are broken into pieces and plugged, your easiest tracking opportunity may be to try to follow just one plug. Nor is it uncommon to find shuffle routines that break the cutoffs in two, then top one half and bottom the other. So long as you can get a good eyeball estimate of the size of these segments, you can follow them through the shuffle.

This is also true when the cutoffs are broken into three pieces, then topped, bottomed, and middled. In a two-pile shuffle with plugs like this, some dealers will consistently remarry that middle cutoff plug with either the top- or bottom-cutoff segment.

The most important thing is that you open your eyes when the dealer shuffles. You will sometimes see moves so obvious, so consistent, and so easily trackable that you will wonder how long it might be before someone in the pit notices and puts an end to it. Fortunately, no one in the pit ever does.

Best Counting System

Any valid card counting system for casino blackjack will work fine for shuffle tracking. In practice, I've found that unbalanced counts, such as the Red Seven Count, aren't great, because you have to keep adjusting your estimates for the imbalance. With variously sized segments and grabs, this adjustment can be pretty confusing. For tracking, I would suggest you use the Hi-Lo Lite.

Estimating Your Advantage

Your shuffle tracking advantage over the house, within any particular slug, is identical to your card counting advantage, assuming you have the same number of high cards remaining in a similarly sized group of cards. In other words, whether shuffle tracking or card counting, if you have 8 excess high cards in a one-deck segment, your true edge is +4, which indicates an advantage of about 4% above the house edge off the top of the shoe.

The main difference with tracking is that this type of advantage is not rare in a 6-deck shoe game, while it is extremely rare if simply counting cards. If using the Hi-Lo Count, you would need a running count of +24 if three decks remained to be dealt, or +16 if two decks remained. And although you would only need a running count of +8 if one deck remained, the dealer would be unlikely to deal another round if he had already dealt 5 of the 6 decks. The tracker will not only see regular true edges of +4 in a 6-deck shoe game, but will also be able to play through the entire segment without fear of the dealer shuffling up.

Your overall edge at shuffle tracking depends on your skill and the shuffle you are playing. For details, I'll refer you to *The Blackjack Shuffle Tracker's Cookbook.*

In any case, this should give you a pretty good handle on shuffle tracking and its logic. If you have access to some fairly simple shuffles in the casinos where you play, you may even find profit opportunities using the very simple tracking methods I've described.

But if shuffle tracking is a playing technique you want to get serious about, then get *The Cookbook,* as it goes far beyond the cursory treatment of this subject here. Shuffle tracking is an advantage play technique best left to the pros. The most important thing is that you know your abilities, and your limitations.

19

MORE SECRETS OF THE PROS

This chapter is especially important for counters who play green ($25) and black ($100) action and higher. Small stakes players will find some of this useful, especially the toking guidelines and the information on preferential shuffles, but some of the other concerns addressed have little to do with low-stakes play. Big players, though, need all of this information to ensure their survival.

Versatility

Heres a story that takes place in Las Vegas, Nevada. Sometime in the year 2000. Max Rubin's Blackjack Ball.

The new millennium had just kicked in and, for the first time in my life, I had made the final four. For a blackjack player, this was an honor beyond compare. Max announced the next event—throwing a playing card into a bowl from a distance of ten feet. I remembered the stories of the legendary Titanic Thompson, who could fling cards into a hat from a distance of 30 feet. And Ricky Jay, the actor, magician, and eccentric author of *Cards as Weapons*, who could sail playing cards hundreds of feet across an auditorium to hit a target.

Ten feet. Ten measly feet.

As much of an honor as it was to be in the final four, I really didn't want to end up fourth. The contest was set up as a pari-mutuel event, with the top three finishers—win, place, and show—in the money. To come in fourth was no better than coming in fortieth as far as the payout, which was zilch. And, with this crowd, the only thing that mattered was the payout. Some of those present had put their money on me. I didn't want to let my fans down.

Ten feet.

Ten measly feet.

I swaggered up to the starting line and, with a devil-may-care flick of my wrist, launched an eight of clubs toward that bowl that appeared to be so close I could almost reach out and touch it.

The eight of clubs did not cooperate. Like an autumn leaf on a windy October day in Michigan, it flitted and fluttered in the air, deciding in the last moments of its wavering descent to reverse direction. It came to rest on the floor behind my foot—a full eleven feet from that bowl that was just ten feet away.

A small voice in the otherwise hushed crowd summed it up perfectly. "That was pathetic, Arnold."

My bruised ego was salved by the equally feeble efforts of the next two contestants. Alas, it is not easy to hit a target with a playing card, even at a measly ten feet. My forlorn look was slowly transforming into a smile of smug satisfaction.

Then Mark Dace approached the starting line. Max handed him a six of hearts and cautioned him to keep his feet behind the line. Mark shrugged, then casually crumpled that six of hearts in his fist, until it was a small, tight projectile. Just as casually, he tossed it into that beckoning bowl that had proven so elusive to the rest of us. No flitter. No flutter. At that distance, who could miss?

That same small voice in the hushed crowd once again broke the silence. "Is that fair?"

But we all knew it was just as fair as glimpsing a dealer's hole card, or check-raising with the nuts. This was war, and all's fair in war and gambling.

Although Mark scored all the points for that round, I did ultimately manage to show in the competition, and I was ecstatic to finish in the money. I took third place by beating a professional card counter in the left-handed arm-wrestling event. I no longer remember exactly what Max's justification for this event was—I mean, all of the contests were supposed to have some kind of a gambling angle. I only remember looking at the puny twerp I was going to be arm-wrestling with, knowing in advance that although he was earning half-a-million a year from the casinos, he was about to lose his shot at the hallowed Blackjack Cup that probably meant more to him than money.

Mark Dace didn't win that year either, and the following year Max instructed all contestants in the card-throwing competition that they could not "alter" the shape or form of the playing card. Kind of like a casino installing auto-peek devices after a spooking team had already beaten their brains in.

But none of those present at the millennium Blackjack Ball ever forgot the lesson that Mark Dace taught us: the most important trait of the professional gambler is *versatility*. You've got to be able to change with the times, adapt to the games, and let your strategies evolve with the playing conditions.

Johnny Moss, poker legend and three-time champion of the World Series of Poker, didn't start out his gambling career as a poker player. Instead, Moss spent twenty years hustling golf. He only turned to poker in his later years, when the younger golfers could drive farther and had better eyesight than he did.

To the average person, golf and poker may seem like extremely different activities. Skill at one would not necessarily translate to skill at the other. To Johnny Moss, however, they weren't really all that different. In his youth, though he'd been a very good golfer, he had never thought of himself as the world's greatest. Instead, his talent lay in sizing up his opponents, matching his strengths against their weaknesses, and getting them to bet against him only when he had the best of it. That is how he beat a lot of better golfers for a lot of money.

Poker is a game where, in the long run, everybody gets the same percentage of good hands and bad hands. The successful pros are the players who can read their opponents and make those with stronger hands fold, while keeping the weaker hands in the game. To Johnny Moss, there wasn't much difference between winning money from golfers and winning money from card players. He simply adapted to conditions.

For blackjack players, this ability to adapt is just as crucial. When Thorp exposed the secrets of card counting in the '60s, it took a few years for the casinos to catch on. But they did catch on—most pit bosses today know basic strategy, and they know the common changes from basic that card counters most often make.

For a while, the casinos felt they were safe again when they started dealing shoe games. Thorp's ten-count wasn't designed to work against a four-deck shoe—it was just too difficult to apply at game speed. But the pros turned to easier point-count systems, Lawrence Revere's revolutionary "true count" method, then to concealed computers, shuffle tracking, hole-card strategies, ace location—the shoe games were being attacked by pros from a dozen different directions.

The successful players will always adapt to the latest conditions. Forty years after Thorp, blackjack remains one of the most beatable games in the casino. The thing is, you're not going to be able to beat the game by using Thorp's ten count. The game itself has simply changed too much.

Every time a gambling pro publicly reveals his methods, the value of that information has a shelf life. That shelf life is based on how widespread the dissemination of that information is.

When Doyle Brunson published his *Super System* in 1978, a book that revealed, among other things, how he played no-limit hold 'em, Brunson found that he had to change his strategies. His opponents read his book and he'd lost his edge. Once he realized that the players who read his book would assume he played in certain ways because his hand was strong or weak, or because he believed their hands were one or the other, he could use their assumptions against them. He adapted.

The casinos have read all the blackjack books. They know about counting. They know about shuffle tracking. They know about front-loading, first-basing, ace-sequencing, warps, tells, spooking—you name it, they've read it all. And because they've read all the books, they assume they know what all of these strategies look like. But the pro doesn't quit because old secrets have been revealed; he simply uses the casinos' assumptions against them.

Today, an amateur blackjack player who has read all the books is usually like the amateur poker player who just finished reading Brunson's book 20 years ago. He goes out and plays "by the book," wondering why his competition seems to read his every move!

When a blackjack pro reads a book that reveals a new method, his first thought is not, "Hmmmm, I wonder if I should give this a try?" Instead, it's "Hmm, interesting, but the casinos have probably read this too...How can I pull this off without looking like this is what I'm doing?"

If you play by the book, you'll never make it as a pro. You've got to write your own book, and then, whatever you do, *don't publish it!* If you don't have the versatility to adapt quickly to changing conditions, give it up.

You Don't Know Me

Card counters must be very careful about their associations with other card counters in the casinos. It is not wise to socialize in the casinos with other card counters. Even if you are traveling with a fellow player, in the pits you should be strangers.

If one of you is identified as a card counter, you do not want suspicion cast upon the other. Most big money players also avoid associations with other counters in the casino restaurants and other public areas. Pit bosses and hosts, as well as other floor and surveillance personnel, eat in the casino restaurants and buy magazines in the gift shops. You never know whom you'll run into, or where.

Don't take unnecessary chances.

House Phone Hang-Ups

Although most counters feel that the casino hotel room phones are unlikely to be bugged, as that would be a federal crime, many still feel it is unsafe to call other counters room-to-room within the same casino. I won't even use my room phone to call another counter even if his room is in another room. The worry is not so much that the private conversation may be monitored, but that surveillance may review the electronic record of the numbers you call.

Does this sound overly paranoid? It's happened. There are teams of players who have been identified like that.

The solution? Use cell phones for all of your calls. If for some reason your cell phone is dead, or you can't get a connection, then leave your room and call your friends via any white courtesy phone, many of which are located throughout the casino. Naturally, if you're the paranoid type, and you believe all casino phones are bugged, federal regulations be damned, then you'll just have to call from pay phones and speak in a code that only you and your friends understand.

Shift Change Vanishing Act

All 24-hour casinos have three work shifts—day, swing, and grave. The hours of each shift may vary somewhat: Day shift generally begins between 10 AM and noon, ending eight hours later between 6 and 8PM; swing starts immediately after and ends between 2 and 4AM; then grave takes over and goes to 10 AM or noon. You can always figure out a casino's shift changes by noting when you see a group of new dealers milling around the perimeter of the pit. If you intend to play for any length of time, ask the dealer how long until she gets off when you first sit down at the table. Although it sounds like you're making small talk, what you really want to know is when the shift change is, and if the bosses change when the dealers do, and if the change is "staggered" over a period of time. Once you learn this information, you should keep a record of it so that whenever you return to that casino you don't have to go through this process again.

The reason you want to know about the shifts is that you do not want to play through a shift change. Whether you are winning or losing, and regardless of whether you think you may be suspected of counting, playing through a shift change is generally a bad idea. You just don't want the swing boss discussing your play with the grave boss. Let the grave boss form his own opinion.

If you intend to play a few more hours that day, the shift change is an excellent time to take a break, grab a snack, take a shower, and come back refreshed. If a shift change suddenly takes you by surprise, you look up and new suits are standing around gabbing with the old suits, you blew it. But remember what time it is and you'll know when all the shift changes take place. Next time, you'll be long gone for the changing of the guard.

The best time to disappear is actually about forty-five minutes before the shift change, because surveillance shift changes usually are scheduled a half-hour before the one on the casino floor. By timing your disappearance this way, you avoid any shift-change conversations about your play that might occur not only on the floor but upstairs in the surveillance room as well.

Going South

One art form that every advantage player must learn is the art of "going south" with chips, or "rat-holing," as many counters call it. **Ratholing,** also called **going south,** is taking chips off the table and putting them in your pockets. The idea is to give the impression that you lost money, or won less than you did. Continually winning money in a casino may be very nice from your perspective, but the casino isn't so enthusiastic. So, you must do what you can to change their perspective.

Unfortunately, one of the signs of a card counter that surveillance watches for is a player who rat-holes chips. Normal tourists and gamblers never try to hide their winnings. In fact, most players are very proud to display them. So you must be very careful—just because the boss isn't looking doesn't mean you're safe. You are always on camera.

It's not a bad idea to go to a magic shop (most big casinos in Vegas have one!), and pick up a book (and video) on coin magic. You are especially interested in the art of "palming" coins, then getting rid of them inconspicuously by dropping them into pockets—without anyone noticing at all!

Casinos keep records on the wins and losses of their big players, and many card counters eventually find themselves barred simply on the basis of too many wins over too long a period. If you intend to stick around in the casinos, you must learn to make it look like you're losing at the tables. If you have a great record at a casino, then take the time to generate some losses on paper. This is not hard to do when the casinos are crowded, and the bosses have trouble keeping track of every individual's result. When you leave the table, be sure to tell the boss how much you lost (or appeared to have lost) so he'll get the total you want in the computer.

You can also use other games—like craps, baccarat, roulette—to generate losses on your play record, which will make you look like more of an all around gambler, and therefore less suspicious. Casinos do keep track of their big chips, but there are many ways you can appear to lose large amounts of money at crowded tables if you use friends to help carry out your scheme. Think about it—use your noggin. Some top pros spend almost as much time generating paper losses as they do winning. We should all have such problems!

By the way, if you are a rated player, it is very easy to find out what the casino record shows—just ask! Most bosses will pull your play record up on their computer screens, and tell you your number of hours, average bet, and win/loss for your current play session. Before you check out and go home, your host will tell you your totals for your whole trip, if you ask. These are the numbers the casino uses to qualify you for comps. Many big players, including lots of regular gamblers, ask the bosses and hosts for these totals, so it won't look unusual or suspect if you ask for your numbers. You should keep a complete record of what the casino record shows, so that you know when you should generate losses, and also to see if your rat-holing efforts are working.

Toking Guidelines

Toking is casino slang for tipping. Some card counters believe their tokes can be used to obtain more advantageous conditions, but they're often mistaken. Let's examine the value of tokes to a card counter.

General Tokes

A general toke is a toke made to maintain or improve the player's long-run playing conditions. Placing a bet for the dealer shortly after beginning play in hopes of favorably influencing him is an example of a general toke. This dealer may be less suspicious, more apt to deal deeper into the deck, and more likely to ignore a betting spread. Tips made solely for the purpose of camouflage, in order to give the appearance of a high roller, would also fall into the category of general tokes; this type of tipping is recommended by Ian Andersen in *Turning the Table on Las Vegas*. It's always a good idea to do whatever you can to keep the dealer feeling friendly toward you. If you're not the outgoing talkative type, nothing speaks louder to a dealer than a toke. Dealers in most casinos are paid minimum wage, and their livelihood depends on tokes.

To avoid excessive general toking, a player must realistically consider his expected average hourly profit, based on hands per hour, average bet size, and approximate advantage over the house. The expected hourly win is estimated by using the Profit Formula from Chapter Twelve. For example, with an average bet of $50, at 120 hands per hour, with a long-run advantage over the house of 1% from card counting, the expected hourly win is $60. Using that figure, you can decide how much you wish to "give back" to the dealer in tokes.

A frequent error of rookie card counters is to toke excessively. I have seen many players betting quarters, using a moderate spread, and playing a solid game, suddenly toss a $25 chip to the dealer after a lucky 20-minute run and a win of a few hundred dollars. Paying a dealer so lavishly for a winning streak is a sure road to the poor house. Winning streaks occur frequently, and toking after every one is expensive. Losing streaks occur just as frequently, though I have yet to see a dealer toke a player who has just lost a few hundred dollars. Toking after a win should be classified as a general toke, and should be figured according to long-term expectations.

Consider a casino with crowded six-deck games, where a table-hopper with a moderate betting spread enjoys an advantage of about 1%. If this player makes $25 average bets, it would be stupid to toke at all under such conditions, as his expected rate of profit is only about $15 per hour.

You must be realistic in estimating your hourly win rate. It would be wise to budget your total tokes per-hour, based on how much of your potential win you feel should be reinvested, either for camouflage or otherwise. Tips to cocktail waitresses and any other expenses incurred in casino play should also be factored into the same equation.

Some general guidelines: If you bet quarters, but never more than $100 on a hand, then dollar tokes are fine, with an occasional nickel if you have a particularly good run of cards. If you are betting black chips, then $5 tokes are sufficient. If you are frequently placing bets of $500 or higher, then an occasional quarter toke will keep any dealer happy.

Specific Tokes

Specific toking is tipping for an immediate potential gain. Toking a dealer in an effort to influence him to deal one more round before shuffling at a high count is a specific toke. The size of the toke must be determined on the basis of the potential gain from one specific hand. The player advantage from card counting rarely exceeds 3% on a high count, and in most multi-deck games, an advantage over 2% is uncommon. Players who make specific tokes should closely monitor results. How often does a bet placed for a dealer fail to influence his action? If a dealer does not suspect you of counting cards, he may shuffle anyway, unaware of the toke's purpose. With a 2% advantage, a single hand will earn you $2 for every $100 you bet. Toking the dealer $1 for every $100 bet would split the profit 50-50 between you and the dealer, but he will likely think you are a cheapskate, betting $100 and only toking him a buck. Toking the dealer $5 for a $100 bet would be paying him more than twice your expectation.

Specific toking is of no practical value to most players. General toking, as part of an act, may occasionally be useful. Such toking should be carefully planned to increase profits, not eat them. Card counters making average bets of less than $25 should not toke at all, unless, of course, you are a generous person and it makes you feel better to give money to people. Don't think of it as part of your counting strategy.

Hole Card Play

Hole card play is a method of advantage play in which a player obtains his advantage by figuring out the dealer's hole card.

There are both legal and illegal methods of hole card play. First, let's get the illegal methods out of the way quickly, as you won't be using them. They could land you in prison. That's too much risk for too little reward.

Illegal Hole Card Strategies

It is illegal to mark the cards in any way.

If you nick the edges of the aces in hand-held games, or rub grease (daub) on the backs of certain cards so that you can identify them when they're being dealt, this is illegal. Obviously, with marked cards, you could determine the dealer's hole card. But you might also learn a little too much about the state penitentiary.

It is illegal to work in collusion with a dealer to get information.

It would be illegal, for instance, for the dealer to purposely "flash" his hole card, or the next card to be dealt, as part of a partnership deal with you. It is also illegal for the dealer to peek at the hole card himself, and then "help" you to play your hand, either blatantly or through some secret signal.

It is illegal to use any device to "see" the dealer's hole card.

You cannot place a mirror on the table, nor can you have a video camera up your sleeve. And, yes, players have gone to jail for using these types of methods.

So, if all of these methods are illegal, what exactly *is* legal?

Legal Hole Card Strategies

As a general rule, it is legal to use any information about the dealer's hole card that's available to anyone who happens to be seated at the table, usually due to sloppy dealing procedures. Let's consider how each of the illegal hole card strategies described above might be legal in different circumstances.

Marked Card Play

Although it's illegal for a player to mark the cards in any way, if certain cards become marked during the dealing process, you're allowed to use anything you pick up from those inadvertently marked cards in making your decisions. For instance, in the old days, casinos rarely changed their decks of cards. Over the course of days of play, some cards developed scratches, nicks, bends, stains, and the like. Astute players found that they could sometimes use these dinged-upcards to their advantage.

Also, dealers used to manually check beneath their tens and aces to see if they had a blackjack and this constant bending of the cards sometimes warped the tens and aces in the same arch. This flaw was best put to use by players making insurance or hit/stand decisions. If, for instance, the dealer's facedown hole card showed the arch typical of a card that has been repeatedly bent, the player might assume it was more likely to be a ten-valued card, and take insurance if the dealer's up-card was an ace, or play his hand under the assumption that the dealer's hole card was a ten. Most casinos today, however, put new decks into play every few hours, before any serious nicking or scratching can take place, and most casinos also use auto-peek devices to check beneath tens and aces, so that the dealer does not have to bend the cards. So you have to be observant for new types of opportunities.

Again, a player may legally use "marked" card information, provided that he didn't mark them in any way. The casinos have taken great measures over the past couple of decades to make this type of legal play obsolete, but it's not dead. There are still small casinos in little Nevada towns where dealers manually peek under tens and aces, and decks of cards are not frequently changed. Also, some of the modern countermeasures have brought their own problems—in sliding cards into an auto-peek device to look at a hole card, inept dealers sometimes nick the edges on the device itself!

Flashed Card Play

Although it's illegal for a dealer to purposely "flash" cards at someone during the dealing process, it is not illegal for you to use whatever you see if the dealer inadvertently flashes his hole card. In fact, this is the most common type of hole card play engaged in by professional blackjack players today.

In Nevada, the courts have found that it is the job of the dealer to conceal his hole card, and not the job of the player to look away if the dealer accidentally flashes it at him. It's not easy to find dealers who are that inept, but some pros make a good living exclusively from this type of play.

The Danger of Hole Card Play

The primary danger of hole-card play is that, if caught, you may be accused of using an illegal strategy. As a result, hole-card players must be careful about how they use the information they obtain. For instance, if you are dealt a hand totaling 18, and you know that the dealer has a total of twenty—since you literally saw his hole card—it would be very unwise for you to hit your 18 total, even though you know hitting is your only chance at winning. Several weird plays like this would alert the casino that you are obviously getting the dealer's hole card. They might accuse you of working in collusion with the dealer; or they might accuse you of marking or bending the cards; and even if you ultimately win in court, when it's proven that you don't know the dealer personally, and examination of the cards reveals no marks or bends, your playing career may have been seriously damaged. Your name and mug shot will be disseminated among casinos, and you will be identified forever as a serious professional player.

The Advantages of Hole Card Play

Hole card play provides a much stronger advantage to the player than card counting. It is usually inaccessible to those who do not live in casino areas, because professional hole-card players must often scout large numbers of tables to locate a flashing dealer. Hole card players do not look like card counters to game protection personnel because they do not need to alter their bets as the count goes up and down. Therefore, if they are careful, they can often play for many hours at the same table without being suspected.

Also, although most hole card players specialize in beating blackjack games, hole card strategies can be employed against most casino card games, including SuperFun 21 or Spanish 21, as well as many of the new tourist traps like Caribbean Stud, 3-Card Poker, and Let It Ride. Many hole-card players appear to be all-around gambling fools to the casinos!

A few blackjack authors have described various hole-card techniques, along with strategies and cursory analyses, but there really isn't any good book for beginners on the subject. It's unlikely that any pro hole-card reader would ever write something like that, as it is a secret art, known only to the practitioners, and too valuable to make public. The hole-card player's "bible" is James Grosjean's *Beyond Counting* (RGE, 2000), a book that has been out of print for a year or so. You might look for copies on the Internet or in used bookstores. But don't expect a how-to book—it's primarily a mathematical analysis of the value of hole-card strategies, along with a number of other unusual professional gambling methods, with little information on how you go about finding dealers who flash in the first place.

Dealers Who Cheat

Cheating does exist in casinos. Unfortunately, there is little anyone can do to protect themselves, except walk away from any suspicious table.

Bear in mind that low-stakes players will be less likely to be cheated than high stakes players, and that players in single or double-deck hand-held games will be more likely to be cheated than those in shoe games.

The long-held conventional wisdom among casino players is that cheating was a thing of the past, that it would be so expensive to any major casino to be caught cheating that they would make every effort to prevent it. A casino license is worth as much as hundreds of millions of dollars a year to a big casino. Since they could lose their license if caught cheating, why would they ever take such a big gamble?

But players seem to forget that while casino owners and upper management may be wary of cheating, the people who work the games may very well be conniving bastards, and not a few are downright idiots. To argue that no casino would ever cheat its customers would be like arguing that no major investment corporation would ever engage in insider trading, or that no bank would ever bilk its stockholders by filing phony quarterly reports. Enron, MCI, and Tyco all say different.

It's a known fact within the casino industry that hundreds of casino employees are fired every year for theft. Dealers, cashiers, floor personnel, security guards—casino employees at every level are tempted by the vast quantities of money that pass in front of their eyes every day. And, unlike most businesses, casinos rarely prosecute employees they catch cheating. If a floor manager in a department store is caught embezzling funds, he can expect to be dragged to court. Casinos, however, are terrified of bad publicity. They do not want the public reading articles in the newspapers about cheating dealers in their casinos. So, a suspected casino cheat is often simply fired. (If a player is suspected of cheating the house, however, that player will absolutely be prosecuted to the full extent of the law!)

Blackjack pros and cardsharps agree that most casino blackjack dealers are honest. If cheating dealers were common, it would be impossible to profit from high-stakes card counting year after year. Cardsharps are among the few who can recognize cheating moves, and most will tell you that you have to be able to perform any of the dishonest tricks yourself in order to recognize them. They will also tell you that some of the most common cheating methods are not detectable by anyone.

A talented card cheat would not perform any detectable moves and would not resort to any device that could be used as evidence if discovered, such as hidden or marked cards. If he stacks the deck, performs false shuffles, peaks at the top card, or deals the second card from the top, all of these movements will appear natural. Unless you have personally witnessed close-up demonstrations of these techniques by expert card manipulators, you would be amazed at some of the "miracles" a sleight-of-hand artist can perform with a standard deck of playing cards.

There are only a few basic signals that are easy for the player to detect and would tell him that a dealer's cheating. Probably the easiest, and most common cheating technique is simply to make incorrect payoffs. Always pay attention to the amount you have bet and the amount of your payoff. Especially watch for incorrect payoffs on blackjacks and insurance bets. If both you and the dealer take many small hit cards on the same hand, be sure you add up both totals. If the dealer collects your money before you finish adding, stop him. Make sure all payoffs are correct. You'll get faster at this as you gain experience.

The most common payoff "error" that crooked dealers make is the incorrect color-up on a blackjack payoff. For example, let's say a player bets a stack of seven nickels, and gets a blackjack. Dealers who specialize in short pays watch for these types of opportunities. Instead of paying the player by matching his seven nickels and then adding another three nickels plus two-fifty to complete the payoff in a very clear fashion, the short-pay specialist will decide to color-up the nickels to quarters in the process of paying the bet. He'll simply grab three quarters from his rack and stack them next to the player's bet, while quickly picking up the player's seven nickels. Then he'll add a couple of nickels, plus two-fifty to the payoff, leaving the player with a total of $77.50. The short-pay dealer does this so fast that the player doesn't even think about what the correct payoff should have been. In fact, the dealer just stole $10 from the player, because the correct payoff on a $35 blackjack is $52.50, so the player should have been left with $87.50 in front of him, not $77.50.

I recently watched a dealer at a downtown Las Vegas casino make five short-pays in the course of an hour at a crowded table where all players were betting less than $50 per hand. All of the short-pays were done during color-ups, one of them while coloring up the chips of a player who was leaving the table. In two of the short-pay incidents, the boss watched the transactions and said nothing.

Many major casinos prevent dealers from paying off bets while simultaneously coloring up the player's chips. By requiring dealers to pay the bet as placed, incorrect payoffs are avoided. Casinos that allow dealers to pay bets in this fashion should always make you wary.

A false shuffle is a difficult cheating move to detect. It may be used in either single or multi-deck games. No sleight-of-hand is necessary—the dealer simply locates a clump of high cards by noting their approximate position when he places them in the discard tray, or his hand, if single-deck. Then, when later shuffling the cards, he controls this clump and positions it where it will be cut out of play. This may seem impossible, but it's actually not that difficult. Dealers know that players are creatures of habit; players who cut dead center on one shoe can usually be depended upon to cut the same way every time. Likewise, some players announce their cutting "strategy" to the table with cute sayings like "Cut thin to win!" The dealer can assume this player believes in this "thin-to-win" superstition, and this player is a perfect candidate to cut those high cards out of play.

By causing high cards to be cut out of play, the dealer doesn't have to do anything else to get a big edge on the players. This type of shuffle is undetectable to players, pit bosses, and the eye-in-the-sky. Yet, the dealer will completely nullify any potential gain from card counting and, over the long run, will win a greater amount of money from all the players who play against him.

This type of cheating is particularly devastating to card counters because it causes the count to ascend as the excess low cards are dealt. The counter raises his bets, but the expected high cards never come out.

The easiest way to handle this type of cheating is to leave the table. Your only clue that this false shuffle technique is being used will be that you will notice the count is always high when the dealer shuffles. If this occurs shuffle after shuffle, leave the table.

In most Nevada casinos, it could be difficult for a dealer in a shoe game to steer a clump of cards anywhere in the shuffled decks because most casinos have house shuffle routines that must be followed. Most players who have reported suspicious games to me, where the count always went up, ended high, and never came down, shoe after shoe, have experienced this disturbing phenomenon in foreign or Indian reservation casinos; in one case the practice was later confirmed by a person who worked at a suspected casino.

At really crooked casinos, where there would usually have to be a boss, and probably a shift manager, involved in the scam, a counter might notice that the count always ends very high, but no false shuffle is used. Instead, a "short" shoe, which actually had aces and tens removed (or extra low cards added) is in play. For years many professional counters have reported that they think short shoes are used in some Puerto Rican casinos, but I've also had confirmed reports of short shoes being used in two Las

Vegas casinos in the past few years.

The second warning signal that you may be being cheated also involves a false shuffle. Again, the mechanics of the shuffle will be undetectable, but the result of the shuffle will be that the dealer will get a natural on the first hand. This type of cheating is most easily accomplished by crooked dealers in hand-held games. There are dozens of methods a card expert could use to control just one ace and one ten to be dealt to his own hand after the shuffle, and you will not see any of them. Just remember that a dealer should get a blackjack about once out of every twenty hands. If he gets a blackjack first hand after a shuffle, it's probably just luck. The odds against him getting a natural in two consecutive first hands after shuffling are more than 400 to 1, and the odds against it happening a third time in a row are more than 8,000 to 1. It's still probably just luck, but I'd find another dealer.

One other bad sign: Be wary of any dealer in a hand-held game who accidentally deals two cards instead of one. This could be a sign that the dealer was attempting to hold back the top card and deal the card beneath it. In fact, any time you feel uncomfortable about the honesty of a game, leave the table. Don't take chances. If you think a dealer is handling the cards in an unnatural or suspicious manner, don't try to catch him in the act of cheating. You will probably be unable to spot it, and if you do, you will probably not be able to prove it. Reporting suspected cheats to the casino will get you nowhere. Unless you can provide solid evidence, and you have witnesses to back you up, you will be viewed as a troublemaker, a paranoid nut, a sore loser, or possibly a scam artist.

Most casino blackjack dealers are honest. If you are on a losing streak, don't blame cheating dealers. If you're playing for high stakes, you would be wise to seek a demonstration, and possibly an instructional course, from a card expert who thoroughly understands cheating moves, especially those used in casino blackjack. There are also books and videotapes available on the subject. (See the Appendix for some recommended titles.) Still, don't expect to see a good cheat. I've had personal demonstrations by some of the best cardsharps in the world; I've had the moves explained to me in detail and performed in slow motion. All a card sharp can teach you is how to spot a sloppy or inexperienced cheat. An expert is undetectable, and unless you have proof, your best defense is to quit that table as soon as you think something's amiss.

You should avoid getting involved in "private" illegal blackjack games. If you play for high stakes, and especially if you take junkets with other high rollers, you are liable to be invited to play in risky private games. I know one pro who couldn't resist such an offer, and he didn't realize he was being cheated until he'd lost $15,000. Stick to the legal casinos—you're less likely to be cheated.

In some cases, bosses will castigate dealers when they go on losing streaks. Likewise, bosses in some casinos are called on the carpet when their pit does not perform up to expectations. There is very little job security in the casino industry, and the pressure to show a healthy profit for the company can be great. The dealer who learns to short-pay is often just trying to keep the boss smiling. The boss who never notices the payout errors simply wants the shift manager off his back. The danger to the industry, however, is that any dealer who can short-pay can just as easily overpay. Such a dealer might be tempted to collude with friends who can pick up a few overpays every shift.

If you are ever short-paid, simply bring it to the dealer's attention. Never accuse a dealer of purposely short-paying you. If you ever notice a short-pay to another player, you should probably say nothing. Remember, you are trying to look like any other idiot at the table, not someone who knows the correct payout on a $35 blackjack. You don't want to get their attention. If the boss knows about the short-pays, but simply ignores them, he will immediately dislike you. If it's a good count game, then stick with it, and just watch out for errors on your own hand. If you correct a dealer once on your own hand, he's less likely to attempt another short-pay on your bet. But continue to watch, just in case.

Cheating by Any Other Name

The most common form of cheating at blackjack in Nevada is "preferential shuffling." This is widely practiced at the hand-held games, and it has become especially popular since the state Gaming Control Board ruled that it was legal. It does violate the Nevada cheating statutes, but it would be very difficult for a player to win a court case against a casino in Nevada, especially when the Gaming Board opposes the law as written.

Preferential shuffling is when a dealer counts cards, then shuffles up if the deck favors the player, but deals when the deck favors the house. Obviously, no card counting system can beat this house strategy, since the counter will never be able to place a big bet when he has an advantage. Card counters, though, need not worry about being cheated this way, because counters immediately recognize it, but some casinos use it to milk their big players. If big cards come off the top, the dealer will continue to deal, knowing that the deck favors the house. But if small cards come off the top, leaving the deck favorable to the players, the dealer shuffles. It's very obvious. So, the smart counter leaves and goes to another casino. Preferential shuffling is not so much an anti-counter tactic as a way that the casinos cheat non-counters who don't recognize what is happening.

Again, you cannot complain to the casino, or to state gaming officials, if you see this occurring in a casino. Because it is legal in the state of Nevada (and I presume most other states), you will see it frequently if you play in hand-held games, and especially when there is a player at the table betting a lot of money. To complain, however, is to announce that you are a card counter! All you can do is leave the table and let the casino have their way with the rich suckers who think they're getting a fair deal.

High-Tech Surveillance

Many of the betting camouflage techniques that have been offered thus far will not fool the new high-tech surveillance computers. These computers can be used to track the count, and rate players according to their skill levels. Traditional card-counting strategies will be recognized, including just about any form of bet variation that involves players betting more on advantageous hands, and less on hands where the house has the advantage.

This type of software allows the unseen surveillance operator to enter all players' bets and playing decisions either while play is in progress, or afterwards from the surveillance videos. The analysis feature then evaluates the skill levels of all players at the table.

The normal types of betting camouflage that card counters have traditionally used with great success will not trip up the computer. Even the most radical forms of opposition betting, which will fool most pit bosses and surveillance observers, will not fool a computer tracking program.

A simple but effective counter-strategy for card counters is to move around frequently, changing tables often, and not playing for extended periods in the same pit. This type of table-hopping will not totally foil the computer, but it will take a very dedicated analyst to follow your play.

Team strategies, where a big player gets called into games, plays a few hands, then moves on, also work well. Again, someone could use the software to evaluate this type of play, but every table that the suspected counter plays would have to be studied from the beginning of the shoe in order to know whether the table-hopper is, in fact, betting into rich decks or just moving around.

Shuffle-tracking strategies are probably least likely to be recognized by this type of software. The shuffle tracking analysis features are very crude, and would likely only recognize players using computers to track shuffles. Shuffle-trackers won't play so consistently or precisely to be recognized by computer tracking programs.

Many major casinos now use this type of software, though I suspect that many of them use it haphazardly, not universally. It is simply too time consuming to evaluate all players this way.

Once there was a time when the pit boss was king. He knew the games better than anyone, and his value to the house was immense. He truly was "the boss." His decisions were final; his word was law. He was the only man with the "power of the pen." If you wanted a comp, you had to ask the boss. You didn't talk to a host, or a marketing exec, or plead your case at the "VIP lounge." There was no VIP lounge. There was no computer program that estimated your average bet, your hours of play, your expected loss—your "theoretical," in casino jargon. If you wanted show tickets, or a room compliments of the house, you asked the boss. Period. The surveillance guys were lackeys of the boss. They did what they were told, watched who he said to watch, and looked for the moves he told them to look for. He was the protector of the games. The guys on the catwalks worked for him.

Over the years, these functions have been taken away from the pit bosses. No boss can give you a room for the night anymore. He's lost the power of the pen. Most bosses don't understand the games anymore. Surveillance protects the games. The once all-powerful boss has been reduced to a bookkeeper. He records totals, counts chips, watches payouts, calls the cage when a table needs a fill.

Says one exec who has watched this change through the years, "They're not really bosses over anything any more. They're just clerks. The old timers remember the power the bosses used to have. It was all-encompassing. If you wanted a job in the casino, the fastest way to get it was through the boss. They had the juice. They could hire and fire dealers at whim. In some joints, the cocktail waitresses were like their private harems. These days, nobody thinks of them as 'bosses' any more. It's a title, but it's an anachronism. They're 'pit clerks,' and they know it. They're grossly overpaid for what they do, and they know that too. For all the talent and knowledge they need for the job they do, they could be check-out clerks at Seven-Eleven."

Now, it appears, the days of the boss may be numbered. MindPlay is a technology that identifies and eliminates the threat of card counters, while simultaneously eliminating the need for pit bosses. MindPlay is owned and distributed by Bally/Alliance Gaming, the same company that is big in the slot machine industry. Prototype MindPlay tables have been tested at casinos in both Las Vegas and Reno, and it is expected that Gaming Control will approve the system for widespread casino distribution in Nevada soon.

According to one Las Vegas casino exec I talked with:

> The primary purpose of the MindPlay system is not to eliminate card counters, but to eliminate pit bosses, floor persons, surveillance personnel, and a good portion of marketing people, namely the small army of hosts that every casino employs. If gaming tables can automatically oversee the games, what do we need bosses for? Most floor personnel are no longer involved in game protection. All they do is monitor the buy-ins, make sure there are no payout errors, and watch the check trays to visually verify the transactions. The only thing they do is count the checks and count the money. With MindPlay, the table counts the checks and the money. The table verifies correct payouts. The table even alerts the cage when a check tray is low and needs a fill.
>
> How many bosses do you see in the slot department? All you see are change girls and an occasional security guard. The pay scale for these employees is not comparable to what pit bosses make. The dream with MindPlay, as the top execs envision it, is that the only supervisory casino employee needed will be a shift manager. 99% of players don't need a boss or a host. Look how it works for slot players. Their slot card keeps the records and tells the house how many points they've earned. There's no fudging. MindPlay does that for table games. Either your player card says you've earned the comp, or you didn't. If you can replace a hundred executive positions with a couple dozen change girls and cashiers, you are looking at a huge increase in profits. It makes no difference if MindPlay can't catch a card counter. Most pit bosses can't recognize advantage players any more. Their only game protection function anymore is to make a phone

call upstairs if they're suspicious about a player. Now, MindPlay makes the phone call. And it will probably be more accurate in recognizing a threat than most bosses or surveillance monitors.

The idea will be sold to players as a technological solution to payout errors and making sure that all the cards are being used. It will also be described to them as a surefire method for making sure that they get all the comps they deserve. On the other hand, it will be sold to pit and surveillance personnel as a solution to card counters, cheaters, comp abusers and other advantage players.

There's an old saying: "Age and treachery will beat youth and brilliance every time." This is so true in gambling, yet it's not something that is understood by the corporations that are running the casinos. They believe in youth and brilliance. I'm old school. I think if you want to make money on your games, and protect your games, you hire a bunch of ex-card counters, ex-hole-carders, ex-crossroaders, and you let people who know how to take off games keep people from taking off your games. These corporate types actually believe that machines can protect the games better than people. In my opinion, this is lunacy. This MindPlay system is so fraught with potential for abuse it's insane.

For instance, the computer will know the exact order of the cards in the shoe prior to the deal. This information can be accessed by anyone with the proper authority, meaning the password to get into the data screens. The casino manager can actually access this information from his home, over the Internet, if he wants to. I don't care how many firewalls and layers of encryption they're using, a couple of smart-ass humans who want to take millions out of a joint could pull an Ocean's Eleven without any explosives. One password is literally the key to the vault.

And how is it that some numskull in Gaming has actually authorized the casinos to use marked cards? Is this nuts, or what? They really believe this system will be impenetrable? Do they really believe everyone on the inside will always be squeaky clean? Do they really believe no outsiders will ever get a hold of one of these systems in order to take it apart and find the weaknesses, the bugs, the backdoors?

The discard holder reads the card order. After the shuffle, the dealer has to place the cards back into the discard holder before placing them into the shoe. The discard holder reads the complete stack, top to bottom, in a second. The dealers will be instructed to tell players that they're just making sure all the cards are still there, that the discard holder checks to see that six full decks are in play. They will be unlikely to tell the players that the central computer now knows the exact order of the cards to be dealt. The dealers themselves may not know this.

Gaming has already approved MindPlay as a legal device in Nevada. Whether or not Gaming will come out and say "You can't use this function of this device in this way," has yet to be seen...At this point, the casinos can do anything that they are not specifically prohibited from doing, and shuffling up is always a legal option. Dealers in Nevada are currently allowed by Gaming to count cards and shuffle away player favorable decks, and MindPlay would not really be doing anything that dealers are not currently allowed to do; it would just be doing it with extreme accuracy. No one in the industry wants to talk about these features out loud right now, but with MindPlay, imagine this: If the high cards are about to be dealt, and a player is sitting there with a table-limit bet, MindPlay would know if the best hand would go to the player or the dealer. MindPlay knows the exact order of the cards. If a dealer blackjack is coming, to beat a bunch of player 20s, why should the dealer be instructed to shuffle up? The current preferential shuffling practices have no accuracy. MindPlay can make these decisions with absolute precision. As soon as you see dealers placing the decks back into the discard tray, after the shuffle, before putting them into the shoe, get out of the game. That's a MindPlay table, and it may not be safe. The only reason for a dealer to do that is so the computer can see the exact order of the cards to be dealt.

So, the casino industry continues in its never-ending quest to turn blackjack into a random game, with a built-in house edge that cannot possibly be beaten in the long run by skillful players. If you look at some of the MindPlay tables in Nevada casinos, you will see that they are most unusual in that the discard holder (the device that reads the order of the cards after the shuffle) is built in to the table in such a way that it holds the discards beneath the table. That is, it looks like a rectangular hole in the tabletop, so that you cannot actually see the cards that are placed into it. I suggest avoiding these tables.

Traveling With Cash

It has become quite dangerous to travel with large amounts of cash, say $10,000 or more. And it's not the robbers you must fear, but the cops. In the U.S., many police agencies will confiscate cash in this quantity as "drug money," with no questions asked. Even though you may not be in possession of any drugs, and will not be charged with any crime, current laws do not require the police to prove their accusations. Unless you can prove that the money you were carrying was not the result of illegal activities, your money will not be returned to you. Should this happen to you, you will have to hire a lawyer, and it could be expensive. It could also take many months until you get your money back, if you get it back.

Traveling through airports is especially dangerous, even on domestic flights. If for some reason you match the profile of a drug courier, or you just happen to be one of the lucky randomly chosen passengers on your flight, you may have your luggage searched. Never carry large amounts of cash in your luggage. One feature of that profile is that you are traveling on a one-way ticket. For this reason, if you plan to travel by air with cash, consider purchasing a round-trip ticket, even if you do not need the round trip. You can always cash in the return trip later. Even though you may know you are innocent, it is much cheaper and easier to avoid confiscation of your money than it is to try and get it back from the feds.

Also, buy your airline ticket with a credit card. It is considered highly suspicious to authorities when airline tickets are purchased with cash. You must take this stuff very seriously. Although professional gamblers often carry very large sums of cash, six and seven-digit bankrolls, and use these funds to buy into big games, the rest of America thinks of that as "abnormal."

Also, when traveling, wear the money on your person. Your bags are far more likely to be searched (or lost, or stolen), so you should get a couple of money belts that you can wear inconspicuously underneath your clothing. Make sure that these money belts do not have metal zippers or snaps or anything that might set off a metal detector. There is nothing illegal about carrying money; it's just that the U.S. government is now allowed to relieve you of it if they have any suspicion. And, unfortunately, the only cause for suspicion they need to cite is that you are carrying a large amount of cash.

If you travel internationally, always declare any cash you are carrying over $10,000. If you do not declare it, and it is found, it is history. Don't attempt to hide it in your luggage or on your person. It is legal to carry cash provided you declare it. If you don't declare it, it will be confiscated. You will probably never get it back.

Some countries will not allow you to exit with large sums of cash in their currency, and you may find it difficult, if not impossible, to convert some currencies into U.S. dollars, or into any other easily negotiable currency. Always check local laws regarding these issues before you spend weeks hammering some casino for money you can't take with you. In most such countries, there will be black markets for currency exchange, but this could prove both dangerous and expensive.

One way to transport large sums of money both domestically and internationally is American Express traveler checks. If they are confiscated at the border—which is highly unlikely—no problem; American Express will replace them for full value when you report them lost. Most countries have an American Express office, where they may or may not sell you travelers checks in exchange for the local currency. This is not a paid advertisement; this is a warning and a suggestion.

Most pro gamblers keep much of their gambling money in cash, either in private safes in their homes, or in safe deposit boxes at local banks or casinos where they can get quick access to it. The reason for this is that we no longer live in a cash society. Even if you have $100,000 in your savings or checking account, you cannot just walk into your local bank and take it out as cash. In fact, if you try to take out even $10,000 or $20,000, the bank may flat out tell you that they do not have that much cash on hand. You will be required to wait at least a few days to get your money, as the bank must place an order for it from wherever their central vault is located.

Big teams often supply their players with notarized letters from attorneys that can be shown to police, federal agents, or airline officials, stating that the person in possession of the cash or chips is, in fact, a professional gambler. Whether or not you play on a team, if you ever carry large amounts of cash on your person, it might be wise for you to carry a letter like this.

If you are playing under your own name in a casino, and staying in the casino hotel, it may be more convenient and safer for you to either wire funds from your bank to the casino cage, or to get a cashier's check from your bank and deposit this check at the cage when you arrive. There can be problems with this approach, however. First of all, the casino must contact your bank to verify the cashier's check. If you arrive on Saturday night, you may not have access to your funds until Monday morning.

Also, if you arrive with a check, the casino will not let you leave with cash. For instance, let's say you arrive with a cashier's check for $20,000 that the casino verifies with your bank. In the course of playing over the next few days, you lose $4,000. The casino will not give you $16,000 in cash when you leave. They will give you a check for $16,000, and it will not be a cashier's check, just a normal bank check. If the casino is not in the same state as your local bank, you may have to wait days until their check clears in order to have access to these funds again.

All of these problems can be avoided if you learn to live with cash the way most pro gamblers do. When you deal in cash, there's no time lag on obtaining or transferring funds, no bank verifications. You may take your money in various quantities to play in multiple casinos. With cash, you pretty much come and go as you please. But bear in mind that carrying cash is the one perfectly legal activity in the United States in which, if detected, you are guilty until proven innocent.

One other word of advice: Never pull out large sums of cash to deposit at the regular casino cage window used by the general public. And especially never get your money out of deposit at a casino cage at the public window. All major casinos have private rooms for large cash transactions. You do not want strangers milling around the casino cage area to see you putting tens of thousands of dollars in cash into your pockets.

Also, whenever you are carrying cash, always use the casino's valet service to park your car. You do not want to be wandering around a casino's parking garage at 2AM looking for your vehicle with $50,000 in your coat pocket. Always think safety. The valet service will cost you a couple bucks, but when you leave the casino, you will wait for your car in an area where there are valets, security guards, doormen, bellhops, and other customers. This is not an ideal environment for a mugger.

Cash Transaction Reports

All casinos now file daily cash transaction reports (CTRs) with the federal government on cash transactions of $10,000 or more. You should know that banks also file these reports any time you withdraw or deposit at least $10,000 in any 24-hour period. This is in compliance with the U.S. Treasury Department and the IRS, who are always on the lookout for tax dodgers and money launderers. It is very dangerous to make multiple transactions below $10K in order to avoid these reports. The IRS calls this "structuring," and it is a crime. Even if there is no evidence that you avoided a penny of your taxes, structuring is a crime in and of itself.

The filing of many CTRs, in and of itself, will not get you into trouble unless the feds have reason to believe that the cash deposited came from illegal activities. Card counting is not a crime, but attempting to dodge CTRs on your large cash transactions is. The casino must get your name and social security number from you in order to file a CTR.

So, what if you don't want to give your name to the casino where you just won fifteen thousand dollars? It is not a crime for a card counter to arrange casino cage deposits and withdrawals for the purpose of keeping under the casino "radar," and possibly being identified as a professional gambler. After a big win, many pros choose to cash out smaller amounts over a period of time. No law is being broken, but if you take this approach, it could be difficult for you to convince the IRS that this was what you were doing. If you file your taxes as a professional gambler, and the wins and losses in question agree with the records you provide in the case of an audit, your explanation to the IRS that you were not structuring but avoiding identification by the casino will more likely be believed. Which leads us to ...

Suspicious Activity Reports

If a casino believes you may be structuring cash transactions to avoid CTRs, then they are required to file a Suspicious Activity Report (SAR) with the IRS. So, don't try to beat the taxman in addition to beating the casinos. If you think that just because you never had a transaction over $10,000 that the IRS has no records on you, you could be in for a big surprise. If you are audited and your records do not agree with those provided to the IRS by a casino, you may find yourself in a heap of trouble.

If you gamble professionally, keep perfect records of all wins, losses, and cash transactions by date and casino. To the IRS, you are a self-employed businessman, and as such you are legally required to keep these records.

Comps

Professional gamblers are of two schools of thought on casino complimentaries. Some are of the opinion that comps are so valuable that all serious players should attempt to get all that they can. Others believe that comps are nothing but trouble waiting to erupt. A player must generally provide identification and be a registered guest in the casino hotel to obtain the truly valuable complimentaries, such as room or airfare, and some pros never stay in the casinos where they play.

On the pro-comp side, during long losing streaks, it is extremely helpful to have the casinos paying your travel expenses. Hotel rooms and restaurants, let alone airfare, are not cheap. High-level players will often generate many thousands of dollars in complimentaries every year. And if you are not playing at the highest levels, then the comps seem even more important. Many low-level ($5-$25) players never pay for a meal in a casino. If you're friendly, and you're not playing in the most expensive carpet joints, you can usually find a boss who will give you a coffee shop voucher. Also, low-level players who use their players club cards will get mailers from casinos with coupons for free rooms during off-peak periods, match-play coupons, buffet vouchers, and so on. Some players make as much income from their comps as they do from their blackjack play.

Special Promotions

Occasionally a casino will have a special promotion where they offer a highly advantageous rule or payout for a limited time. Probably the most common promotion that has been offered by many casinos is Blackjack Pays 2 to 1, instead of the normal 3 to 2. If a promotion like this gets much advance advertising, you can be sure that card counters will be flocking to it from near and far. Plan to arrive early if you want a seat.

If the promotion is so valuable that the casino turns into a card-counters convention even before the promo begins, the casino may cancel the promotion. If the promotion allows big bets, say $500 or more, then you should expect that many known counters will be there, and you must be very careful about being seen associating with strangers (or friends) in the casino. The casino game protection personnel may be totally shocked by the crowds of players at their tables, all placing maximum table-limit bets. They will likely believe they are under attack by some organized team of professional players.

Playing Blackjack on the Internet

I know many pro players who make money playing blackjack on the Internet, although card counting is a waste of time in Web casinos because the computerized dealer shuffles after every hand. You make money in Web casinos by hustling the "sign-up bonuses" offered to new players. The details of exactly how you go about doing this are beyond the scope of this book. The only reason I'm even bringing up the subject in this book is because many players who do not have easy access to regular casinos might be tempted to use the methods in this book to beat Web casinos. Don't waste your time. If you are interested in playing online I would advise you to obtain a book by Barry Meadow (yes, the famous author of horse racing books!), titled *Crushing the Internet Casinos*. You will find information on obtaining Barry's on my website at: www.BlackjackForumOnline.com.

And Finally...

Assuming you achieve your goal of making it as a full-time professional gambler, there is one last problem you will face. You must learn to deal with the existential fear of being a replaceable cog in a machine that produces nothing. Human beings, alas, have this weighty fixation on doing something important, producing something of value, making a difference to the world at large, or at least to the few meaningful characters who populate their lives.

Must professional gamblers relinquish this human need to do something of value? According to some, especially casino management, card counters are simply siphoning money from a meaningless cash flow system. They produce nothing, perform no service of value to anyone, entertain no one, and in the true sense of the word, are financial parasites to an industry.

Over the past twenty-five years, I have talked with many gambling pros about how they deal with this feeling that they are contributing nothing to the world, that their life is just a meaningless passing of time with a lot of money. Many successful players who quit the gambling life cite this feeling of uselessness to the world as the reason for their re-entry into society at large. But those who stay, stay for something...Here are some of the reasons they give for choosing a career in gambling:

The Idealist

"I don't feel like I'm doing no good. I really do see casinos as evil entities in the world, and I think beating them is a courageous and moral act."

The Pragmatist

"I never feel like my existence is meaningless. I found something that I enjoy doing, that I'm really good at, and that I can make a living at. Why should I feel guilty for doing what I like to do? What if I was a professional basketball player? All they're doing is playing a game, same as me. Do they feel useless and meaningless? I don't think so. You can argue that their lives are more meaningful because in addition to playing a game well, they entertain us…so they do give something back to society. But really, so do I. People are intrigued by the freedom of professional gamblers. No alarm clocks. No time clocks. A lot of people would love to think that if they ever really needed to make a change, this escape route is there for them. Pros like me are constantly taking new arrivals under our wings."

The Cynic

"I'm a very cynical person at heart. I don't vote. I think all politicians are crooks. The world is run by a bunch of swindlers who would all burn in hell—if it existed. Most of the jobs available in this country add nothing to society, and in fact, they're pretty much all bad if you really want to classify them as good or bad. Maybe a pro-bono lawyer helping wrongfully accused poor people get out of jail is doing something good. Or an independent farmer growing organic vegetables. I used to work in a bank. Now there's a real moral profession. What do banks do except squeeze money out of people and line the pockets of billionaires? Should I work in a restaurant or a grocery store? Have you ever read anything about the food industry in this country? Animals are tortured, the environment is destroyed, most of the food we eat is non-nutritious garbage. This is a screwed up world. Go read about the drug companies, or the medical profession, or real estate tycoons. Human beings are just a bunch of selfish and greedy slobs intent on destroying the planet. Maybe if I believed in God I would try and do something about this world. I don't, so I just stay out of it. Gambling for a living may not contribute to society, but at least I feel like I'm not part of the system that's destroying people's lives."

The Philanthropist

"I'm just fine with this lifestyle. Gambling allows you to build wealth without currying favor with the rich and powerful. I take good care of my kids, and that's important to me. I can afford to be generous to those in need. I've been fortunate enough to be able to help out a lot of my family members and friends. I have enough money to donate to causes I believe in. My contribution to society is to take money from the Trumps and

Kerkorians and spread it around to people who need it more than they do. I love beating the casinos, but my 'job' is helping to make the world more humane."

APPENDIX

COMPREHENSIVE BASIC STRATEGY
FOR ANY NUMBER OF DECKS

STAND

	2	3	4	5	6	7	8	9	X	A
17	S	S	S	S	S	S	S	S	S	S
16	S	S	S	S	S	H	H	H	H[1]	H
15	S	S	S	S	S	H	H	H	H	H
14	S	S	S	S	S	H	H	H	H	H
13	S	S	S	S	S	H	H	H	H	H
12	H	H	S	S	S	H	H	H	H	H
A7	S	S	S	S	S	S	S	H	H	S[-2]

DOUBLE DOWN

	2	3	4	5	6	7	8	9	X	A
11	D	D	D	D	D	D	D	D	D[3]	D[4]
10	D	D	D	D	D	D	D	D		
9	D[5]	D	D	D	D					
8				D[5]	D[5]					
A8					D[5]					
A7		D	D	D	D					
A6	D[5]	D	D	D	D					
A5			D	D	D					
A4			D	D	D					
A3			D[5]	D	D					
A2			D[5]	D	D					

SURRENDER (LATE)

	2	3	4	5	6	7	8	9	X	A
17										¢[6]
16							¢[7]		¢	¢[8]
8-8										¢[9]
15									¢[10]	¢[6]
7-7									¢[5]	¢[9]

S = Stand   H = Hit   D = Double Down   ¢ = Surrender

1 = Stand with 3 or More Cards
2 = Hit in Multi-Deck, or if Dealer Hits S-17
3 = European No-Hole Hit
4 = Multi-Deck or European No-Hole Hit
5 = Single-Deck Only
6 = With Hit Soft 17 Only
7 = Single Deck Hit
8 = Single Deck, X-6 Only
9 = With Hit Soft 17 in Multi-Deck
10 = Excluding 8,7

PAIR-SPLITS

NO DOUBLE AFTER SPLITS

	2	3	4	5	6	7	8	9	X	A
AA	$	$	$	$	$	$	$	$	$	$¹
99	$	$	$	$	$		$	$		
88	$	$	$	$	$	$	$	$	$¹	$¹
77	$	$	$	$	$	$				
66	$²	$	$	$	$					
33			$	$	$	$				
22		$²	$	$	$	$				

WITH DOUBLE AFTER SPLITS

	2	3	4	5	6	7	8	9	X	A
AA	$	$	$	$	$	$	$	$	$	$¹
99	$	$	$	$	$		$	$		
88	$	$	$	$	$	$	$	$	$¹	$¹
77	$	$	$	$	$	$	$²			
66	$	$	$	$	$	$²				
44		$²	$	$						
33	$	$	$	$	$	$	$²			
22	$	$	$	$	$	$				

INSURANCE: NO

SURRENDER (EARLY)

	2	3	4	5	6	7	8	9	X	A
17										¢
16								¢	¢	¢
8-8									¢	¢
15									¢	¢
14									¢	¢
7-7									¢	¢
13										¢
12										¢
7										¢
6										¢
5										¢

$ = Split   ¢ = Surrender

1 = European No-Hole Hit
2 = Single Deck Only

COMPREHENSIVE HI-LO LITE STRATEGY
FOR ANY NUMBER OF DECKS

	2	3	4	5	6	7	8	9	X	A
STAND										
17	S	S	S	S	S	S	S	S	S	-2
16	-4	S	S	S	S	4	4	2	0	4/2
15	-2	-4	-4	-4	S	H	6	4	2	6/2
14	-2	-2	-2	-4	-4	H	H	H	H	8/4
13	0	0	-2	-2	-2/-4	H	H	H	H	H
12	2	0	0	0	0/-2	H	H	H	H	H
A7	S	S	S	S	S	S	S	H	H	0/H
DOUBLE DOWN										
11	D	D	D	D	D	D	-2	-2	-2	0
10	-4	D	D	D	D	-2	-2	0	2	2
9	0	0	0	-2	-2	2	4			
8	6	4	2	2	0					
7			6	4	4					
A9	6	4	4	2	2					
A8	4	2	2	0	0					
A7	0	0	-2	-4	-6					
A6	0	-2	-4	-4	D					
A5	8	2	-2	-2	D					
A4			0	-2	-4					
A3			0	0	-2					
A2			2	0	0					
SURRENDER (LATE)										
16						6	2	0	0	0/-2
8-8								4	0	
15						6	4	2	0	0
14							6	4	2	4/2
7-7									2	
13								8	4	

S = Stand   H = Hit   D = Double

Note: Table entries with slashes (/) indicate different decision numbers for Stand Soft 17 and Hit Soft 17, in format S/H. 4/2 Means the index is 4 if Dealer Stands on Soft 17, or 2 if the dealer Hits Soft 17.

HI-LO PAIR-SPLITS

NO DOUBLE AFTER SPLITS

	2	3	4	5	6	7	8	9	X	A
AA	$	$	$	$	$	$	$	$	$	-2
XX		4	4	2	2					
99	0	0	-2	-2	-2	4	$			2
88	$	$	$	$	$	$	$	$	4^1	$/0
77	$	$	$	$	$	$				
66	2	0	-2	-2	$					
33	4	2	0	0	$/-2	$				
22	4	2	0	$	$	$				

WITH DOUBLE AFTER SPLITS

	2	3	4	5	6	7	8	9	X	A
AA	$	$	$	$	$	$	$	$	$	-2
XX		4	4	2	2					
99	0	-2	-2	$	$	2	$	$		2/0
88	$	$	$	$	$	$	$	$	4^1	$/0
77	$	$	$	$	$	$	2^2			
66	$	$	$	$	$	$^{3}				
44		4	0	0	-2					
33	0	-2	$	$	$	$	2^2			
22	0	-2	$	$	$	$	2			

INSURANCE: 2 (1 in single-deck)

SURRENDER (EARLY)

	2	3	4	5	6	7	8	9	X	A
17									4	¢
16							2	0	-2	¢
8-8								4	0	¢
15							4	0	0	¢
14							6	4	0	¢
7-7							6	2	0	¢
13									2	¢
12									4	-4
7										-4
6									6	-2
5									6	0

$ = Split   ¢ = Surrender

1= Split if below this index; 2= One-deck always split; 3= One-deck only

COMPREHENSIVE ZEN COUNT STRATEGY FOR ANY NUMBER OF DECKS

	2	3	4	5	6	7	8	9	X	A
STAND										
17	S	S	S	S	S	S	S	S	S	-3/-2
16	-4	S	S	S	S	5	4	2	0	3/1
15	-2	-3	-4	-4	S	H	5	4	1	4/2
14	-1	-2	-2	-3	-3/-4	H	H	H	3	5/3
13	0	-1	-1	-2	-2/-3	H	H	H	H	H
12	1	1	0	-1	0/-1	H	H	H	H	H
A7	S	S	S	S	S	S	S	H	H	2/H
DOUBLE DOWN										
11	D	D	D	D	D	-4	-3	-2	-2	0
10	-4	-4	D	D	D	-3	-2	-1	1	1
9	0	0	-1	-2	-3	2	4			
8	5	4	3	2	1					
7			5	5	5					
A9	4	3	3	2	2					
A8	3	2	1	0	0					
A7	0	-1	-2	-3	-3/-4					
A6	0	-1	-2	-4	D					
A5	5	1	-1	-3	D					
A4		2	0	-2	-4					
A3		3	1	-1	-2/-3					
A2		3	1	0	-1					
SURRENDER (LATE)										
16		3				5	2	0	-2	-1/-
8-8							4	0		
15						5	3	1	0	1/0
14							4	2	1	2/1
7-7									1	
13								5	3	

S = Stand   H = Hit   D = Double

Note: Table entries with slashes (/) indicate different decision numbers for Stand Soft 17 and Hit Soft 17, in format S/H. 2/1 Means the index is 2 if Dealer Stands on Soft 17, or 1 if the dealer Hits Soft 17.

ZEN COUNT PAIR-SPLITS

	2	3	4	5	6	7	8	9	X	A
NO DOUBLE AFTER SPLITS										
AA	$	$	$	$	$	$	$	$	$	-2
XX	4	4	3	2	2					
99	-1	-1	-2	-2	-2	3	$			2
88	$	$	$	$	$	$	$	$	2^1	$/0
77	$	$	$	$	$	$				
66	1	0	-1	-2	$					
33	3	1	0	-2	$	3^1				
22	3	1	-1	$	$	$				
WITH DOUBLE AFTER SPLITS										
AA	$	$	$	$	$	$	$	$	$	-2
XX	4	3	3	2	2					
99	-1	-2	-2	$	$	1	$	$		1
88	$	$	$	$	$	$	$	$	4^1	$
77	$	$	$	$	$	$	1^2			
66	-1	-2	$	$	$	^{3}				
44		3	1	0	-1					
33	-2	$	$	$	$	$	2^2			
22	-2	-2	$	$	$	$	3			

INSURANCE: 1

SURRENDER (EARLY)

	2	3	4	5	6	7	8	9	X	A
17									3	¢
16							3	0	-3	¢
8-8								4	-1	¢
15							4	1	-1	¢
14							5	3	0	¢
7-7							5	2	0	¢
13									2	¢
12									5	-3
7										-3
6									6	-2
5									6	0

$ = Split   ¢ = Surrender

1 = Split if below this index
2 = One-deck always split
3 = One-deck only

Recommended Source Materials

These are the books on gambling I really like. Not all of them are blackjack specific, but they have at least some material on the game. Some are out of print, but most can still be located in used bookstores. There are 29 books listed. If you read all of these, you will know a lot about professional gambling. The books marked with an asterisk (*) should be read by every serious blackjack player.

*Andersen, Ian. *Turning the Tables on Las Vegas*. New York: The Vanguard Press, 1976.

*Andersen, Ian. *Burning the Tables in Las Vegas*. Las Vegas: Huntington Press, 1999.

*Auston, John. *World's Greatest Blackjack Simulation (AOII, Hi-Lo, K-O, Red Seven, and Zen Count editions)*. Oakland: RGE Publishing, 1997.

Baldwin, Roger, Cantey, Wilbert E., Maisel, Herbert, and McDermott, James. *Playing Blackjack to Win*. New York: M. Barrons and company, 1957.

Canfield, Richard. *Blackjack Your Way to Riches*. New Jersey: Lyle Stuart, 1979.

Carlson, Bryce. *Blackjack for Blood*. Santa Monica: CompuStar Press, 1992; revised, 1994.

*Cellini, D.V. *The Card Counter's Guide to Casino Surveillance*. Las Vegas: Huntington Press, 2003.

Chambliss, Carlson R., and Roginsky, Thomas C. *Fundamentals of Blackjack*. Las Vegas: GBC, 1990.

Dalton, Michael. *Blackjack: A Professional Reference*. Merritt Island, FL: Spur of the Moment Publishing, 1991; third edition, 1993.

Epstein, Richard A. *The Theory of Gambling and Statistical Logic*. New York: Academic Press, 1977.

*Forte, Steve. *Read the Dealer*. Oakland: RGE Publishing, 1986.

Griffin, Peter A. *Extra Stuff: Gambling Ramblings*. Las Vegas: Huntington Press, 1991.

*Griffin, Peter A. *The Theory of Blackjack*. Las Vegas: GBC, 1979; 5th edition, Las Vegas: Huntington Press, 1995.

*Grosjean, James. *Beyond Counting*. Oakland: RGE Publishing, 2000.

Haywood, Bill. *BeatWebCasinos.Com*. Oakland: RGE Publishing, 2000.

Humble, Lance and Cooper, Carl. *The World's Greatest Blackjack Book*.

APPENDIX

New York: Doubleday, 1980.

Malmuth, Mason, and Sklansky, David. *How to Make $100,000 a Year Gambling for a Living*. Las Vegas: Two Plus Two, 1997.

*Marks, Dustin D. *Cheating at Blackjack*. San Diego: Index Publishing, 1994.

*Marks, Dustin D. *Cheating at Blackjack Squared*. San Diego: Index Publishing, 1996.

*Meadow, Barry. *Blackjack Autumn*. Las Vegas: Huntington Press, 1999-2002.

*Meadow, Barry. *Crushing the Internet Casinos*. Las Vegas: Huntington Press, 2003.

*Mezrich, Ben. *Bringing Down the House*. New York: The Free Press, 2002.

*Munchkin, Richard W. *Gambling Wizards*. Las Vegas: Huntington Press, 2002.

Noir, Jacques. *Casino Holiday*. Berkeley: Oxford Street Press, 1968.
Ortiz, Darwin. *Gambling Scams*. New Jersey: Lyle Stuart, 1984.

*Perry, Stuart. *Las Vegas Blackjack Diary*. New York: Self-published, 1995; 3rd edition, Pittsburgh: ConJelCo, 1997.

*Revere, Lawrence. *Playing Blackjack as a Business*. Secaucus: Lyle Stuart, 1969; last revised, 1980.

*Rose, I. Nelson, and Loeb, Robert A. *Blackjack and the Law*. Oakland: RGE Publishing, 1998.

*Rubin, Max. *Comp City*. Las Vegas: Huntington Press, 1994; revised 2002.

*Schlesinger, Don. *Blackjack Attack*. Oakland: RGE Publishing, 1997, revised 2000, 2004.

Sklansky, David. *Getting the Best of It*. Las Vegas: Two Plus Two, 1982-89.

Sklansky, David. *Sklansky Talks Blackjack*. Las Vegas: Two Plus Two, 1999.

*Snyder, Arnold. *Beat the 1-, 2-, 4-, 6-, 8-Deck Game (5 editions)*. Oakland: RGE Publishing, 1987, revised New York: Cardoza Publishing, 2004.

Snyder, Arnold. *Blackjack for Profit*. Oakland: RGE Publishing, 1981.

*Snyder, Arnold. *Blackjack Wisdom*. Oakland: RGE Publishing, 1997.

Snyder, Arnold. *The Blackjack Formula*. Oakland: RGE Publishing, 1980.

*Snyder, Arnold. *The Blackjack Shuffle Tracker's Cookbook*. Las Vegas: Huntington Press, 2003.

*Thorp, Edward O. *Beat the Dealer*. New York: Random House, 1962; revised, New York: Vintage Books, 1966.

Uston, Ken. *Ken Uston on Blackjack*. Secaucus: Lyle Stuart, 1986.

*Uston, Ken. *Million Dollar Blackjack*. Hollywood: SRS Enterprises, 1981.

*Uston, Ken. *The Big Player*. New York: Holt, Rinehart and Winston, 1977.

Uston, Ken. *Two Books on Blackjack*. Wheaton, MD: The Uston Institute of Blackjack, 1979.

*Wilson, Allan. *The Casino Gambler's Guide*. New York: Harper & Row, 1965-70.

*Wong, Stanford. *Basic Blackjack*. La Jolla: Pi Yee Press, 1992; revised 1993.

Wong, Stanford. *Blackjack in Asia*. La Jolla: Pi Yee Press, 1979.

*Wong, Stanford. *Blackjack Secrets*. La Jolla: Pi Yee Press, 1993.

*Wong, Stanford. *Professional Blackjack*. La Jolla: Pi Yee Press, 1975; last revised 1994.

*Wong, Stanford. *Casino Tournament Strategy*. La Jolla: Pi Yee Press, 1992-97.

*Wong, Stanford. *Winning Without Counting*. La Jolla: Pi Yee Press, 1978-80.

*Zender, Bill. *Card Counting for the Casino Executive*. Las Vegas: Self-published, 1990.

*Zender, Bill. *How to Detect Casino Cheating at Blackjack*. Oakland: RGE Publishing, 1999.

5 PROFESSIONAL REPORTS TO TURN
AMATEUR CARD COUNTERS TO PROS

NOT FOR BEGINNERS—FOR CARD COUNTERS ONLY

NEW AND REVISED! - These are the **groundbreaking** reports relied upon by **professional blackjack players** for more than 25 years. And now they are completed updated! This is a **very big event** for winning and pro blackjack players.

THE LEGEND REVEALS HIS SECRETS - These professional strategies are the personal work of Arnold Snyder, **legendary** blackjack player and guru to thousands of serious players. Snyder, **one of the greatest players** in history and a member of the **Blackjack Hall of Fame**, is the author of nine books and advanced strategies including his national best-seller, *Blackbelt in Blackjack*.

THE PROFESSIONAL COUNTERS SECRET STRATEGIES - Start **winning** by applying the strongest betting strategy with the lowest risk. Good for all valid counting systems, some of the technical questions answered are:

- What's my advantage if the dealer deals out 4 1/2 decks instead of just 4 decks?
- Should I raise my bet at a count of +3 or +4?
- Can I beat the game if I use a betting spread of 1-to-4 units, or do I need 1-to-8?
- What's the best betting strategy if I only have $1000 and the minimum bet is $10?
- What's my win rate if I quit the table when the count goes negative?
- What's my win rate if the house uses eight decks instead of six?

You **don't need** to run computer simulations to get the answers, and you don't need a degree in probability and statistics. You simply need a set of charts where you can look up the answers —the math has already been worked out. **Accurate for all counting systems** and any size bankroll, each report is 64 pages, with 44 pages of charts. There are five separate reports for games being dealt with 1, 2, 4, 6, and 8 decks. With any betting spread, the charts show the fluctuations you can expect in an hour of play, ten hours, a hundred hours and more, so you can estimate your **best approach** to any game based on your actual bankroll. Get just the Reports that cover the games you currently play in, or get them all (and save $$$) to **be prepared** for *any* blackjack game *anywhere*.

Beat the 1-Deck Game: $25   **Beat the 6-Deck Game:** $25
Beat the 2-Deck Game: $25   **Beat the 8-Deck Game:** $25
Beat the 4-Deck Game: $25   **All five reports:** $95 (You save $30.00!)

To order, send $95 for all 5 reports (or $25 per report)—plus postage and handling to:
Cardoza Publishing, P.O. Box 1500, Cooper Station, New York, NY 10276

FROM CARDOZA'S EXCITING LIBRARY
ADD THESE TO YOUR COLLECTION - ORDER NOW!

SUPER SYSTEM *by Doyle Brunson.* This classic book is considered by the pros to be the best book ever written on poker! Jam-packed with advanced strategies, theories, tactics and money-making techniques—no serious poker player can afford to be without this hard-hitting information. Includes fifty pages of the most precise poker statistics ever published. Features chapters written by poker's biggest superstars, such as Dave Sklansky, Mike Caro, Chip Reese, Bobby Baldwin, and Doyle—two world champions and three master theorists. Essential strategies, advanced play, and no-nonsense winning advice on making money at 7-card stud (razz, high-low split, cards speak, and declare), draw poker, lowball, and hold'em (limit and no-limit).This is a must-read. 628 pages, $29.95.

SUPER SYSTEM 2 *by Doyle Brunson.* The most anticipated poker book ever, SS2 expands upon the original with more games and professional secrets from the best in the world. Superstar contributors include Daniel Negreanu, winner of multiple WSOP gold bracelets and 2004 Poker Player of the Year; Lyle Berman, 3-time WSOP gold bracelet winner, founder of the World Poker Tour, and super-high stakes cash player; Bobby Baldwin, 1978 World Champion; Johnny Chan, 2-time World Champion and 10-time WSOP bracelet winner; Mike Caro, poker's greatest researcher, theorist, and instructor; Jennifer Harman, the world's top female player and one of ten best overall; Todd Brunson, winner of more than 20 tournaments; and Crandell Addington, no-limit hold'em legend. 672 pgs, $34.95.

CARO'S BOOK OF POKER TELLS *by Mike Caro.* One of the ten greatest books written onpoker, this must-have book should be in every player's library. If you're serious about winning, you'll realize that most of the profit comes from being able to read your opponents. Caro reveals the the secrets of interpreting *tells*—physical reactions that reveal information about a player's cards—such as shrugs, sighs, shaky hands, eye contact, and many more. Learn when opponents are bluffing, when they aren't and why—based solely on their mannerisms. Over 170 photos of players in action and play-by-play examples show the actual tells. These powerful ideas will give you the decisive edge. 320 pages, $24.95.

CARO'S GUIDE TO DOYLE BRUNSON'S SUPER SYSTEM *by Mike Caro.* Working with World Champion Doyle Brunson, the legendary Mike Caro has created a fresh look to the "Bible" of all poker books, adding new and personal insights that help you understand the original work. Caro breaks 36 concepts into either "Analysis, Commentary, Concept, Mission, Play-By-Play, Psychology, Statistics, Story, or Strategy. Lots of illustrations and winning concepts give even more value to this great work. 86 pages, 8 1/2 x 11, $19.95.

MILLION DOLLAR HOLD'EM: Winning Big in Limit Cash Games *by Johnny Chan and Mark Karowe.* Learn how to win money consistently at limit hold'em, poker's most popular cash game, from one of poker's living legends. You'll get a rare opportunity to get into the mind of the man who has won ten World Series of Poker titles—tied for the most ever with Doyle Brunson—as Johnny picks out illustrative hands and shows how he thinks his way through the betting and the bluffing. No book so thoroughly details the thought process of how a hand is played, the alternative ways it could have been played, and the best way to win session after session. *Essential* reading for cash players. 352 pages, $29.95.

THE POKER TOURNAMENT FORMULA *by Arnold Snyder.* Start making money now in fast no-limit hold'em tournaments with these radical and powerful strategies! These never-before-published concepts and secrets for beating tournaments can turn any "fish" into a dangerous shark. For the first time, you'll learn why cards don't matter as much as the dynamics of a tournament—your position, the size of your chip stack, who your opponents are, and above all, the structure. Poker tournaments offer one of the richest opportunities to come along in decades. Every so often, a book comes along that changes the way players attack a game and provides them with a big advantage over opponents. Gambling legend Arnold Snyder has written such a book. 368 pages, $19.95.

ADVANCED BLACKJACK TITLES
• For Serious Players Only •

THE BLACKJACK SHUFFLE TRACKER'S COOKBOOK - $49.95
In this 110-page professional report, Arnold Snyder reveals techniques never-before disclosed on the advanced and dangerous form of card counting known as shuffle tracking. These powerful techniques, known only to a few professional players, are way below the casino radar and allows players to use their winning skills long before the casinos ever get wind that there is an advantage player taking their money.

Powerful Winning Data
Included are numerous practice and testing methods for learning shuffle tracking, methods for analyzing and comparing the profit potential of various shuffles, the cost of errors; and much, much more. The hard data is organized into simple charts, and carefully explained. Note: If you are not currently a card counter, this book is not the place to start as shuffle tracking is not easy. This is for serious players only.

THE CARD COUNTER'S GUIDE TO CASINO SURVEILLANCE - $99.95
Learning the subtleties of playing winning blackjack undetected is an extremely difficult skill. It's hard enough to fool the casino employees you can see—dealers, floormen, pit bosses, and casino managers—but then there's the "eye," the behind-the-scenes surveillance department, with its biometric-identifying software along with the surveillance agents themselves. But now, for the first time ever, a long-time surveillance agent with vast experience and knowledge has emerged from the deep and dark recesses and exposed the inner workings to the light of scrutiny.

Powerful Weapons for Professional Players
This 135-page special report by D.V. Cellini is packed with inside advice on solo and team-play tactics; how to fly below the radar screen; how to confuse the agents and software; successful camouflage and counter-offensive techniques; and even sure-fire ways to get busted. This is a mighty weapon in any card-counter's arsenal—and it's fascinating reading for anyone interested in how casinos really work.

323

NEW BLACKJACK TITLES
BOOKS YOU MUST HAVE

THE BLACKJACK SHUFFLE TRACKER'S COOKBOOK
by Arnold Snyder
$49.95

In this 110-page professional report, Arnold Snyder reveals techniques never-before disclosed on the advanced and dangerous form of card counting known as shuffle tracking. These powerful techniques, known only to a few professional players, are way below the casino radar and allows players to use their winning skills long before the casinos ever get wind that there is an advantage player taking their money.

Included are numerous practice and testing methods for learning shuffle tracking, methods for analyzing and comparing the profit potential of various shuffles, the cost of errors; and much, much more. The hard data is organized into simple charts, and carefully explained. Note: If you are not currently a card counter, this book is not the place to start as shuffle tracking is not easy. This is for serious players only.

THE CARD COUNTER'S GUIDE TO CASINO SURVEILLANCE
by D.V. Cellini
$99.99

Learning the subtleties of playing winning blackjack undetected is an extremely difficult skill. It's hard enough to fool the casino employees you can see—dealers, floormen, pit bosses, and casino managers—but then there's the "eye," the behind-the-scenes surveillance department, with its biometric-identifying software along with the surveillance agents themselves. But now, for the first time ever, a long-time surveillance agent with vast experience and knowledge has emerged from the deep and dark recesses and exposed the inner workings to the light of scrutiny.

This 135-page special report is packed with inside advice on solo and team-play tactics; how to fly below the radar screen; how to confuse the agents and software; successful camouflage and counter-offensive techniques; and even sure-fire ways to get busted. This is a mighty weapon in any card-counter's arsenal—and it's fascinating reading for anyone interested in how casinos really work.

Win at Blackjack Without Counting Cards!!!
Multiple Deck 1, 2, 3 Non-Counter - Breakthrough in Blackjack!!!

BEAT MULTIPLE DECK BLACKJACK WITHOUT COUNTING CARDS!
You heard right! Now, for the **first time ever, win** at multiple deck blackjack **without counting cards**! Until I developed the Cardoza Multiple Deck Non-Counter (the 1,2,3 Strategy), I thought it was impossible. Don't be intimidated anymore by four, six or eight deck games - for **you have the advantage**. It doesn't matter how many decks they use, for this easy-to-use and proven strategy keeps you **winning - with the odds**!

EXCITING STRATEGY - ANYONE CAN WIN! - We're **excited** about this strategy for it allows anyone at all, against any number of decks, to have the **advantage** over any casino in the world in a multiple deck game. You don't count cards, you don't need a great memory, you don't need to be good at math - you just need to know the **winning secrets** of the 1,2,3 Multiple Deck Non-Counter and use but a **little effort** to win $$$.

SIMPLE BUT EFFECTIVE! - **Now the answer is here.** This strategy is so **simple**, yet so **effective**, you will be amazed. With a **minimum of effort**, this remarkable strategy, which we also call the 1,2,3 (as easy as 1,2,3), allows you to win without studiously following cards. Drink, converse with your fellow players or dealer - they'll never suspect that you can **beat the casino**!

PERSONAL GUARANTEE - And you have my personal **guarantee of satisfaction**, 100% money back! This breakthrough strategy is my personal research and is guaranteed to give you the edge! If for any reason you're not satisfied, send back the materials unused within 30 days for a full refund.

BE A LEISURELY WINNER! - If you just want to play a **leisurely game** yet have the expectation of winning, the answer is here. Not as powerful as a card counting strategy, but **powerful enough to make you a winner** - with the odds!!!

EXTRA BONUS! - Complete listing of all options and variations at blackjack and how they affect the player. ($5.00 Value!)

EXTRA, EXTRA BONUS!! - Not really a bonus since we can't sell you the strategy without protecting you against getting barred. The 1,000 word essay, "How to Disguise the Fact That You're an Expert," and the 1,500 word "How Not To Get Barred," are also included free. ($15.00 Value)

To Order, send ~~$75~~ $50 (plus postage and handling) by check or money order to:
Cardoza Publishing, P.O. Box 1500, Cooper Station, New York, NY 10276